LETTERS TO THE WORLD
POEMS FROM THE WOM-PO LISTSERV

LETTERS TO THE WORLD

Poems from the Wom-Po LISTSERV

Editors in Chief

MOIRA RICHARDS   ROSEMARY STARACE   LESLEY WHEELER

Preface by

ANNIE FINCH

Introduction by

D'ARCY RANDALL

Editors

Margo Berdeshevsky, Rachel Dacus, Ann Fisher-Wirth,
Ellen Goldstein, Eloise Klein Healy, Ann Hostetler,
Louisa Howerow, Lillian Baker Kennedy, Athena Kildegaard,
D.O. Moore, Ren Powell

Red Hen Press  Los Angeles

LETTERS TO THE WORLD

Book design by Mark E. Cull
Layout assistance: Stephanie Halpern, Nicelle Hughes and Ben Mesirow.

ISBN: 978-1-59709-099-5
Library of Congress Catalog Card Number 2007938217

The City of Los Angeles Department of Cultural Affairs, Los Angeles County Arts Commission, California Arts Council and the National Endowment for the Arts partially support Red Hen Press.

Wom-po LISTSERV
www.usm.maine.edu/wompo

First Edition

Red Hen Press
www.redhen.org

This is my letter to the World
—Emily Dickinson

For Annie Finch and the members of the Wom-po Listserv

Contents

Preface: On Wom-po, Womponies, and the Wompology

You never know what's going to happen next on the Wom-po LISTSERV . . . One minute, people are speculating on motives women have for changing their names when they marry, arguing the merits of a seventeenth-century British "poetess," and making plans to translate from Farsi the poems of Afghan poet Nadia Anjuman. The next, a relatively new Wom-po subscriber in South Africa, Moira Richards, causes cyber-chaos. Moira lays out a plan for an anthology of poems by womponies (yes, womponies, a term long-time subscribers will recall being coined by Terri Ford)—and moreover, Moira offers to coordinate the project. Though Wom-po has spawned a web site, another listserv or two, at least two online poetry workshops, and numerous collaborations on books, journals, and conference panels, as well as tentative plans for various anthology projects, this is the first time anyone has put forth a concrete proposal for an anthology of Wom-po poems.

Moira's proposal causes a definite stir. Though the list is, thankfully, usually quite reasonable in volume, over the next few days dozens and dozens of posts flood our e-mailboxes as subscribers weigh in about the editorial process, design, and format. There is conflict, disgruntlement, agreement, appreciation, and finally something resembling consensus. Moira calls for volunteers for various tasks and more than a dozen people quickly organize to collect biographies, advise contributors which poems to send, and otherwise edit the collection.

Poems start to pour in for the "wompology," as it is soon nicknamed. Not so many at first, then gradually more and more, finally 259 from all walks of Wom-po-dom: eminent poets such as Marilyn Hacker and Alicia Ostriker; young poets just starting out such as Hadara Bar-Nadav and Amy King; experimentally leaning poets such as Heidi Lynn Staples and Elizabeth Treadwell; formalist poets such as Tara Betts and Molly Peacock; free-verse poets such as Aimee Nezhukumatathil and Ann Townsend; nature-oriented poets such as Ann Fisher-Wirth and Peggy Shumaker; poets of the personal such as Debra Bruce and Crystal Williams; politically outspoken poets such as Judith Arcana and Kristin Prevallet. There are rhapsodic poets such as Renée Ashley and Rachel Zucker; poets of the vernacular such as Eloise Klein Healy and Kathrine Varnes; performance-oriented poets such as Mendi Lewis Obadike and cin salach; poets who work with visual arts such as Sharon Dolin and Shin Yu Pai. There are blogger poets such as Catherine Daly and Luisa Igloria; poets who run their own listservs such as Alison Croggon and Robin Kemp; poets who do translation such as Anny Ballardini and Ellen Moody; poets who edit journals such as Glenna Luschei and C. J. Sage. There are irreverent poets such as Amy Lemmon and Rachel Loden; poets who write of history such as Nicole Cooley and Diane Thiel; poets ranging in age from MFA student Mary Alexandra Agner to octogenarian Margaret Rockwell Finch.

There are poets from all regions of the United States: west coast poets such as Aleida Rodríguez and Judith Barrington; east coast poets such as Moira Egan and Katha Pollitt; southern poets such as Jilly Dybka and Beverly Rainbolt; midwestern poets such as Elise Paschen and Marilyn Taylor. There are internationally known poets such as Farideh Hassanzadeh-Mostafavi from Iran and Rati Saxena from India; South African poets such as Liesl Jobson and Crystal Warren; Australian poets such as Barbara A. Taylor and Caroline Williamson; Canadian poets such as Louisa Howerow, Rachel Rose, and Sina Queyras; U. S. poets now living on other continents such as Adrianne Kalfopoulou in Greece and Ren Powell in

Norway; poets whose careers span continents such as Meena Alexander and Margo Berdeshevsky; poets from Palestine, the Philippines, New Zealand, Romania, the United Kingdom, Ireland, Cuba, and Mexico; and David Graham, one of Wom-po's few but loyal male subscribers, who remind us all that men indeed can listen to and support discussion of women's concerns with civility, dignity, and good humor. In short, the poems, like the listserv, represent a seemingly endless variety of often conflicting and always outspoken points of view.

At one point, I suggest that the themes of the submitted poems might focus on women poets or women—but that idea is soon plowed under along with many others into the general merry fertility of the list culture. And that is as it should be. Rather than the editors attempting to favor any common themes or threads, each poet here has chosen the one poem they would like to be represented by, for whatever reason. (I use the generic "they" for the genderless singular here, as recommended by Miller and Swift's definitive *The Handbook of Nonsexist Language).*

As the poems begin to pour in and the editors to compile them, another surprise ensues: longtime womponian Eloise Klein Healy is inspired to invite Kate Gale, publisher at Red Hen Press, to subscribe and check out the project. Kate subscribes to Wom-po, sizes up the situation immediately, remarks, "You're a scrappy bunch—I like that"—and the rest, as they say, is herstory.

The piece of herstory you are holding in your hands, published just about the time of Wom-po's tenth anniversary, is a remarkable document, perhaps the most complete cross section currently available of the great range of women *writing* poetry in English today in the United States and beyond—not publishing, mind you, but writing. Unlike other anthologies, this book is not restricted to poets who have already been accepted by the literary establishment—nor is it confined to poets who have not. Since the listserv by definition has a feminist bent, political conservatives here are of the kind with a high tolerance for progressive discourse. And since the only criterion for inclusion was that the poet be a subscriber to the Wom-po LISTSERV, the poets are limited to those with computer access and so tend to be of a certain minimum economic level. Given these caveats, it is accurate to say that this group of poets and poems does not reflect any one editorial aesthetic bias, nor does it reflect the regional or aesthetic bias of any group of people or "club." Instead, we have here the combined poetic gifts of 258 women and one man, all engaged in the common endeavor to write the best poems possible in a time of wildly conflicting aesthetic messages and great political pressures. The poems here are given in the spirit of our shared joy in the art. We hope that you will share that joy in return.

Annie Finch

April 2007

Introduction

1.

Letters to the World is the first book publication from the Discussion of Women's Poetry List (WOM-PO), commonly known as Wom-po. And its birth has been breathtaking, but hardly a surprise. Wom-po, the leading listserv in women's poetry and poetics, has for nearly a decade inspired poems, blogs, essays, readings, syllabi, conference presentations, and spin-off lists. It has become a significant force in contemporary poetry—so much so that when *Poetry* published an "Exchange (on Women's Poetry)" in January 2006 that neglected to mention Wom-po (O'Rourke), subscriber Robin Kemp promptly educated them (2006).

Annie Finch invited me to join Wom-po in February 1998, when I was a graduate student seeking a hospitable e-mail discussion list about poetry. I had seen Annie Finch and Kathrine Varnes at the West Chester Poetry Conference in 1996, and the following year I found both contributing to another online poetry discussion. At one point, Finch posed a question about women's poetry, and I emerged from "lurking" with a post that quoted a relevant paragraph from Sandra M. Gilbert and Susan Gubar's *No Man's Land*.[1] Scarcely twelve hours had passed before a male on the list "flamed" me, denouncing Gilbert and Gubar as having absolutely nothing to offer any literary discussion. I responded in a placatory manner: in an earlier career as a literary editor, I had grown accustomed to harangues from misogynist poets, and I thought that engaging them wasted time. So I was surprised by Finch's response. She not only sent me a private e-mail thanking me for my suggestion, but also posted a sharp retort to the flamer: Would Yale University Press bother to publish a series of massive scholarly volumes from writers with nothing to offer? The flamer apologized to Finch, but not to me. Now, I was angry. So when Finch asked if I'd like to join her women's poetry discussion group, I gratefully moved camp to No Man's Land.

Finch had founded Wom-po two months earlier, in December 1997. That month, the list membership grew from an original cluster of five to approximately thirteen. In addition to Finch, those posting the first month include Wendy Battin, Catherine Daly, Marilyn Hacker, Rachel Loden, Gwyn McVay, Marilyn Nelson, Judy Roitman, Susan Schultz, Kathrine Varnes, and Elizabeth M. Waldner. Several of these poets subscribed to other poetry and poetics listservs, but, like me, objected to aggressive grandstanding and longed to channel their energies toward developing an informed and lively discussion about poetry. In her first official post, Finch brought up a "procedural" question: Wom-po had been originally conceived as a "woman-only space," but should it remain that way? (18 December 1997). Consensus supported the original plan, and the conversation quickly turned to one of Wom-po's goals: giving women poets and their poetry the attention they deserved.

---

[1] This introduction uses terms commonly employed by Wom-po and other electronic mailing lists ("listservs"). One listserv subscriber normally communicates with others by "posting," or sending a message ("post") to the host server, which then forwards the message to all subscribers. Subscribing to a listserv and reading the posts without contributing is known as "lurking." Online communities use the term "flame" to signify "an angry or abusive e-mail message from one user to another" ("Flame," 2004). See Susan Herring for research on flaming, gender, and online rhetoric in the 1990s (1999).

Yet before Finch could add "women-only" to the official invitation, a "guy" posted to the list in March 1998 (Paris). He soon unsubscribed, but not before making a valid point. Although Wom-po needed to spring from the words, the lives, and the spirits of women poets, keeping men out of the garden as a rule would be both unenforceable and counterproductive. Males quietly joined and lurked, and Jeffrey Levine finally revealed his presence with "Fear and Trembling" (4 April 2000). By Wom-po's fourth birthday, Finch spoke for most of us when she welcomed the "supportive, thoughtful and tactful company" of not only Levine, but also Ron Silliman, David Graham, and Gabriel Gudding (15 December 2001).

Now with over 600 subscribers, Wom-po has developed into a rich and inspiring literary culture, facets of which shine in the short essays set among these poems. One of the list's particular strengths is its multigenerational mix of poets, critics, and poetry readers who vary in degrees of experience and fame. A young activist poet like Tara Betts finds networks of experienced artists in Wom-po, who greet her with "an opening of arms, a firm hand on the shoulder." For Judith Arcana, Wom-po is a zone in which she is "imagining [herself] into a generative old woman who spends her days making art with words." Joyce Nower historicizes the list in the context of the feminist movement: Wom-po continues the legacy of Second and Third Wave feminism in its "affirmation" of women's "sense of internal authority." In addition, "the rich sources of information that Wom-po members offer one another daily forge the connection between being a woman and a poet."

At its best, the list encourages reflective conversations that stimulate creativity. As Jean Anaporte-Easton writes, "One of the great gifts of Wom-po for me has been the women who have described the struggle to grant themselves permission to do their own kind of creative work, conventions and traditions be damned." Wendy Vardaman recalls one hot debate over the color pink ("this seemingly innocuous color") in defending her own aesthetic choices and arguing for more "tolerance, not to mention imagination" in discussing women's creativity. Online writing workshops draw from list subscribers: Patricia Brody and Kathrine Varnes each celebrate their thriving sonnet groups. Sharon Dolin and Glenna Luschei show Wom-po as a generous resource of poems for teaching and ceremonial occasions, and Arielle Greenberg traces her poet-moms listserv to her years on Wom-po. Every Monday the "Gazette," edited by Diane Lockward, lists wompos' readings and events for the week, as well as recent publications and prizes.

In addition to its inspirational force, Wom-po functions as a virtual community, supporting women poets in our historical struggle with isolation, both social and geographic. As Charlotte Mandel explains, even much-published poets may want for colleagues if they begin publishing later in life, without formal networks. Helen Ruggieri, who lives in a small town near the border of New York and Pennsylvania, remarks that "Wom-po was a step out of the isolation ward into visiting hours." Ann Fisher-Wirth describes having felt "eclipsed" as a woman poet in Oxford, Mississippi, until she found Wom-po's "poetry family." Kelli Russell Agodon appreciates the way wompos participate in "conversations that stretch from Seattle to England and down to New Zealand." Farideh Hassanzadeh-Mostafavi writes from Tehran. Expatriate and English-speaking poets such as Anny Ballardini, Margo Berdeshevsky, and Ren Powell post from Europe, and Moira Richards initiated this anthology from South Africa. Of course Wom-po hosts plenty of lurkers, but Athena Kildegaard and Lois Roma-Deeley prefer the term "listener." As Roma-Deeley puts it,

I guess what I love most about this forum is the listening in—my ear against the door of this great gathering of poets who share my passion, my will, my love of craft, and the constant thrill of poetic astonishment.

Despite Wom-po's primary focus on women's poetry and poetics, the sense of community among "unacknowledged legislators" inevitably provokes discussion about the languages of public life and contemporary culture. Here, Margaret Ricketts expresses her concern for American civil liberties. Ana Doina, who grew up in Ceausescu's Romania, reflects on common western literary conversations concerning the "death of poetry," and she argues "Whoever doesn't think of poetry as changing the world does not consider the world I know."

Wom-po has sought an inclusive membership from the start, and wompos often illuminate and challenge one another's unspoken or unquestioned assumptions. For Shayla Mollohan, Wom-po and a spin-off writing workshop enable her to "enjoy in my daily life all the companionship, education, resources, and ordinary human connections available to any able-bodied person I know." Many wompos seek and offer language to overcome a white, western cultural inheritance in poetry, art, and criticism. Although, as Lesley Wheeler points out, "[m]ost wompos know each other only as disembodied text on glowing screens," she and Mendi Lewis Obadike write insightfully about how race and racial awareness manifest themselves on the list. Deema K. Shehabi asks if Wom-po, being of its time in history, is "also prone to the empire's complex prejudices." She hopefully imagines a "blending of values between East and West, North and South so that there's a wide, inclusive agenda distilled from our diversity."

As a poetry resource, Wom-po deepens members' understanding of well-known foremothers such as Gwendolyn Brooks, Edna St. Vincent Millay, and Muriel Rukeyser. This anthology's title, "Letters to the World," honors Emily Dickinson's opening lines "This is my letter to the World / That never wrote to me—". Talk of Sylvia Plath emerges and submerges as new generations of wompos join the list. Contemporary writers Anne Carson, Jorie Graham, Ann Lauterbach, Harryette Mullen, Marie Ponsot, and C. D. Wright (to name only a few) are also discussed. Recurring themes in women's poetry—sexuality, maternity, women's reproductive lives, women's spirituality—are explored with a depth and candor found nowhere in print. One of the more profound features, the "Friday Foremother" custom, resurrects the lives and works of women poets from earlier generations, poets whose books were lost and names forgotten, until now. Each week, one wompo introduces the rest of us to a new "Foremother," thus slowly and meticulously drawing us closer to one of Finch's hopes for the list: to reconnect women poets with their traditions (10 March 2006).

2.

As Finch indicates in her Preface, Moira Richards—in active collaboration with listserv members—first planned and then implemented the compilation of this anthology. Richards' original intent was to create a print-on-demand (POD) book, and with this purpose in mind, she established a temporary blog ("CWJ: form," 17 November 2005). Entitled "Community Wom-po Journal" (CWJ), the blog comprised poems and biographies from wompos who contributed as they saw fit. Submissions guidelines were simple:

> The cwj is accepting one poem, previously published or unpublished from every wompo (man or woman) who wishes to be part of this book.[2]
> (Richards, 1 December 2005)

---

[2] In block quotations, I quote the original listserv postings as originally typed, although I have corrected obvious typos, and line and paragraph breaks vary from the originals. Ellipses in square brackets are mine.

Wompos volunteered to "advise, mentor, encourage" (Richards, 1 December 2005), and those volunteers eventually became the editorial teams for this anthology. In the Afterword, Richards, Rosemary Starace, and Lesley Wheeler discuss the unusual collaborative nature of this anthology and its production, from blog to book.

Richards' initiative sprang from a long discussion about editorial and publishing practices, a discussion that included the kinds of complaints we poets often make when fighting frustration at the hands of our unseen editors and judges. Yet editors and publishers also contribute to Wom-po, and two responded with constructive comments. Susan Bright, a poet who runs Plain View Press, urged that wompos rethink their attitudes toward the conventional mode of seeking publication. She dismissed the idea of authors who wait passively for a publisher to discover them, and who expect that publisher to manage all the hard work of editing and promoting:

> Waiting to be "picked" is not empowering. Expecting to have everything done for one is even less so. And it doesn't insure good art. I favor a model in which people work together in a community to create art [. . .]
> (12 November 2005)

Jeffrey Levine from Tupelo Press agreed and added,

> Poetry is a sacred trust. If we want to keep it alive and vital we need to stop complaining and recognize that each and every one of us needs to participate in this mission as fully as humanly possible—in the writing, reading, and support of poetry, of our journals and our presses. [. . .] Want more responsive journals? Want poetry presses that can afford to say yes more often? Want a renaissance of poetry in America? Determine to make it happen. Make it happen.
> (12 November 2005)

Two days later, Richards took up Levine's "gauntlet" and proposed "a WOMPO anthology produced by us, a collective venture." In less than a week, the CWJ blog was ready to receive poems (Richards, "cwj—the blog," 17 November 2005). Rachel Dacus submitted the first poem, and other wompos quickly followed.

The blog, its guidelines, and publication plans unfolded together as a highly charged conversation. After a vexed exchange about editorial screening, Richards considered the majority's leanings and wrote:

> So, I'm going to try running with [the] least possible editorial screening and see how the book looks on the blog. If we find that we have ended up with an undisciplined, vanity, sub-standard, unprintable mess, then we can relook the submission guidelines : -)
> (1 December 2005)

Finch encouraged wompos to consider the focus of the list and to send

> poems about women poets, about being a woman poet, or reading women's poetry, or discussing women's poetry, or, barring that, about poetry in general, or women in general. I know I will

keep that theme, the discussion of women's poetry, in mind when thinking about which poem of my own to send.

(5 December 2005)

During the first two weeks of December, Richards continued fielding questions, suggestions, and challenges concerning the blog and POD production.[3] Meanwhile, volunteer Eloise Klein Healy was thinking that a "serious publisher" should be considered; she informed her own publisher, Kate Gale, of the work-in-progress (2007). After reviewing the initiative online, Gale found that it matched her "passion as an editor for promoting women's work" (2007). On 14 December, Finch hinted to the list that a "real publisher" was interested in the anthology, and the following day, Gale introduced herself and announced that she "would be willing to publish it."[4]

Although the poems included here have not been "picked" or thematically arranged, threads of Finch's suggested themes do appear. Finch's poem, "Letter for Emily Dickinson," considers the poet's profound influence on her, and her struggles under that influence. As the speaker crafts her poem—cutting and pinning like a seamstress—she finds that her words cannot be pinned down, and still in some ways belong to foremother Dickinson: "I take from you as you take me apart." Like Finch, many of us contributed poems clearly acknowledging sources of influence and inspiration in other foremothers or contemporaries. Patricia Brody cites Lady Caroline Lamb; Diane Gage, Anne Sexton; Maryanne Hannan, Audre Lorde; Carol Peters, Lyn Hejinian; Karen L. Lewis, Adrienne Rich; Evie Shockley, Gwendolyn Brooks; and Caroline Williamson invokes both Marianne Moore and Elizabeth Bishop. (And, yes, Walt Whitman and Lawrence Ferlinghetti merit mentions too, thanks to Kim Roberts and Catherine Daly, respectively.) Do we suffer from Harold Bloom's "anxiety of influence," or Gilbert and Gubar's "anxiety of authorship"? I would like to think that Wom-po has guided us toward a wiser attitude, in which we may openly pay homage to our foremothers and forefathers, perpetuating their names and works, while patiently working toward what is distinctively ours.

The blog home page urged wompos to "watch the cwj grow!" That invitation, Wom-po history, and the nature of any blog prompted us to contribute poems that responded to themes, images, styles, and forms discussed on Wom-po, or evident in works already submitted. Here, one can find poetic connections the way one finds poems. Eloise Klein Healy and David Graham bring teaching poems, echoing multiple Wom-po threads on poetry education and performance. Alicia Ostriker's famous "Everywoman Her Own Theology" holds a special place here, given that women's spirituality has always been a popular Wom-po topic. Poems by Kate Bernadette Benedict, Marcia Falk, Kathleen Flenniken, Cindy Williams Gutiérrez, and Susan Firghil Park are among many that relate to this theme—in Flenniken's case, hilariously.

Another correspondence derives from the first poem submitted to the blog, Rachel Dacus's ekphrastic "Femme au chapeau," which meditates on Henri Matisse's brilliantly-colored painting of his wife. The speaker observes the *chapeau's* "crushing fruit, its dour antiquity," then imagines the subjected wife anticipating a life even more dazzling and explosive than the painting itself:

---

[3] For some examples, see archival discussions from December 2005: "Anthology, non-profit: what next?" and "cwj—pleasing some, some of the time."

[4] See Finch, "using the wompo name," (14 December 2005), and Gale, "CWJ: Vote Tallying," (15 December 2005).

Who will I be, Henri, when I come to fruition?
As a woman all rainbow atomic ignition.

Both Jessica G. de Koninck's "Chagall's Windows" and Felice Aull's "Alice Neel Paints a Portrait" speak to "Femme au chapeau" in that they share the ekphrastic strategy: "Chagall's Windows" also finds an objectified female figure in a male artist's work, and conjures an inner life for her. But "Chagall's Windows" expands the feminist aesthetic theme by transforming Chagall's famous dream imagery into a nightmare of 9/11. Aull's poem raises another question about the role of gender in ekphrasis: what happens to the representation of women when a female poet writes of the work of a female artist? Thus, these three poems, like any good conversational exchange, meet, connect, and take off in new directions.

Yet this anthology also reflects an immediate context, of Thanksgiving 2005. Three months prior to the blog's inception, Hurricanes Katrina and Rita slammed into the Gulf Coast, and ruptured levees flooded most of New Orleans. The city and region were still devastated, and wompos directly affected were preoccupied with survival and hurricane relief. Thanksgiving brought occasion to reflect on spiritual and poetic as well as material need. Where to find the words for what happened? Beverly Rainbolt's "The Text Is Dead—Long Live the Text" suggests that we start with the "random" poetry of magnetic kits to "explain the way / things change so quickly." Mendi Lewis Obadike's "Strut" resurrects joyful New Orleans nights of times past, while Malaika King Albrecht, Wendy Taylor Carlisle, Carolyn Whittle, and Abe Louise Young bear witness to the disaster, observing its horrors and miracles, and praying passionately for Home.

Rosemary Starace's essay declares, *I belong to Wom-po because I say I belong*, a rallying cry that embodies the rambunctious, eloquent, and generous spirit of the list. And I believe her concluding words best wrap up this Introduction:

I, or anyone, can participate in this vibrant, vital, credible world arena on the merit of words alone, without having to brandish particular credentials or think or write in a particular way. Knowledge, experience, insight can fly across the great divides—in both directions. All of us individuals, and poetry itself, may benefit from this exchange. This is a personally empowering and perhaps world-changing situation—and a most significant aspect of this anthology.

D'Arcy Randall
March 2007

Works Cited

"Anthology, non-profit, what next?" Online discussion. Discussion of Women's Poetry List. December 2005. (Accessed 25 March 2007.) <http://lists.usm.maine.edu/archives/wom-po.html>

Bright, Susan. "Lit Journals—Community or Hierarchy?" Online posting. Discussion of Women's Poetry List. 12 November 2005. (Accessed 3 October 2006.) <http://lists.usm.maine.edu/archives/wom-po.html>

"cwj—pleasing some, some of the time." Online discussion. Discussion of Women's Poetry List. December 2005. (Accessed 25 March 2007.) <http://lists.usm.maine.edu/archives/wom-po.html>

Finch, Annie. "Anthology, non-profit: what next?" Online posting. Discussion of Women's Poetry List. 5 December 2005. (Accessed 3 October 2006.) <http://lists.usm.maine.edu/archives/wom-po.html>

———. "happy birthday wompo." Online posting. Discussion of Women's Poetry List. 15 December 2001. (Accessed 3 October 2006.) <http://lists.usm.maine.edu/archives/wom-po.html>

———. "here we are !!" Online posting. Discussion of Women's Poetry List. 18 December 1997. (Accessed 3 October 2006.) <http://lists.usm.maine.edu/archives/wom-po.html>

———. Personal interview. 10 March 2006.

———. "using the wompo name." Online posting. Discussion of Women's Poetry List. 14 December 2005. (Accessed 25 March 2007.) <http://lists.usm.maine.edu/archives/wom-po.html>

"Flame." Def. 1. *Oxford Dictionary of Computing*. Oxford: Oxford University Press, 2004.

Gale, Kate. "CWJ: Vote Tallying." Online posting. Discussion of Women's Poetry List. 15 December 2005. (Accessed 25 March 2007.) <http://lists.usm.maine.edu/archives/wom-po.html>

———. Personal correspondence. 12 March 2007.

Gilbert, Sandra M. and Susan Gubar. *No Man's Land: The Place of the Woman Writer in the Twentieth Century.* New Haven: Yale University Press, 1988–1994.

Healy, Eloise Klein. Personal correspondence. 12 March 2007.

Herring, Susan. "The Rhetorical Dynamics of Gender On-Line." *Information Society.* 15.3 (July–September 1999): 151–167.

Kemp, Robin. Letter to the Editor. *Poetry.* March 2006. (Accessed 3 October 2006.) <http://www.poetrymagazine.org/letters/archive/0306.html>

Levine, Jeffrey. "Fear and Trembling." Online posting. Discussion of Women's Poetry List. 4 April 2000. (Accessed 3 October 2006.) <http://lists.usm.maine.edu/archives/wom-po.html>

———. "Lit Journals—Community or Hierarchy?" Online posting. Discussion of Women's Poetry List. 12 November 2005. (Accessed 3 October 2006.) <http://lists.usm.maine.edu/archives/wom-po.html>

O'Rourke, Meghan, J. Allyn Rosser, and Eleanor Wilner. "Exchange (on Women's poetry)." *Poetry* January 2006: 318–329.

Paris, Michael. "another discussion." Online posting. Discussion of Women's Poetry List. 24 March 1998. (Accessed 3 October 2006.) <http://lists.usm.maine.edu/archives/wom-po.html>

Richards, Moira. "cwj—the blog." Online posting. Discussion of Women's Poetry List. 17 November 2005. (Accessed 3 October 2006.) <http://lists.usm.maine.edu/archives/wom-po.html>

———. "CWJ: form, purpose, content." Online posting. Discussion of Women's Poetry List. 17 November 2005. (Accessed 24 March, 2007.) <http://lists.usm.maine.edu/archives/wom-po.html>

———. "Lit Journals—Community or Hierarchy?" Online posting. Discussion of Women's Poetry List. 14 November 2005. (Accessed 3 October 2006.) <http://lists.usm.maine.edu/archives/wom-po.html>

———. "Submission guidelines + call." Online posting. Discussion of Women's Poetry List. 1 December 2005. (Accessed 3 October 2006.) <http://lists.usm.maine.edu/archives/wom-po.html>

WOMPO—Discussion of Women's Poetry List. <http://www.usm.maine.edu/wompo/index.html>

DIANA ADAMS

Trees

Deep in the lungs of green, a catch
of knives so sharp—yet we keep
putting bright things in their hair.

No one talks to them anymore. Thieves
don't come out, no one naps or spreads out
red squares for chicken bits. No, nothing

marches out into the sun after being lost
or led by leopards. A shelter for fat
country beasts that eat themselves—

I don't like it. I see how they're tall
amidst squabbles, or bent low
to catch grave whispers. Waving

dead arms in air they probe
our dark hotels, grow children
close to their feet.

Longest Night

The shadows name me. They pull me underneath their tide,
their raven waters trap me in their depth and thrust.
The small dark hours throw the soul full wide.

The window glass reflects the twilight dyed
with chalky grit. I watch bright whorls of frost
outline my shadow, then shatter in the unnamed tide.

I look away. I know what waits inside
my heart on winter days when I have lost.
The small dark hours throw the soul full wide

into the frozen waves. Snowflakes glide
to earth, fill emptiness—despite the cost—
even the nameless, shadowed furrows of the tide.

In drowsy light, I push away my pride.
It billows out like curtains full of dust.
The small dark hours throw the soul full wide.

In pairs, pier lamps blink on. Powdered snow slides
past the yellow pools to vanish as it crosses
shadowed solstice light. I name the tide,
the small dark hours. Throw the soul full wide.

KELLI RUSSELL AGODON

In the 70's, I Confused Macramé and Macabre

I

I wanted the macabre plant holder
hanging in Janet and Chrissy's apartment.
My friend said her cousin tried to kill himself
by putting his head through the patterns
in his mother's spiderplant hanger, but
the hook broke from the ceiling and he fell
knocking over their lava lamp, their 8-track player.
His brother almost died a week later when
he became tangled in the milfoil at Echo Lake.
I said it could have been a very
macramé summer for that family.

II

When I looked outside for sticks to make a God's Eye
to hang on my bedroom wall, I found a mouse
flattened, its white spine stretching past its tail.
And a few feet from that,
a dead bird with an open chest,
its veins wrapped tightly together.
This neighborhood with its macramé details
crushed into the street. I wanted
my mother to remind me
that sometimes we escape.
But when I returned to my house
it was empty, except for the macabre owl
my mother had almost finished, its body left
on the kitchen table, while she ran out to buy more beads.

We Can't Step into the Same River Twice

My daughter's worried that the Live Oaks in City Park
can't breathe underwater,
and the ducks that bit her small hands full of bread,
"Who will feed them?"
She imagines the Aquarium fish swimming away
quick as the silver flashes
of our pond's minnows, only freer. The elephants,
large as memory, will wade out
like ships from the zoo and rescue smaller animals.

But a poem's not a life line,
and the poet, not a boat. These places burning
and flooding at the same time,
these buildings where I've said to my daughter,
"This is where you were born,
and your father and his father. Your great grandparents
were married at St. Louis Cathedral.
Grandma Cherry used to say the gardenias in New Orleans
bloomed so sweetly that the bees
flew drunkenly into her kitchen windows all afternoon.
And here, here's where your father
and I met. Because this is there, we are here."

But we aren't *here* anymore.
Nobody predicts when it will stop, and no one
when anything will begin again.
My friend's daughter kneels, thanks God for her house
that has a tree on it.
She'll start kindergarten elsewhere in borrowed plaid uniforms.
On TV the city's sounds
are dozens of dogs calling for someone across this filthy
slow moving water.
A man and a pregnant woman paddle an air mattress with brooms
to anyplace else. "The city is a bowl."
An anchor says again, "The city is a bowl" until I too
am too full.

MEENA ALEXANDER

Triptych in a Time of War

I.
Why hunch at the screen chipping syllables, chewing up rhyme?
You're no Forugh Farrokhzad, registered 678 in the sun's throat—
counting out jewels in the city street, dead in a car crash, aged thirty-two.

You're older by far, thrice failed your driving test,
never visited a leprosarium or Zahir al-Doleh cemetery in Tehran
where trees leak snow.

Where she whispers as a child might, smoking burnt-out tips,
a slip of a thing dressed in white rags
filled with light—

I did it, I got myself registered,
dressed myself up in an ID with a name.
So long 678... O rattling law!

II.
O the bomb is fear's flower
there is no love in the bomb,
only chaos, the sea must swallow.

The flowers of Mesopotamia are tiny, blue edged,
driven under the skin of earth. But where can children hide?
The mouth of the cave is rimmed with red.

Spring brings the golden mustard seed and clouds of war
float over the ziggurat of Ur.
Enheduanna is poised on an alabaster disc.

She has nose breasts hands a poet needs, also
that sweet etcetera, dark flower who sheds blood and eggs and praises
to be sung at twilight into the high hold of heaven.

You remember her and Forugh too who fought against pain.
Their stanzas flicker on the internet,
you flee a windowless office,

climb the stairs to the eighth floor, enter a high room.
Light spills through sloping glass,
clouds drift and float,

you hear the clatter of knives in the cafeteria.
On an eastern wall the Dove of Tanna,
wings raised, mute blessing in a time of need.

The artist born a year after Forugh, cut up aluminium for the dove's tail
infolding fire, icon of earth struck free of flood waters,
pediment of peace beneath the arrow's flight.

You have come to a high room
in search of language that could tell of love,
of love alone, uncumbered, and to search for it, as for justice

even in the guise of what has no words and cannot speak
and must lie down in the dark
hungry and unappeased.

III.
Out of the spotted beak of the dove,
out of the olive tree axed into bits,
out of blood a child touches to her lips murmuring words no one else can hear,

out of the eyes of the woman who stands shock still in sunlight
and flings open the door
and Bombay rushes in a tiger that brings her to her knees:

a vividness of island sky and wind,
(she strolls by a slurry wall that held back island waters after catastrophe)
visionary company, electric water, fiery wind

where what is torn and severed slips out of soiled skin,
is seized in simple nakedness,
named and healed.

So turning to little bits of wisdom—do not hurt, do not cut,
love in all the right places and the wrong.
There is no fault in love.

The boughs know this cracking free of winter
in the cemetery where Forugh's body lies,
so too the Dove of Tanna.

It takes flight from the eastern wall of 365 Fifth Avenue
and settles on the ziggurat of Ur
by a crater where a bomb burst.

Returning to the office without walls
you hear Enheduanna cry
O the ziggurat of Ur is crowned with doves!

You hear her words unfurl on the screen,
bare sound, filled with longing,
syllables of raw silk, this poem

Composed March 7–26, 2003, New York City.

The poet Forugh Farrokhzad (1935–67) lived in Teheran and wrote fierce, dazzling poems; the lines in italics in section 1 are taken from her poem "O Bejewelled Land." I have drawn on the translation by Hasan Javadi and Susan Sallee in their book Another Birth, Selected Poems of Forugh Farrokhzad (Emeryville, Albany Press, 1981) Enheduanna (circa 2300 BCE) is the earliest poet known in recorded history. She lived in Mesopotamia—her likeness is to be found on an alabaster disc preserved in the University of Pennsylvania museum. The creator of Dove of Tanna is Frank Stella; the artwork hangs on the eastern wall of the atrium at 365 Fifth Avenue, CUNY Graduate Center.

REN POWELL

Essay

Last night a friend of mine said that, as a writer, like all writers, he was in a kind of exile before he ever became a political exile. I would never describe myself as exiled because I have several friends who have been imprisoned for their writing, who live here because going home might mean death. They live in exile. I live in a self-imposed double enclave: the enclave of the writer and the enclave of an American living abroad.

I belong to the writer's union here in Norway, I'm active in PEN and other writers' groups, but even after 13 years the subtext of discourse is still sometimes incomprehensible to me. Deciphering conversations peppered with cultural allusions is like trying to read around the blackened parts of a censored document.

I guess I don't need to say that writing poetry—publishing poetry here, where I live—sometimes seems futile, or egocentric. But what is worse, is that when I read a poem that touches me deeply, it's difficult to share. There's no local community that understands the specifics, the subtleties of the language, the cultural references that provide poignancy. I can't share a joyful little "hmm" with a group of people. That's why Wom-po is important to me. It's the link to my literary culture. I can feel the vibrations of the virtual "hmm."

The women (and men) on the list have given me my literary education. Given is the key word. They have and continue to give freely out of their love of the language. Poems, poets, booklists. And they've forgiven misdirected e-mails, knee-jerk outbursts, misspellings, and rotten grammar.

I know that at times the list is too political for some members, but I like that aspect of the group. I enjoy the passion and activism. Things do get tense now and then. I "go digest" for a few weeks. Then I come back. I have to come back.

KELLY LENOX ALLAN

Untitled

Beyond the window
a garden blooms in full sun—
fly beating the glass.

CELIA LISSET ALVAREZ

What It Takes to Be Lois Lane

At twenty-one she graduated magna cum laude
with a degree in English. Her first apartment
had a leaky faucet that kept her up nights
and a view of the bridge to Metropolis.

Her shoes pinched as she walked
handing over typed carbon copies of her resumé
explaining once again that she was not interested
in the secretary position, although she was
good at steno and really appreciated
that comment about her legs.

Late nights with the stray cat
who got in through the fire escape
(she called him Elroy), she looked
out the window and dreamed of uncovering
corruption in the city government.

Her first week at the *Daily Planet*
they made her get coffee for the fellas,
and assigned her a story on the Junior League.

Writing back to Sam and Ella, she asked
about the weather in Pittsdale, said hello to Lucy,
and could you please send a little money,
although I'm doing just fine.

When those naked pictures Jimmy Olsen took
somehow wound up in *Playboy,* she went missing
for three days. Some say they saw her with Lex Luthor
in Detroit, sipping screwdrivers and go-go dancing
around the Metro area in white cowboy boots.

At work in her ruffled collar and solid pumps
she looked only at her typewriter. Promptly at five,
she walked into the phone booth, closed the door,
and screamed for fifteen minutes. Nights with Elroy
and the faucet, she meditated on her chakras, placing
the green crystal Lex gave her on her flat,
grumbling navel.

IVY ALVAREZ

length

I could collect
basketfuls of my hair
knit a little rug from
what I've shed

you could weave a carpet
lay down whole rooms
a house
down the street
and out into the highway
with yours

a full twenty years on me
plus the chemotherapy
you've got a head start

the miles you could've covered
with your hair

JEAN ANAPORTE-EASTON

poem for the new year

Orange flower Blood blossom Heart pulse
stand for our sun in the marbled winter sky.

I awake in dark.
Small harness bells
chime as if nestled

in clusters of long-needle pine
bobbing like necks of restive horses.

Work days i wake a long train coming at me,
the things i have to do. So that's what i become
when i'm done hiding in bed.

My fears like knives at my throat
my right to breathe a question.

                    Breathe then. Anyway.

Can i wrap my arms around that?

Orange flower Blood blossom Heart pulse
straight from the body
breathe.
                    I surrender my tiny polished
silver knives my ignorance my anger my bags of poison.
Let them fizzle up into the veined sky.

Let the pine trees with the bells and the orange sun
those blossoms
let them weave me a hammock of light.
I lie down, i surrender.
I give myself to this net of light i first saw when it caught my daughter and
                                        held.

Let the drawing in of breath be a blessing. Let the expelling of breath be a
                                        blessing.

Lie back in this hammock of light.

JUDITH ARCANA

Facts of Life

—for Ruella

You don't have to stand in the street, six-guns
glinting high noon sun; you don't have to be
American, sixteen and angry at the teacher.
All that we do, living, is killing; birth
and death the pumping hearts of life.
What's born is born from death. Every cell
inside us, every cell that makes us; skin
of our faces, facing each other with cells
falling away, cells rising: lips, eyelashes,
cheekbones dying, being born.

Beyond these facts of life, involuntary
cellular facts, what counts is the voluntary
thinking creature living beyond fact,
inside metamorphosis. Crucial in moments
of transition (all moments being
moments of transition) is that inside
the taking and giving, you are conscious.
You are responsible. You know.
So when you decide to open the bottle,
count pills out with your fingers, turn
up the morphine with your thumb,
switch the electric current off – or on,
push the plunger of the syringe,
shoot straight fast into the body
of someone you don't know, release
the catch of the bomb bay, cut down
the field of ripened rye, pull off
all the berries, pluck the reddest apples,
cut the throat of the biggest ram
or the smallest lamb, close the eyes
of the very old dog, the senile cat
who slept years in the curve of your back,
you know. You know everything.

MARILYN ARNOLD

Messages

Mummy's run away from daddy.
She's in the women's shelter
obsessing over leaving;
He's stalking her with text messages.
She replies, hoping to appease;
All night I hear the music of her mobile phone.

My sister scratches runes, cuts secrets
into fresh skin, skips school;
says she knows enough already—
Teachers can't read her future like she can.
All day she whittles away at fear
till her arm's a map of hidden journeys.

And I have dreams—our house on fire,
all of us running to dowse the flames
with tiny cups of water;
the red queen surrounded by hundreds of children;
phone in hand, she's calmly pressing buttons,
O.......... f.......... f..........
Off with their heads,
Off
with
their
heads.

RENÉE ASHLEY

The Weaving: Her Voice
(Another Poem About Penelope)

How little I understand! at best, the rhythm of the dependable sun on the flinty water, the weaving
of the steady moon amidst the waves — yes, and time like a shower of arrows. The sea
changes. But what makes men wander? Neither unspent lust nor lack of love! Ripe with rumor, men
crawl, promise laid out behind them like slime behind slugs, penises tucked in their dark places
like bags of wine or salted meat slung below deck — and off they go, the swine. Tell
me — what dreams must they run from? what can they be thinking of? Not wives. Not sons.

Even long before the boy was born, his father's eyes cast out to sea, and our shared sun
strung ribbons of light on its surface, threw them down on the waves, wove
the sticky net. And he watched it like a blind man watching — no telling
what he imagined there, or what his weak gods showed him. I looked too, and saw the sea —
just that. Water and light, in depths like barrows. Idiocy in honor's guise: to displace
lovers, fathers—Bah! We are not fishes, not fishes' wives. The sea's no place for men

at all! But husbands are such royal asses. They can't just look. Oh, those women
are no secret. And I'm no fool. I'm a pretty wild ride myself, and still those liaisons
suck him merrily downstream. He comes back. I take no pride in that. It's commonplace.
But, still, it's the wives that rate a crown: insufferable weaving,
the waiting like thirst, the ravenous welcome with the dog looking on. Oh I can foresee
all that: a beggar's disguise, the long fires of the greedy dead, some tell-

tale music in the emptied hall. Why else would I wait? Some hearts bear witness and never tell
a soul! We are the ships our husbands should cling to! Our tongues are the omens
those men should heed: there is nothing beyond their dreadful sea
but more sea. They're shirkers and stinkers! And what can we tell their sons?
that we stay home? wear our long hair up — and wait? that we bind the strands tightly, weave
them into the dull pattern of our days? Not likely. The mind of a man is the dwelling place

of mystery. No answers there — they're moved by gods, for heaven's sake! Place
your ear here, in the curve of this breast — hear the whisper? That tells
more than seaborne men can ever know. It's the patient heart that weaves
the miracle, not the sunstruck or the loveless. Tell your sons that! What men-
dacity to blame the gods! What cowardice! We build our own prisons.
We make the choices that bend us at the knee. If we wear crowns of sea-

wrack, it's by choice. Such monsters we create! Men drown in a sea
they fill themselves! It's the heart that is the sturdy god. I place
my faith on dry land, then deep in the body. This I'm sure of: it's treason
otherwise. And sacrifice: men pay huge ransoms for their salty lives, then tell
tales, justify their grief with piddling joy, return, spread their semen
thick in the furrows of their wives and assume we've

borne, with grace, their absent seasons — as if we were mere bagatelles to barter
for cocks and cravings! Such ill-placed hope! No acumen at all! Dead men
see more: the risk, the thousand threads of poison woven in persistent hearts — unraveled.

FELICE AULL

Alice Neel Paints a Portrait

of herself at 75, nude, working it
for five more years while breasts
sag lower, belly grows more lax,
body following its own path.
She is seated with weapons—
paint brush and rag. Look
at her watching you, the wall
in blue pastel, blue shadow
on leg and face, her old woman's
whiteness, the eyeglasses
for relentless vision. Look
at Alice seeing herself, knowing
what you will see.

LANA HECHTMAN AYERS

Near Winter Solstice

—for Chard deNiord

A man stands in his yard facing
the gradient of pine
that eventuates to deep woods.

A quiet night as always
in this far from city-lights hamlet.
Cold, but not unpleasant.

The ice in the glass he's holding
rasps, sighs.
He tilts back a long swallow.

The sky has the deep sheen
of crafted mahogany, the stars
are a multitude of fine crystal bells

he can almost hear
summoning him.
Inside the house

there will be cake,
trick candles, singing.
There will be flowing wine,

companionable words.
Soon he will join his party,
but for now he's thinking

about the wind,
how its voice
through the tall dry grass

on this clearest of eves,
sounds so much like rain, so much
like want.

ANNY BALLARDINI

Apples

I remember it was Xmas

                when you arrived
                        arms full with
                                a round wicker basket
                      mistletoe on the threshold
                your hair white with snow
        an electric thrill in the air
"This is for you," you said,
        a broad smile on your face

as happy as a child I looked in & there were
                        some little red and white apples on the bottom
                        covered by short moving gray and black vipers,

"Be careful," you said, "don't touch them—"
at my awe you added,
           "—the apples might be poisoned."

December 2003

HADARA BAR-NADAV

Night with Wings

A fairy drowning
    in a glass of milk
        and a chandelier
    posing as the god

of diamond earrings:
    translucent,
        dangling,
    indifferent.

I've touched
    the fairy's skirt,
        felt the pink
    silk thrill and

gauze of it with my hands.
    (How I envy
        the cat at the bowl,
    rapid white mouthfuls.)

The three old women
    in The Conversation Club
        won't help us.
    So near death

in pointy hats and scarves,
    it may as well be Tuesday,
        the mailman, or any
    ordinary glass of milk.

I'm delighted when
    the milk fairy rises,
        a minikin woman shaking
    the dampness from her wings.

Late for her date
    at the palace of Versailles
        she rushes the heavenly ballroom
    of glass and garish glitter.

The chandelier opens and closes
    its claw of merciless light.
        Alas, I only have my glass
    of milk to kiss goodnight.

JUDITH BARRINGTON

Souls under Water

No longer tumbled by currents as when
long ago they were lodgers in frail bodies,
now they drift free of the flesh that was sucked
and nibbled from bones and the blood that swirled
away, its quick red streaking the deeps.

Souls mingle in the democracy of weed.
Passing through great barnacled bulkheads,
once-passengers, transparent without furs or jewels,
glide through the shiver that marks the presence
of stoker or convict, or the drunken oilman

who one night staggered to the edge of the spider-legged rig
and dreaming of his girlfriend—unusually tender
in his mind at that dizzy moment—plunged through cans
and plastic trash, into the arms of another.
Welcome, said the souls, though his ears heard nothing.

No longer sailors nor slaves, still they remember
the struck bell piercing sleep, the darkness
below decks where rats splashed in the bilges,
the wide-eyed newborn who flew over the deck rail
saved from the plantation by her mother's arm.

Oceans are thick with them: submariners floating
free of their vaults and pilots whose planes dropped
from the sky like giant guillemots but failed to surface
with a catch of fish. The careless were snatched
by sneaker waves, the joyful by cruising sharks

who dispatched them with a lunge and spat out
their splintered surf boards. Some are surprised
to find themselves here, having thought they'd ascend
to the heaven of upper airs or deep star space. But
these *are* the heavens, say the souls: the heavens below.

Lois Roma-Deeley

Essay

I do not post on the Women's Poetry LISTSERV.

I may *never* post—though I often want to. Sometimes I compose whole essays in my head that I would like to post but know I never will. Sometimes, during the day while I am cleaning my office at school or washing clothes at home or taking a walk through the Phoenix desert, I make list of questions I would so much like to ask my sister/brother poets on this list.

I value their answers. Indeed, I am hungry for their thoughts.

Is it shyness? Is that the reason I refuse to post? Yet I seem to have no problem addressing 500 people at a poetry reading, lecturing to a class of 125 students, publishing poems, articles, and books that go into the world and find themselves in the hands *of perfect strangers*. I have no talent for small talk yet have allowed myself to be involved in all the kinds of public relations/poet events connected to television, radio or newspapers. On many occasions, I have—with a respectful tone of voice that would make my mother proud—even answered the question—*so what do you write?* Yet, this list is somehow different. I love listening to not only what is said on the list serve but how it is being said. I love the use of language and the passion behind the language. I love the themes and threads. I even love those moments when the writer has *completely* forgotten that *this* really *is* a conversation which just happens to involve about 600 "writers of distinction" and will be—*forever*—etched inside the internet—I love that moment when the writer forgets all this and—with fierceness of will—*hits* the *send* button *anyway*.

I guess what I love most about this forum is the listening in—my ear against the door of this great gathering of poets who share my passion, my will, my love of craft, and the constant thrill of poetic astonishment.

JEANNE MARIE BEAUMONT

Home in the World

Sometimes when I'm in countries alone
    I look at the stars.
        Once, in San *whatwasit?* (oh, already I'm losing

my travels), where I had placed my feet
    on the footmarks to pee,
        hung

a huge ecstatic red-orange moon
    the kind a god would sink
        his shiny teeth into.

It's sky always and everywhere,
    and gravity, too
        that holds me to the skin

of the planet, but not so stringently
    that I cannot lift my feet
        to wander

a little along a path Etruscan soles
    might have trod.
        Entering a domed tomb room

with my meager travel flashlight
    I found niches, bunks in the walls
        for their bodies, that seemed

sensible and cozy, and I climbed
    back out, and there—sky,
        and the sun winked loudly,

my eyes juiced like grapes
    and I'd burst my skin, also
        delicious, also food

for a god as the earth will one day
    consume me entire
        and refashion my atoms into

a leafy garment for itself. Which is okay.
    Our lives must be shaded, must be tilled.
        These heavenly bodies never leave me.

KIMBERLY L. BECKER

The Fallen Apples

Target fodder for BB guns,
the fallen apples
once were used for apple butter,
pies, dumplings,
or drying—shriveled faces on a rack.

The fallen apples
are fewer now.
The orchard,
once dense with bees,
is sparse.

The fallen apples
fit in the snug of your hand
like the skull of a fetus,
squash under your shoe,
core crushed like soft bone.

How long can trees bear?
Kenosis of growth.
And we lowered the branches
and ate until we were as gods,
knowing good and evil.

The apples, no longer picked, but fallen,
fall with a soft thump.
They roll down the hill and halt.
Like us, they are both sweet and tart.
Like Schiller's apples, their very rot is inspiration.

So much has fallen into ruin:
the house, the barn, our lives, our overripe intentions.

Look: two apples have fallen beside each other.
They look to be red but instead are striated with discoloration.
Companions, they lie and ripen where they fall.
A still life
is still a life.

LYNN BEHRENDT

A Portmanteau Kind of Quiet Evening Filled with Exit Words

—for the Poets

I thought maybe if I could lower my expectations for art—assume that rather than an objective standard of goodness existing 'out there somewhere' I could reconcile myself to a subjective and fickle vehicle for our desires, built on shifting sands, and having more to do with our erotic needs and psychic wounds than some idea of magnificence—then I could release some of this pain. —Ange Mlinko

we try to tithe the words
to fill up this new page

with branches that
winter, shift around, then destroy

the even texture
of the unyielding disease of Language

"I am the forger," God said
but argonauts are all a little mad

whereas in whiteness
a poet is born
with a huge watery head
and the world so real and full of itself.

But let me think now.
What was this evening's designated transcription?

Why is poetry these days always
an anagram of a chronogram
of the hyperhypnogogic to cryptically express
that which is eternally internal?

a clock and its invariant cawing
The gulls

no sleep for cynics

Even the trees are annoyed, Joan Houlihan.
While we dream of living
we're governed by dicks.
dishrags.
The new antibiotics.

then there's this bandage called religion
inserted into the calendar
every April
which is supposed to cleanse
the body of illness
or make a work of art

but the crops fail, and children
are cleft

and you'll never understand

Listen. In a season of stethoscopes
Foucault stepped off the cliff face
unaware of the old measure
taught us that
a star never sets so
we follow Polaris
in our trek
cross the Great Prose Plains

bring a gift
for the angels
and their diatribes

words these days mere
Methodist snake-handling

system broth

beautiful leaves

ba ba blood ram

Psyche watched the stars
fall into a lagoon-shaped vessel called doubt

as the cruel lamp was lit

Is *this* not a waxen hiding place also?

emerge from products
oh ye economic prey

burn the living wood

I've been wandering too far
Odd symbols purport meanings other than what I type
and I worry worry worry worry
I speak to the dead
send inquiries by dream
into a medieval crypt notebook
and I wait for answers . . .

. . . a nest
    a lizard
        a well-known field

           bird before emerging

out of clouds

and into view

these kinds of things I write in the book

here I sit at

a table
hitting objects

the sound and the

fury of fate striking
a percussive pencil tapping on paper

meanwhile a perfect white sphere in the sky

I respect spirits and long for a religion
I, an ancestor of apes, come from the original orchard.

Are we vessels with oars
glowing particles headed in the wrong direction
necessarily oak trees oblivious to our own roots

words from the soil
form the soil

trees to ashes

wash off the machine soot

I remember there was always
suet in the back yard for birds
and a little wooden castle
in the sandbox

Neither the metaphoric asphalt
nor the symbolic family mixture would harden,
so the whole damn batch was ruined.

Why are there jawbones of small dead animals
collected at the edge of every memory?

the human body
is kept safe
only by love

a child
is a star
not included in any constellation
baked in haste
for the gathering

watch for a loss of taste
metal lining of the mouth
pesticide poisoning
let them say we

Rang rang against the vapidity of the Right

The Idea of a Field—
full of reeds
and dried animal urine,
the only sign it had ever been a pasture—

still empty—

behind the river

the flattened coin-like sun sets,
our final offering
to the *Illuminati*

KATE BERNADETTE BENEDICT

Sheela-na-gig

Disquieting, this spectacle of flesh:
hunching hag with massive nether lips.
Her two hands spread them open in a gaping nether leer.
She puts the fear
of God in all who look. All look.

She's said to be a sign of mortal sin,
a warning to the penitent: keep chaste
or fall into a mouth like Sheela's mouth, insatiable.
Monk, layman,
beware the awful chasm of desire.

Or is she more a totem or a charm
whose magic may avert the evil eye?—
for such depictions cast away the devils of the night,
it's said,
who stalk the undefended souls of travelers.

Appalling mouth and mouth beneficent,
portal of death and portal too of life,
you impart a vital power even as you horrify.
That's why
laboring women keep a Sheela near.

If Sheela's mouth could speak! But she is mute,
her open maw of stone, stone still.
Statue strange and numinous, guileless, grotesque,
lewd, squat,
most holy, most unholy, unstatuesque.

MARGO BERDESHEVSKY

But a Passage in Wilderness

i

But a woman prepares to cross the perfumed
river, little crying.

She has left candles placed like birds with folded wings.
When they are lit, she will watch their heartbeats burn.

Sings,
night-sphinx of rivers, am I eye to eye with your light,
or closer to your claw,   tell me this.

Sings the thousand prayers like ponies vying with winners, how
they know the course, but cannot stretch their white-downed spines
to gallop, can't span the fathoms with kicked   light.

Broken-eyed roses, colts, don't fall!
Dark matter of the daily heart, do something beautiful.   Do this.

Between soul and stone, there is grass, its mere and pushing green.

Once, there was a wind heavy as a wilderness, made in its soul to
be without ground, and with song.   Incantation, magic, serenity,
each, so near.

ii

Do not abandon me. (Louise Bourgeois, at 90.)

iii

Here is an autumnal phrasing: Though all
the crimson windows of the season are symphonic,
only the viol's carousel can speak.

Now they veer toward bone, toward tin. These leaves. These
small red hands. But now they burn. Now they grow fine claws,
and spread them. Now they say Our Father, in every language
including silence. How they ask for one true sentence, and a
woman says it: "For sale: love, hardly used." She is no
Renaissance mystic.   Never meant to be.

MARY ROSE BETTEN

My Voice

My voice goes where I'm afraid to go
I tell it *Go on this is America*

It climbs in the driver's seat
I ride shotgun mouth agape
It arrives with me
at the scene
climbs out
sniffs a bit
scratches
moves things around

On its own it begins to speak
Never checks to get my okay
just blurts it all out

It plasters my signature
like a bumper sticker on the fender
jumps in the driver's seat
slams the door and
makes me search for the address

While it drives like a maniac
toward the next happening

KATHRINE VARNES

Essay

Acting quickly before I could talk myself out of it, on March 6, 2005, I posted to Wom-po inviting sonneteers to collaborate in a group crown. I'd written a few crowns myself and enjoyed how the linking refrain between the sonnets served as another volta. Turning so often got me a little dizzy, I'll admit, but in a good way, nothing a little ballet-style spotting couldn't solve.

At the same time, I'd long wanted to try writing Japanese linked poetry but felt too daunted by the many rules to lead such a venture myself. It seemed natural to put the tradition of one with the collaborative nature of the other, but I wasn't sure if anyone else would agree. I expected two replies, hoped for six. I got nearly 30—and from good poets, too, as I learned, with talent, commitment, wild humor, and impressive skills at revisions. From those replies, and with some inevitable drop-outs, we shook out into four collaborative crown writing groups, including wompos Pamela McClure, Charlotte Mandel, Julie Enszer, Marcus Bales, Lana Ayers, Mary Agner; Lesley Wheeler, D'Arcy Randall, Julia Lisella, Julie Kane, Annie Finch, Judith Barrington; Marilyn Taylor, Tatyana Mishel, Emily Lloyd, Amy Lemon, Moira Egan, Patricia Brody; Rosemary Winslow, Meg Schoerke, Robin Kemp, Ann Fisher-Wirth.

Since the last three of the four groups continue in one form or another—one with a seven-part crown titled "Intertidal" forthcoming in *Prairie Schooner*, a second very active group with a circulating 21-sonnet crown "What Lips," as well as three independent off-shoot crowns, and a third more methodical group putting together sonnet seven of ten or 15 as I write—I'm happily in no position to get historical. But our thriving sonneteer subgroups strike me as a testament to Wom-po as a resource, meeting source and community. Long may she wave. And turn.

TARA BETTS

Another Unwilling House

Softened skin from salty sweat as lotion.
Flesh finds sparks for abrupt genesis when
cells race toward guessing games—daughter or son.
No money creases against debts contend-
ing with her copper hopes minted daily
with clock punch, pages turned, grades and checks earned
Latex tears its climactic finale.
Letters pop CLOSED on her brain's blank screen burned
as punctuated sentence and shackles.

Each penny squeezed into her bank of dreams
squandered on uncommitted kisses that
lock her in, heave her beneath parent beams
beyond blueprint drafting her architect
sketches mother once wanted to collect.

PAULA BOHINCE

Acrostic: Queen Anne's Lace

Quietly tatted, silent, they edge the snowball bush—
unlit, without judgment. Theirs is a vision I've always wanted:
eiderdown-colored, stained as lace in a cupboard,
emblems of a softer life.
Neglected, they lean neck and neck with each other.
Audit of sixty years: one tablecloth, one draft card, one confession . . .
No one else to do it: emptying his house of its sorry
nests, cubbyholes filled with flannel and moth-eaten deer heads.
Entropy and decay, he said. *A house is a kind of bondage.*
Strangled, the weeds have no one to kill them. Difficult to
leave them alive, these last witnesses to his last days, who
act blameless, cowering beneath brambles, who
cannot tell me a fraction of what happened. Who did this? You
ears, you idiot eyes that cannot close.

LISA BOURBEAU

Collage

—for Jeka

where you begin   where what is proffered is as much

      what is withheld

white eggs in a blue bowl   impassable sky, transparent —

      each hour's imprint

on the next,   and all trajectory it seems a withdrawing from

      one's own black border. . .

where beginnings   it seems a withdrawal from and, stillness,

      broken like an offered branch

from all intention,   the begun. you want what the nail wants,

      for being driven, place

within itinerate place, morning coffee   as a variant of wind,

      and wood smoke

tangled in a shift of cloud   behind the tethering tree linesyours

      a last lone light.

which was, is, would forever   in its long bones of reflection be

      trapped, offered up, lost,

found, deflected, still,   sparked by the flint of its shadows,

while the shadows, intercepted,   become unstrung, estranged. . .

this is not

how you were meant, not why the river,

which spoke in too many syllables

to gather in any one lifetime,   forswore your being

other than

this, isinglass,   refulgent, increased. beneath

a hundred strokes of night,

the etiolated moon   you thought un-named you

tenders tousled cheeks and childfret,

white roots stirred to waking,   heartchords, stammer,

the inevitable

leap. you accept   each half breath, replication—

beyond name, beyond naming:

custodian of the unslept sleep.   in time there is

no moon not a riderless horse,

burnt pillar. . . seaweed. . . smoke,   no door opened

not a whisper, no feather

not a knife.

KAREN BRAUCHER

Medusa in the Checkout Line

No milk in the fridge
      so here I am,
            pantyhose bunched
    in my dainties.
Hellish day, hemorrhoids,
     and the boss demanded
          umpteen spreadsheets.
     I focus on breathing,
like my shrink always says,
     but still I feel my hair
          lift and sway, spiral, writhe.
     I get jazzed
on the tongues, little red flickers
     in the periphery,
          then the glorious hiss—
     I could go to the front
of the slime! Everyone's
     turned to stone,
         and the cashier
     with averted TV eyes
faints dead away.
     I grab my milk and float
         through the door. Another
            serpentine holiday.

SUSAN BRIGHT

Enheduanna Wrote on Stone

Born ca. 2300 B.C., Enheduanna was a moon priestess, daughter of King Sargon of Agade,
who reigned over the world's first empire, extending from the Mediterranean to Persia.
Enheduanna is the first writer, male or female, in history whose name and work have been
preserved. Her personal history survives in highly political poems. We have a stone disk
which contains a detailed likeness of the high priestess, revealing her particular features
and dress, flanked by three of her retainers. The poetry we have has been preserved on
cuneiform tablets.
—Quotation above and within text are taken from adaptations by Aliki and Willis Barnstone of
"The Exaltation of Inanna," Yale Univ. Press (1968) by William W. Hallo and J. J. A. Van Dijk.

Enheduanna wrote on stone.
The first poet in recorded history was a woman
who wrote political poetry, a woman who gathered symbols,
mysterious and strange for us to see, a woman who cut clay
glyphs in order to catch thought, cut stone words to throw
at the goddess. How dull and heavy the medium, sculpture to
chase fleet passages of mind, heartbeat.

She said:
Like a dragon you have filled the land with venom.
Like thunder when you roar over the earth,
trees and plants fall before you.
You are a flood descending from a mountain,
O primary one,
Moon Goddess Inanna of heaven and earth!
Your fire blows about and drops on our nation,
Lady mounted on a beast.
An gives you these qualities, holy commands,
but you decide.
You are in all our great rites.
Who can understand you?

Enheduanna wrote on stone,
questions about divinity and human suffering,
questions about the vibrant green of spring,
the black green of thunder, the violent green
of torrent, mountain emptying into ocean,
wars so violent earth trembled—

She said:

> *Storms lend you winds, destroyer of the lands.*
> *For you the rivers rise high with blood*
> *and the people have nothing to drink.*
> *The army of the mountain goes to you captive*
> *of its own accord.*

Her stone words fall out of history, pour and tumble,
rough and fierce, into our lives.
It has always been so.
I have been singing this song for so long
my tongue grows thick, numb, cold and sullen,
snake hair, stone face, over and over,
since there were words
we have used them to unmask savage gods.

She said:

> *You have lifted your foot and left*
> *their barn of fertility.*
> *The women of the city no longer speak of love*
> *with their husbands.*
> *At night they do not make love.*
> *They are no longer naked before them,*
> *revealing intimate treasures.*

Words are fast now, fast words:
Words: Deny the violent gods.
Words: Leap through the fire of your soul.
Words: Conquest kills passion.

Words are fast now—
fly from river to sky, continent to ocean, parent to child,
page to heart. In an instant, the entire world could change
its mind. Everything is possible, planets converge,
populations emerge, change, revolt, but it doesn't do any
good—

We worship violent gods.
Enheduanna wrote on stone.
That is what she said.
She said we worship violent gods.

PATRICIA BRODY

Dangerous to Know, Even after Death

Mad, bad, and dangerous to know
—Lady Caroline Lamb's journal entry, on first meeting Lord Byron, 1812

Oh!
was it in woman's nature to hear him,
and not to cherish every word?
It was Glenarvon—that spirit of evil
whom she beheld; her soul trembled within,
and felt its danger.
—Glenarvon, Lady Caroline Lamb, London, 1816

I've been chilling with these dead people,
        not just reading their letters and poems
but going to their balls.

I've been under their clothes
        in their skins,
sticking to dampened petticoats

and floaty muslin.
        I'm at Devonshire House;
Lady Someone is my mother.

At Brocket I'm running through the trees,
        a lordly satyr at my heels, his lip
curled, his brow furred, pale skin agleam,

his hair black as the moors, of course.
        "I know not," I say in some confusion
"but this I believe; the hand of heaven never

impressed on man a countenance
        so beautiful . . ."   Oh if it falls on me—
"What, is it even so?—Heaven defend us!"

There are parties and morning calls,
        dances from Allemagne and Spain
swirling the halls. These *most nervous* affairs!

Fly me, says the mad corsair.
Deep-drugged in the night
I creep from bed, Lord M stretched

senseless beside me.
Down through Georgiana's garden
I fall, down to the white hawthorn

as the mist rises from wet petals
and opium swells in syrupy draughts,
I swoon: For God's sake, sherry!

(Sips from Spain revive me.)
And the susurrous leaves will
waken the heat in my reborn thighs.

Over the moonstones I leap, snapping twigs.
Grass clings to my wingèd soles.
"Do you know what I've done?" sneers he.

"I've heard but I know it is false," I breathe.
"No, I've done what they say," he boasts.
How can I not cry out?

He reaches to crush me into his coat,
his thigh strums through my gown,
I drink his sighs in the moonlight—

broken gasps—*Greek and natural*;
we are so gone, we are so pale,
and his maimed foot throbs in the soil.

ELAINE BROWN

View from the Golden Gate

For Gita

Imagine Oscar Wilde half-naked,
drinking sherry in a pin-striped, pin-leg
suit with pen in hand,
even though it's the angels that record him
now as he recites the plays he wants performed
first in heaven and then on earth. He rides,
occasionally, bareback, on a flying angel
with enormous genitalia (still intact),
its white feathered wings stained crimson,
spots from all the kisses its stone counterpart
receives in Paris. My life's being written
by Oscar Wilde, only now, in heaven,
he's forgotten to be funny. His plays, my life,
now only ironic, clever, and let's face it, biting.
He's bitter being force-fed joy in heaven because
frankly, ecstasy's a little boring.

                                    Cut to you:
flying full swan dive, your black hair
almost-iridescent, your arms spread while you fall
through the mercy of such thin air,
each leg kicking   *tat katta kat tat*
as if you mean to *Kathak* dance
your way to heaven. But this is the part Oscar Wilde
didn't write. They don't want you there,
and you, tricked for a moment into *thinking* you wanted peace,
chose to jump. So, let's stop pretending this is pretty.
Falling from two hundred and fifty feet
(read that: twenty-five stories), you hit
the water going eighty and slam to almost-zero
in a nanosecond (Oscar never heard of *nano-*).
Your face rips clean, split from brow to chin
by that sparkling bay.
Your organs smash as your ribs snap
and you drown in the dark underwater

of your own blood.
Six thousand, four hundred, and fifty feet wide,
you chose the bridge, your last step facing East

                                    O cool, grey city of love!
as you dove for Angel Island.

And this reminds me:
that afternoon in your living room, dancing *Kathak*
to your son's techno, spin after spin *chakkar,*
your feet *tatkar* tapping so fast   *tat katta kat tat,*
your arms bent-arc angles like wings, the light
from the window gold all over you. This
is the closest I get to forgiveness: leaving you
like this spinning   *pat katta tat pat,*
so beautiful then. Spin after spin

                                    tat patta kat tat

                                                tat.

DEBRA BRUCE

The Unmothering

Because her absence is now a presence
wherever you go, although it's true she never
approved of what you live by,
knew what you're most moved by;
because you are as capable as she
was culpable, you now consider dropping
all charges against her, notwithstanding
the decades it took to make
an impeccable case.

Who among us has not been summoned
to watch you, at seven, spiral
in terror down cellar stairs, hurrying
to heave into her arms with a fact
you couldn't unlearn.
But she kept on ironing even while you pleaded:
Does everybody really have to die?

Whatever kept her from looking at you,
from touching you whose wingbeats
backed you harder and harder away
from her until you were trapped
against the wall—it's time
to let it go—her shoulders rounded down
as she smoothed over surfaces, folding, closing
herself around what would not, could not fly.

BEVERLY BURCH

Referred Pain

Season of hot-and-cold: winter months
leach into April: steely fog, honey locusts
shivering. Then yellow heat returns.

It's confusing: the past confuses things.
And distance, the ache I feel if you're away.
The way the shoulder I need to ice—
my crimped rotator cuff—causes burning
in my biceps, six inches down:
where the heart grips in a cardiac event.

What isn't a cardiac event?
Someone refers to self-deception in love:
I think of you: I meant me. Harm from how
we're built, intimately tied. Invisible threads.
Nerves, streaking down the arm.

Rebecca Byrkit

Number Four Is Heroin

If God made anything better, He saved it for Himself.
—Charles Mingus

No one knows more about the music I am into than I. Heavy bees,
Listening, and the

Stupefied copper of color
Can all just thrust their humid

And mobilized buzz into the aching amber hammock of my
Heart. Please. I have the wings of an escalator on. I am a rising man. When

God wakes, rubbing out of his snooze on the thirtyninth afternoon
The rain is raining. The rain is raining hard. I get up. I get on down. Another

Day my own sharp body, electric
With jazz in guitar shops, stops.

Every note I deliver disengaged from its chord
Hovers, soaked, in its own honey ochre over

The salted city, and sails the musical, salt sea of myself.
This beautiful mess of mainline I've made is mine.

Hell, I can't believe it. He saved me for Himself. Is it time?

WENDY TAYLOR CARLISLE

In the 9th Ward

Let there be winds Lord,
and let them blow,
you know how.
And Lord, blinding sun,
but make that later on.
And standing water too.
And let the dead float up
against porch railings, Lord,
with the Spanish moss
and let the chiggers there
be many and hungry for blood.
And Lord,
let there be busses
and kings of the city
to commandeer them
for drives through
the front of Frady's One Stop
and the Winn-Dixie on Almonaster,
Lord. Let the days then
roll like a river
over the levees, and over
the dry tongues of the people.
But could there also be song
in those peoples' mouths
and in their ears
One-A-Chord singing harmony
and the Joyful Gospel Choir's
"O Happy Day," or anything
by Miss Mahalia from Water Street?
And may there always be
a walking bass, a cornet
and drumming Lord, drumming.
And last, Almighty,
if you please, let my son,
the other sons and daughters,
walk from the parted waters
onto a dry land.

NANCY NAOMI CARLSON

What Floats through Me

Under a veil of morphine, I want to look away,
not see the doctor, scrubbed and gloved.
I count each labored step he takes

across the sterile field—thick with risk
like yesterday's raspberry field with thorns
scratching pink each inch of exposed skin.

I chose one berry, so lopsided it collapsed
between my fingertips, its feel imagined
on my tongue, rolled over and over,

every angle examined inside out
like a difficult choice,
until I crushed the cells flat against my thumb—

fingerprint a crimson stain.
I count backward from one hundred,
and feel him reach across blue sheets

for the hypodermic needle—
the saline solution.
The needle buries itself into layers of flesh

as if they were not a part of me,
piercing the final membrane.
I taste salt.

In one dream she floats through me,
riding the curve of my hip like a wave,
as chambers of her defective heart—

like a cave worn down by the sea—
fill and empty in a rhythm
that almost catches hold.

In another dream she is face down
in a riverbed swollen by recent rain,
her tangle of black hair pooled

on the surface like an oil spill.
Her infant gown traps a pocket of air
that keeps her bobbing on each ruffle.

I pull her out, thumping her back,
and wait for breath to sputter and start.
Morning comes, so clear I can follow

its thin string of causality:
events hold their place, explanation
has the solid logic of stone.

SHERRY CHANDLER

Skin Out a Woman

Callisto is a bear now.
Pigeon-toed, nearsighted,
rippling with muscles and fat,
she births, suckles in her sleep,
lives on human trash and honey,
fur too thick to feel the sting of outraged bees.

That string of nightingales, trees,
and bears the gods left in their trail—
was there no desire?
Can even a god make you into some
thing you don't want to be?

When I rise up from the bed and
        must walk bent until
                my muscles stretch and
                        I can walk straight,
I would be a bear and go on four legs,
rise only to nibble grapes from the high vine.

My father was a bear,
growling through my nights,
taciturn, given to sudden rage.
My mother was something lighter—
a mockingbird perhaps—fluttering,
singing through her days.

When I bend and try to rise and
        must wait until
                my hip pops
                        cracking in its socket,
I would be a bear—no frilly apron,
no sweet-smelling garden with orderly borders—
throat-ripping big fat honey-licking black-fur
living in a cave full of rabbit bones.

LAURA CHERRY

The Nurse and the Principal

"Mr. Carpenter to the nurse's office" was the secret faculty code
for a bomb threat — an announcement
that interrupted class, and paused, and repeated,

and we hooted and whistled at this raunchy development,
the nurse and the principal going at it in the closet
with the asthma medications, alcohol swabs and blood-pressure cuff,

while our French teacher ticked over to the door
in her three-inch heels and stuck her pretty neck out,
looking left and right (these were the expert precautions:

look both ways down the hall to find the bomb) and we
were quiet in the odd static of the moment, until she turned,
snapped her fingers and started warbling transitive verbs;

but after school our English teacher told some of us
what it meant — as teachers whisper everywhere
to their favorite few — so that later, in the dark,

instead of picturing Mr. C., suitpants pooled
at his ankles, bending the nurse over her porcelain sink
to the delighted cheers of the intercom,

the mascots, pets and geeks, privileged with insider status,
fell asleep seeing purple-and-gold pennants in flames, blown
bits of brick and flesh, glass beakers just bursting to sing.

MARY ROSE BETTEN

Essay

The breast specialist, a doctor who looks like Robin Williams, said, as though delivering the punch line to the world's funniest joke: "You don't have to worry about having a mastectomy. At your age, whatever it is, it won't grow fast." By phone his nurse got me on the hospital list for surgery and explained how they'll drop my breast into some sort of pocket (I envisioned the netted ones on pool tables), and how there will be bleeding from poking around for a biopsy. I hung up and felt unexplainable, unshakable rage. Last night I dreamed I made lifelike clay figures lined up on a pool table but no one could see them. They stood waiting.

This morning the *N. Y. Times* and the *L. A. Times* are filled with news of Oscar contenders. One contender will be picked from a list of five for each category. The article suggests we tune in and "Wait with them." I dropped the newspapers and walked over contender-faces to my study. I turned on my computer to the Wom-po list where they are discussing how to pick poems and make sense of them for one's book.

There on the list were ideas, affirmations, calls to action, and answers. Everywhere answers for me while I wait. When I read these poets, these cartographers, these dream-maker women, I wish I might have had access to a similar list before I retired from acting. From past Wom-po offerings: "I am coming to understand that when you are haunted and obsessed, trying to make some sense of the world that won't make sense, some of us have turned to poetry." And I am moved by this Emerson quote from a Wom-po thread: "The beautiful soul of a poet lives and perceives deeply." So I am scared. I am a mature woman, a retired character actress writing poems and claiming good healthy rage, graced by women's wisdom. My membership on the Wom-po list generates ideas faster than I can pull them from my file. I'll clothe my soul in poetry. And I'll never have to depend on a designer to count myself a worthy contender. I might even learn to play pool.

KATHLEEN CLANCY

Maiden Garden with Koi Pond

I am a garden of pretty thoughts and broadening memories,
rippling in a koi pond of silken colors, liquid and lithe.
I am the keeper of my dreams. What else would I want to be?

Look at these buds. How lush my waxy magnolia leaves. Their sheen
calls to the edges of the pool where they will glimmer and thrive.
My garden is full of flourishing thoughts and nurtured memories.

This maiden garden suits me well. I am plump with poetry.
Pregnant with everything I treasure, happy at home like a wife.
I am the keeper of my dreams. I'd be crazy not to be.

Who needs to leave the garden searching for carnality,
temporality? Be still to see the wink of stars at night.
My garden can grow the glitter of thoughts and the mirror of memories.

No need to mess with nature to put more apples on the tree.
The perfect dream won't dare to bloom outright. It longs to lie
sleeping and safe. I keep my dreams or fear what I won't be.

Reflections are lovely and strange. There's nothing else I'm eager to see.
The koi disturb the water where my floating face alights.
My garden is full of ripening thoughts and fertile memories.
I am the keeper of my dreams. What else could I possibly be?

KATHARINE COLES

Outside Newton's House

April 1999
That's what the alchemists want to do: to turn one element into another.
—Copenhagen

1. Abstract:

Error. Crime. No, make that *trespass*.
Disaster. Redemption. Journey by water.
                                    Brackets:
Two wars. Interval: with goat.

2. Question:

How do we know what we're seeing? What sees us?

3. Problem:

Just staying dry in this country. I'd ridden the train
Through rain- and glass-bent light to find—no bus.
"Come all the way from America to see that house,
Didn't you?" the cabby kept saying.
The truth: not exactly. I'd come from Leeds.
Metered now, counted out, timed back,
I marked the moment cost becomes no object. My luck:
They'd changed the closing day.
                                    What I needed:

My own change. Clothes, fortune, or better, element:
Water to gold, cloud to sun. What Newton
Spent his life's coin looking for. I wasn't
Going to get it, but I had on sneakers and jeans
(Still only damp), and the fence wasn't high.
The old glass was undraped against the eye.

4. Hypothesis:

One does what one can: looks for signs,
A trace of any presence; looks for that tree—
Not the original, but scion of its scion—
Though apples are only a fragrant hope, be-

Draggled by rain, and that delicious fall,
The coming into mind of gravity, a bold
Lie, but lovely, its ripening arc all
Fulfillment, late summer, fields gone gold.

But soldiers marched for, against the crown
Just there, on that highway, and in the cities death
Rode the backs of rats, on human breath.
So he lay here, tucked up and thinking. Newton,

Counting blessings, counting the family sheep,
Dreamed not only spheres, numbers, or light
Divided—spectral day from ghosted night—
But of what's elemental, buried deep

In the bred bone. Could he change his fortune?
In this room I peer at, hands cupped to glass,
He dreams on. Rain trickles down my back, as
Newton paces another afternoon

Brilliant with sun. He's thinking nothing great.
No, that's me. How I meet the goat
(Scion of scion?)—he presses against my jeans,
Expelling rainwater like a goaty sponge.

5. Methodology:

Take what comes. So I pet the goat. And,
Even wet, he has a certain sweetness—
At least of face, its pure demands,
And of soft ear, of vibrato voice.

His song rewards my laying on of hands.
You'd never know there still lies, past that hill,
The highway—now the M2—aroar, driven
Wild by hearts that throb with tested metal;

And, beyond that, across the channel,
Boys urge other engines into flight,
Hardly knowing what they drop, battle
Chaos they rise above. They're so light,

And I'm no longer good at the dire, I find,
Or even the sad, as if all my eye touched
Turned to gold, or to gold's illusion—
And there is no difference, or not much,

Is there? So long as illusion holds.
All that glisters, etcetera, but who knows the real
Nugget we want from any fool's gold?
Or, against the world's blast, Newton's idyll.

6. Experiment:

It turns out the other gate was open.
And the caretaker forgives my nose, pressed
To his personal window, my gaze vexed
By his undergarments, futilely strung

To dry across the kitchen. Not on my
Own account, or even the driver's refrain—
All the way from America, didn't she?—
But Henry is never wrong about a person,

Is he?—and Henry, love being blind,
Bleats his after me. A small test:
To change a goat's heart, to turn a mind
From stubborn gristle into tenderness,

Then walk through wet jockeys into history. Say
It all started here—light, attraction,
Every newfangled idea of heaven—but why
This? The past looks safe: so many turns

To choose from: at Cambridge, skipping all those pages,
Newton writes the protest: *Amicus Plato,*
Amicus Aristoteles magis
Amica veritas.

7. Results:

The caretaker thinks I'm nutso,

But harmless, unlike you, Isaac, you
I hardly dare invoke. All of that
Dark creeping under ceilings, beamed so low
You had to divide light to see it

Enumerated. Outside, it just rains harder
On Mrs. Thatcher's hometown, though her drear
Decade's finally over; this country where
Nothing is original anymore

But everything is accurate. Or
Is it the other way? I can't seem
To come to a conclusion. I've got no quarrel
Against you, though your eye ghosts a gleam

Of the human violence we would perfect
In our century, in a flash of brilliance
To put you to shame, its creators shocked
(Against time, against you, they had no chance)

As God must have been, that morning he came
Face to face with his intent, to find
He'd raised the human, light and air from grime,
And his own explosive longing slipped his mind.

VIRGINIA CONN

The Donut Girl

All gum snap and pink
inflection, talking up
a trucker. She slips
a cruller into a bag,
licking icing
off a finger, wiping it
on her smock to show
she's just kidding.

She drums her nails
on the counter to the radio
they won't let her play
but she can stand there
doing nothing, staring
at cars, wishing less
and less to jump
into a back seat, knowing
the world is round;
she'll be back.

The way all good mysteries
are round and turning inward
with a hole in the middle
where the heart ought to be.

NICOLE COOLEY

Grief As Is

In memory of Ruth E. Cooley

A silver gift bag holds the box of ashes beside my bed.
In the closet, flush, butter-colored silk: clothes tell her story,

how fifty years ago the Empire Builder sped East to this city
where I yank her jacket, fingernail pink, tight across

my breasts, where I pretend I'm her, while like a throat
Fifth Avenue floods with light. Where I pretend I'm her.

—Italian Pavilion New York 100% Merino Wool—

I pretend she isn't dead, stand at the closet door, step
into her dress, black acetate shimmering stiff.

Clothes, hold me together. Labels, tell me a narrative of events.

—Miss Liberty Fashions Madison Avenue 60% Gabardine 40% Nylon—

I try everything on, buttons torn off, seams split.
Grief's landscape is fabric: small cigarette burn on a sleeve or

an edge of stained eyelet lace. Mourning is repair: holding
the silver needle, thread wet with spit as I stitch all the holes shut.

HELEN RUGGIERI

Essay

I live in a small town (15,000 or so weary souls) along the banks of the Allegheny River on the New York/ Pennsylvania border. If I mentioned "pantoum," most residents would assume I was talking about a flotation device. No one knows what foetry.com is or a Pushcart or P & W. On the Wom-po list we know all that stuff and if we want more detail, there's someone to help us out. For me, Wom-po was a step out of the isolation ward into visiting hours. Members wrote about things I wanted to know and I could ask questions and get informed answers. Copyright, deadlines, requests for poems, biographies of overlooked women writers, craft talk on line breaks and linked poems, new forms to experiment with, scandals and scams, gossip and guidelines, all the po-biz my lonesome heart hungered to hear. And surely someone would say something about that mixed metaphor.

CHELLA COURINGTON

Summer at Thirteen

Anna Claire and I never like tall grass
afraid we'll step on a cottonmouth.
But water the color of indigo
waits for us the other side of danger.

We shed jeans, shirts, underwear,
mark our place at the edge,
hold hands like Ruth and Naomi
wading into the deep.

With each step, water moves higher,
chills our new breasts.
I throw my arms around Anna Claire,
press against her for warmth.

She pushes away,
plunges deep beyond,
surfaces, arches,
plunges again,
swims under me,
cradles my back in her palms,
lifting me to the air
so I float on her fingertips.

Her hands move gently
touch my shoulder and thigh.
She kisses my lips,
unclosing my eyes with her tongue.

We don't say a word
before we reach the point of mooring
before we venture back through tall grass.

MARY CRESSWELL

Free on Board

They were cut down
squill, succory, styrax
unitised on pallets
silver canisters
wheeled into place
by the bearded iris
the grey man cycled off
whistling in his teeth

We should have picked it
once we checked
export documents
English to English
the pink quotation marks
exchanged anxious glances
moved closer together

It happened in English.
They were cut down
inula, ixora, ilex
never safe at all
laid out in rows
methyl bromide smoked
under metal doors
thin as thoughts of fall.

ALISON CROGGON

Ars Poetica

It will make no difference.
But you'll find you can't speak without love
although it's an imprisonment.
Your voice must be love wrestled to unloving,
the lyre at the moment of catastrophe, a silence
within which another voice opens.

You'll speak as you must, as always,
although you'll never know why you're listening
through the elisions of your stuttering heart.
You'll long to finish, although nothing has happened,
although you haven't begun, as if your mere being
hurt you with abundance. No one will explain.

There are wounds that blind you, sudden voices
splitting into winter, toothed windows, terrors
sifting through white slumbers of corruption,
the wraith that greets you with your shrinking face
at dawn, anonymous and violent,
waiting for Virgil.

Because you have tasted your salt in the blood
of another's mouth, because a small flower
is eating the history of stone,
because you are asleep and all possibility
tilts on the edge of your vision, because you are nameless
and are called, because you know nothing—

a possible music
lifts through the panic of dismay—
it's the blue of all the flowers of your body,
the brain stem, the clitoris, the tongue,
the wrist vein, the channels of the heart, the dying lips,
reaching to their likeness in the sky, in the sky's waters—
you can't lift it out of your flesh
because it won't exist, but it flowers past you.
It opens the places you've always been,
house, fire, glass, bed, water,

tree, night,
the child's glance which strews your transparencies
across a field of colours you have no name for,
the profane ash of touch
darkening your tongue, the dream of imperishable silver
which wakes to another dream, a boat departing
from an unmapped shore, and your crumbling words, unable
to hold even one drop of light.

BARBARA CROOKER

All that Is Glorious around Us

Title of an exhibit on the Hudson River School

is not, for me, these grand vistas, sublime peaks, mist-filled
overlooks, towering clouds, but doing errands on a day
of driving rain, staying dry inside the silver skin of the car,
160,000 miles, still running just fine. Or later,
sitting in a café warmed by the steam
from white chicken chili, two cups of dark coffee,
watching the red and gold leaves race down the street,
confetti from autumn's bright parade. And I think
of how my mother struggles to breathe, how few good days
she has now, how we never think about the glories
of breath, oxygen cascading down our throats to the lungs,
simple as the journey of water over rock. *It is the nature
of stone/ to be satisfied/* writes Mary Oliver, *It is the nature
of water/ to want to be somewhere else,* rushing down
a rocky tor or high escarpment, the panoramic landscape
boundless behind it. But everything glorious is around
us already: black and blue graffiti shining in the rain's
bright glaze, the small rainbows of oil on the pavement,
where the last car to park has left its mark on the glistening
street, this radiant world.

RACHEL DACUS

Femme au chapeau

—after a painting of his wife by Matisse, 1905

She's ready to doff tradition's muff and the cane
on which she stylishly leans. Yeats is about
to write: *The bees build in the crevices.* Her mane
of red is upswept, but wants out.
Hollowed by chaos, her face is Internet
turquoise and neon pink, cartooned as if
she were a television on which we get
the perennial game show, *What's the Dif?*
Miracles of the time are all around her—
the German and his unconscious, Pavlov's reflex—
a patent examiner with a theory that avers
time's not absolute. Matisse goes psychedelic
on a woman's face. Titled *Woman*, like so
many painters' wives, she seems not to see
the changes or first she'd remove that chapeau,
and its crushing fruit, its dour antiquity.
Eyes wild as pinwheels whirl questions:
If we can't escape birth or condition,
what's the point? If not now, when?
Who will I be, Henri, when I come to fruition?
As a woman all rainbow atomic ignition.

Of Hollywood

I set off for Frederick's playing Lawrence Ferlinghetti's underwear poem, taking notes
on the flip side of a book xeroxed and sent to the boys for option — rejected
       and recycled, an extended single joke on *The Rules,*
       how to lose a man, illustrated with stick figures, one page a bra, "32D,"
       the bra that should be left behind, as quickly as possible, in his apartment — it is
Frederick's of Hollywood on Hollywood Boulevard,
the desolate stretch east of Vine. Many of the sidewalk stars are blank, next to
       Little Jack Little and June Havoc,
       Jack Palance and Fleetwood Mac.
          While Lana's soda shop may have been there,
          Hollywood High, at Sunset and Highland, is now considered too far to
          walk.

Nearby copy cat lingerie stores sell tawdrier lingerie, the shortest schoolgirl get up,
       American flag print thongs.
Frederick's pink awnings are flanked by
Hollywood Toys and Costumes, which stocks wigs,
and St. Pierre's Magic Supply, a real magician shop with, in its vitrine, Dlx. Top Hat
       Table, Dagger Head Chest, a dusty wrist guillotine with a rubber hand stuck in it,
       signs decorated with stick figures, like those opposite these notes, hopefully
       drawn but probably not drawn by a child,
Mirage, the hologram maker my Theory of Knowledge professor used,
realistic thumb tips, angel wings, and various manacles that read from stage,
       not those manacles in vitrines farther west.

Frederick's lingerie museum has stage and screen underwear plus a brief
       historical overview.
In von Stroheim's *Silk Stockings,* Cyd Charisse's bustier had
more than 100 garter clips attached since the silk "stockings
       had to be pulled from every angle
       so that at no time
       would [they] wrinkle or show creases."
          Lana Turner, from *The Merry Widow,* Greta Garbo, The *Gorgeous Hussy,*
Pamela Anderson in an old Frederick's catalog during her modeling days.

I have always recognized Frederick's for their 70's shoes, specifically the 5 inch stilettos
     with real spikes in the catalogs my parents occasionally had, since
Dad bought Mom a joke lingerie item each Christmas for her stocking.
While the shoes are like those in the 70's again, the spikes are disappointingly encased in
     lucite.

Joan Collins was in a movie called *The Red Velvet Swing,* which reminds me
that when my Mom worked for *The Chicago Tribune*, she went under cover at a lounge
     called The Velvet Swing, although I had always pictured the velvet as black or
     purple velvet,
with a friend. It was a bar waitressing job except the girls took turns swinging on a swing
     over the bar.

I have always wondered about the "no bra" bra, and see it comes with Sexi-Set adhesive.
Bras with nipples and nippled pads for stuffing bras "have that 'cold weather' look at all
     times," or in slang used by my fiancé and his writing partner, the former lead
     phone salesman at Victoria's Secret catalog, "turn on your headlights."
My favorite, in theory, is the underwire alone — although there is no comfortable
     underwire, there's a rib there — with two strategically placed netting daisies,
although the newest technology is the water bra, or "liquid dream."
Why get implants?

Since I locked my keys in my car, I have the special treat of standing on Hollywood
     Boulevard in front of Frederick's, looking at Musso & Frank's, where Fitzgerald
     hung out during his final decline, home of the overpriced original food and old
     style martinis — a shot and a half of gin and an olive to cling to like a life raft.
A real school girl with a regulation-length plaid shirt walks past with her arms xed across
     her chest, her fists near her shoulders
as I am clutching my scraps to me and getting ink all over the front of my white t-shirt,
     waiting for AAA.

DeLana Dameron

ode to jasmine

for palestine

i dream a lover
whose lips are jasmine

i drift in dreams
towards your scent
your persistent flowering
meandering vines
skirt of delicate yellow petals
a permanence
that outlasts passing seasons
knows no limits

you live in the hearts of lands
where planted

i plant you in my heart

my lover's lips are jasmine
i want to kiss

i praise the earth
that allows your existence
you grow along rivers
in meadows
tickle noses
of those fortunate to reach you

                                        i even love you from abroad

your remembered scent sleeps
just beneath my skin
and i carry you wherever i go
like the honey bee
how beautiful the honey bee
rapt by your petals
attracted to your nectar

flies miles and miles
to catch your letters
dresses of dusted pollen

my lover's lips are jasmine
your roots sip waters from the sands
your fragile leaves wilt when removed from earth
an elegance that cannot be culled
we dream your vines
your relentless vines

and in palestine
you mask
the scent of death
dance fumes away
from our noses seeking
jasmine's familiar tinge

each breath is a beginning
each breath is a beginning

Deema K. Shehabi

Essay

It's not all that we think it is; there's something else lurking beneath the drift and intimacy of a community engendered by belonging to a women's poetry forum. As the Egyptian feminist writer Nawal El-Sadawi says, "Everybody is the son and daughter of their times." The question then becomes: is a women's poetry listserv—despite the seductive humanist agenda—also prone to the empire's complex prejudices as they exist on a social, political, and economic level? Are we really immune from the sharp splinter of racism with its end result of colonialism? How do we face the "colonialist within" and come to terms with our own agenda for liberation?

As a Muslim-Palestinian woman living under the nauseating grip of anti-Muslim, anti-Arab hysteria, can I really enter the realm of sisterhood with Western women poets? In introspection, my sense of uncertainty lies in how my own identity is perceived in the West. By allying myself with what is perceived as liberal Western values, how can I be certain to maintain and reclaim my own cultural prowess (of which I am proud), especially if that culture is seen as inferior?

I feel that perhaps the answer lies in a holistic understanding of the interconnectedness of liberation around the world. If the struggle for liberation points to Tibet, Palestine, or the Indian subcontinent, then we should listen carefully and know that there can be no distances between us "here" and them "there." Maybe the answer also comes from the blending of values between East and West, North and South so that there's a wide, inclusive agenda distilled from our diversity. Only then can we root together and flourish. Only then would there be a union, a remaking, and a rebirth.

KAY DAY

Volunteer Reading Lesson with Mira

She nudges syllables along, then stares
at me when each sentence ends. She always
stops at the sight of words like *slip* and *snare*
because she hates the lisp her mouth obeys.
She likes the pictures best—a girl beside
the sea, the moon, a flower bouquet in tones
much deeper than those that bloom in beds outside.
She wants the picture talk to go on and on.

Persistent prodding gets her back on track,
almost. She leans on me, then takes my hand.
She says her mama's boyfriend hurt her brother.
That's the reason Mira can't go back.
She pulls the book into her lap. A quick scan
and she points. How do you say this one? *Smother.*

MARTHA DEED

Illegal Entry

Note: Each year, the Coast Guard installs an ice boom at the confluence of Lake Erie and the Niagara River to protect the power intakes at Niagara Falls from ice floes from the lake. The ice boom consists of steel drums chained together in three sections and anchored to the bottom of the lake. The sections overlap, keeping out the ice, but allowing movement of small boats between the lake and river.

Immigration officials report
the arrest of a young poem tonight
crossing over from Canada
without passing through customs
or declaring its value in American dollars.
The poem refused to make a statement
to authorities, but flashed a
simile as it exited the ice boom
and disappeared into traffic.
Passersby alerted police
who confiscated it during open
mic at a well-known Elmwood Avenue bar.
Police have yet to release the name of the illegal
poem as fingerprint and photocopy analysis
are incomplete. Officials have scheduled a press
conference at 10 AM tomorrow in the lobby
of the Federal Building. Until then, officials
remind the public that, while extreme fear
is not appropriate, officials cannot guarantee
the safety of those who import or read
foreign poems. INS spokesperson
Guy Laroach told our reporter,
"It's a problem we have every year:
Unauthorized foreign poems
attempting to enter the country
with insufficient documentation,
words sliding willy-nilly across our
ice boom. These poems, often Canadian in origin,
but sometimes from other lands as well,
reduce employment opportunities for our local
homegrown poems. We are doing
everything we can to prevent their entry

with little cooperation from the Canadian
authorities who have an interest in letting their poems
go, in order to enhance employment
opportunities for those who stay behind.
Thank goodness, Spring will soon be here.
The poems will drown if they make any
further attempts, because we are removing
the ice boom tomorrow, and they will be forced
back upon the internet where they will languish
unseen, and pose no threat to our native poets."

SHIRA DENTZ

Poem for my mother who wishes she were a lilypad in a Monet painting

We're in a gray tree (you and I).
Lunging into an orange—not eating it.

I'd like nothing better than to come to another kind of arrangement;
mostly, though, we just don't come apart.

,

Behold
a single contractual mark
to possess and to withhold (contractions),
and the dialogue within the dialogue that began before it.

Black seeds on a white dish
.... (pores)

The sound of your voice has always been a fragment

          organized as a flower,
       a tin can cling-clanging upstream,

the spaces between my heartbeats
          lengthening (like shadows);

You a part of the tough rubbery vine that expands on the skin of the pond (still).

JESSICA G. DE KONINCK

Chagall's Windows

In the dream she falls
from a tall building.
No, she is flying. Guided
by thought, her body floats.
Suddenly she remembers,
only men fly in dreams.
She cannot be dreaming
having willed herself, remain
alert. Sleep means waking
in the future when the past
cannot change. She must remain
in possibility, that today not turn
tomorrow. Always Tuesday.
She floats like dust, like paper
encircling a crystal tower.
No, a cathedral, larger
than any church she remembers.
Hears a crackling. A bridegroom's
foot crushes glass, wrapped in cloth,
the color of paper, the color
of bandages. Around her men fall
from the sky head first, surprised
that gravity does not pull
towards the breach position.
She floats, looking for something
lost, something written down.
Papers keep blowing away.
She cannot propel herself
fast enough. Each gust teases
a page from her eyes.
One sheet burns. Ashes drift
like memory, like sleep. Men drop,
falling like paperweights.
They disappear, as if erased,
as if someone wrote their story
backwards. She must write
the words, but does not
know the language. No time

to learn. She does not know how
to get down. She does not know
how to wake up.

ANNIE DEPPE

The Throat Singers

With a half hour left before closing
and most of the museum still unexplored,
why was I unable to leave

the exhibit on Inuit throat singers?
I kept pushing the button
that played a film of two old women—

are they sisters?—standing nose-to-nose
in what looks like a musical duel.
As one lays down a challenge

with the sounds of muffled snow,
the other improvises riffs like ice
cracking. How deep their voices are,

probing a place far lower than expected.
It's as if by descending,
they can sing from the inside of things.

They sing the metal rod used to chip through ice.
They sing water welling up through the hole.
They sing the wind, the sled, the dogs.

And from somewhere at the back of their throats,
known from a time before their births, they sing fire
to guide the hunters safely home.

Each woman holds the other's gaze. Shoulders
rise and fall together, as they play
a game where everything in their world's at stake.

Now at night, after watching that film so many times,
I seem to hear, right on the edge of my understanding,
the singing of old women

dressed in the flowered clothes of school girls.
I think they're singing the silver fish scooped
from a hole, as well as the crackling plastic bag

they use to carry those fish. They name
the tilt of telephone poles and the sound
of grass pushing up through snow,

and the wind, also, swirling through that grass.
I'm going to sleep to the snowmobile's whine,
to the sound of the prefab home's aluminum door

and the electric can opener's miracle drone.
My prayers hum as the women sing to young girls
who've come to learn their song.

They weave in the girls' names—
Winnie and Sarah. Somehow I'm hearing
the names of my children, too.

Their voices hold the stars of an Arctic sky.
The aurora borealis
on a baby's cap. They hold the baby itself

as it's tucked into fold after fold of sleep.
I give myself to the sounds of voices
singing from the insides of things.

MICHELLE DETORIE

Elegy for a Sleepwalker

I mourned

      the death of my half-
sister long before
           she was born. This

began when I discovered

      a rabbit's frail bones
in a bed of pine straw.
        I began to bury stones

beneath the fringed gaze

      of the perennials—
gladiolas and asters.
        Her breathing

I discerned

      in a bowl of milk.
I chose clothes
        that would be hers

when I outgrew them.

      For months
I drew her inside a belly—
        I drew her—

an outline—a body

            beneath fallen petals.

ARIELLE GREENBERG

Essay

I'd been off of the Wom-po list for about a year when I decided to start my own listserv for poet moms. I can't say that the decision to start poet-moms was a reaction AGAINST Wom-po, but Wom-po certainly inspired both what I wanted and didn't want poet-moms to be. I loved Wom-po for its supportive nature and its frequent brilliance, for its articulate discussions and candor, and in many ways, it helped me get to a place where I could think about being a poet mom, not to mention wanting to start a listserv for poet moms. But on Wom-po I'd felt bogged down by the size and volume of the list; and more than that, I will make this very snotty-seeming admission: I felt a bit exhausted by the mixture of women who were trying to forge careers as poets with the women who already had powerful careers going. I know it sounds elitist, but as someone with an academic job and a couple books out, my concerns were and are very different from those of poets considering or in graduate school, or poets just starting to send work out for publication. I was that poet once, but I'm not now, and frankly, for me, one of the gendered issues about being a woman poet is the issue of giving out too much nurturing energy to family, friends, students, colleagues, etc. To my own detriment, I love to give advice; despite all the friends and wonders I found there, dropping off Wom-po was one way to help myself put up some much-needed boundaries.

So when I started poet-moms, I made it smaller, by invitation only, with the focus on poets who were already active in recognized careers. The issues these women face in juggling motherhood with publishing, editing, teaching, etc. are my own issues, and thus I founded poet-moms as a selfish act, though I'm happy to say that of course it's now serving many needs that are not my own. But I would have never thought to create it if it hadn't been for Wom-po first.

JOANIE DIMARTINO

Ultrasound

I've seen these pictures before.

My womb, swollen, poised on a table;
before me a panorama

of shadows sweeps across the monitor,
single image

sound waves beating: a fetal heart
in fluid, seminal.

My own options flat on their backs
like a canvas, this unborn landscape a sketch

of shoreline. See myself as the pink bride
painted in the distance, a missing

future smothered by bouquet
and silk, to hide my belly

behind.   This beach, this summer's

shell-blushed afternoon, this reflection
of pink sand under my feet;

          I do not ask
for the ocean to pity me:

my child's pink throat will open.

See the transducer reflect a penis
onto the screen,

hear a voice rise in hunger
above the next squall.

ANA DOINA

Romanian Village

—for Dr. John Gilgun

One day uncle sent us to fetch a bucket of argil—
the ash colored clay, wet, sticky and cool.
He promised to make toys for me, a flute
for my brother, some pots for his wife
to use in the kitchen, the old ones were cracked.

He said the best clay
for his pots was to be found further than the last row
of peach trees in the orchard, near a small cemetery
with freshly dug graves, at the edge of the woods,
where thick blades of grass change to dense moss,
and the forest begins its quiet and tall growth
off earth's darker velvet.

Right there we found the stranger—the round shape
of his metal helmet was glistening dark in the sun
like the back of a tortoise. There was a buzz
of insects around him, and a sickening smell,
dizzying and entrapping.

The flesh had rotted,
soaked as he was in the argil earth, only his boots
and his helmet still good. Muddy, but dry. "Not
a sight for a girl" brother said, "God knows
how many days he's been dead." Muck worms
had squirmed through his flesh until nothing
was left but bones

and brown shreds in the rags of his coat still heavy
with war. We went home empty-handed and scared.
But soon, the whole village came to see the dead man.
Children and grandmas rushed first, then women
and men left their fields to come flock to the spot

where a dead soldier had lain
covered by clay, God only knows for how long.
The men said he must have been a soldier left there
during retreat, no doubt a German, considering
his helmet and his boots. They covered him
with a peacock rug my aunt had woven
a few years back, during the war,

and they went for the priest.
But the priest didn't know what to do, "If he's
German," the priest said, numbering prayers
on the argil beads of a rosary, "he's not of our rite."
There was no way to know who he was,

where he came from,
whom he fought for. They knew he was young
by his bones and his teeth. Maybe a peasant
or a shepherd like us. No grades, no insignias,
nothing memorable, heroic or great about him
was found in the mud near the corpse.
So they dug a grave

at the edge of the forest, in the small cemetery,
in the last row. They gave him a proper burial, less
his name and the birth-right ritual of mourning.
The priest led a mixed ceremony with prayer words
from all the Christian rites, making the sign

of the cross from right to left
for us and left to right as he thought the dead man
would have done, and they all prayed, because my aunt
and uncle had asked, for the souls of all mothers
and fathers and sons lost on other foreign lands.
They laid the German—this unknown stranger,
this enemy—

near some of our own dead soldiers. Next day
brother and I had to go further than the last row
of peach trees in the orchard to fetch some potter's
clay. My uncle came with us and touching
the argillaceous earth, pinching it with his agile fingers

he said "this must be
the best clay in the world" and I knew
he would make a vase of this clay, oval shaped
like a nursing breast, like a tear, like an ocean,
like a continuous, enclosing horizon.

SHARON DOLIN

Envy Ghazaled

Hydra-headed, you. No Heracles, I am being slain.
No wonder my favorite color is green—slain.

To slay you I slay myself: Mirrors dilate.
Looking at you I will be last seen slain.

Comparisons caper through my head in bed at night.
Why haven't I scaled the Apennines? Slain.

How many parts of lives I'd exchange: job, book, prize . . .
Emotional landmines at a party? Preen, slain.

Her coat, her house, her love, her life, her reputation.
Did I hear someone's off to the Mediterranean? Slain.

How to slay the heads inside without them
growing back to poison my sheen: slain.

Sometimes you're my younger self: Self-envy
no oxymoron—nor envy of being nineteen: Slain.

Count me happy when I can enjoy the lot I've been given.
Confessing to you, I know it's quite obscene. Slain.

Write to exorcise—or exercise—you with lines, images, rhyme.
If Sharon does not from Envy wean—slain.

CAROL DORF

Liminal

In my hand the stumbling block:

to fall into meaning
        as in the momentary
                joy after illness;
then back to my annoyance
        at mourning doves
                declaring territory
on my windowsill;
        or anxiety about finding
                clothes for the day,
all the undone laundry
        of my childhood piling up
                in that basement.

The blessing where each breath counts:

and I know every answer
        on the exam before I turn
                over the booklet.
If I were a mystic,
        would my day be informed
                by these moments;
a Zen baker mindfully
        kneading whole grain dough
                on a wooden board;
or would I remain the woman
        packing lunches at midnight
                trying to remember
to breathe.

KATHERINE DRABEK

Sliding on Ice

When Harry Winster's dump truck slid on the ice
and spun down the steep hill like a whirling dervish
knocking the hutches to pieces, the rabbits made a noise
like tearing tin. Mr. Winster jumped out of the cab
into a blizzard of woodchips. The Guernsey lay down
fawn and white against the grass and then bawled—not the way
babies do when waiting for dinner—but a deep-throated
howl out of the last weave of wilderness. She lay there collapsed,
sweat running down her cheek like tears, as if she knew
what would happen next. She bawled one more time
as the truck tumbled over again and rested against the barn.

I think most believed it was a good marriage. At first
we shadowboxed alone behind closed doors. Later
practiced our undoing on each other, grappling
with each other's brittle shells. Finally we were so tired,
we just held each other, trying to open our cages of hunger,
and dream ourselves into desire.

The lettering on the truck faded to Ha   Win. Neighbor
kids scavenged some parts of the cab. I clothes-pinned
the wash on the line and it flapped like wings away
from the wreckage below.

CAMILLE T. DUNGY

Almost Like They Wanted It

Because she'd heard him laugh through new moon darkness
and she knew he'd fallen and she knew, before she turned,
he'd be crawling, like a crawdad, rock to loam—

because she tried to love the straight back and neck
he'd erected to recollect the man he'd been
before—because she found herself adding up his usefulness

like some kind of auctioneer—she showed him
the dark coils areoling both her breasts and all the ways
she bent and lifted, bent and lifted, steady, strong.

She let him believe he was past due for a harvest
and her hands were the right ones, now, to hold the scythe.

★

She made quick work of pleasure. The boysmile bunked down
in his eyes, she claimed. Her tongue found the place in his mouth
where the teeth were gone—where he'd hold his corncakes

until they grew soft enough to chew. History had bedded him
in all of this—his own history and failures not his own.
Before he'd tramped in she'd watched another man—a man she'd thought

she'd hated—watched his body opened, opened, opened until
blood had married brine. She'd watched that man be whipped into something
good for nothing more than fertilizing clay and she'd thought

buckshot would have been a brand of kindness if sprayed into him
just then. But even after his hard going, she did not miss him very much.

★

Anyone she chose could be shucked like surplus property tomorrow,
but that hadn't been enough to warn her off of picking him that night.
Because she knew if she set her sight on nothing she'd get nothing

in return, she'd walked with him. But because the night progressed so
—because there were some clouds—no stars—no moon—he'd tripped
over the branch of a dead and down tree. In all that darkness,

there, without a moon, even then, she had not fallen. She thought
to say so, but she did not say so. She did nothing
but say she was sorry for him. She did not use her mouth

to say this. Could he not listen to her hands? They spoke softly,
articulating her condolences, to his torn and bleeding skin.

Rishma Dunlop

Naramata Road

You know this is a landscape that tends to unfasten
you, brings you again and again to the brink of weeping.

No matter how many departures and disappearances,
you are marked by this beauty, astonishment that depends on loss.

As the bitter edges of things slide into memory and flesh, you
claim the meaning of your days on this frayed loveliness.

You sign your name to it.

At these moments something is given back to you, panic
dusted off, calmed by desert heat in the summer, vineyards

heavy with grapes. The body is set to music, carried by rain in
the spring resurrection of orchards. In the fall, the road swells with

harvest, the ripe comfort of apples. Even in winter, the skeletons of
trees dangle gifts, Golden Delicious earrings abandoned to the wind.

The ghosts of dead teenagers and drunks live here, their
voices echo along the curves and bends, in the rocky incisions of

graves, haunted by memories of prom dresses, cigarettes smoked in
the 7-Eleven parking lot and behind the high school.

There is a soft spot in everything.

You drive that road, move into a sky like a late Turner painting, gold
and amber, white canvas dreaming colors of Venice. It makes you believe

there is tenderness in every geography. And this has the power to change you,
unweight your eyelids every morning, as the sky leans towards the absolute.

LISKEN VAN PELT DUS

Broken Things

for Benjamin Bright Ladley

When the boy fell, what
he saw: boulders, scree,

a delicate kestrel
in flight. The sky, this

earth, how it breaks apart,
the urge to shatter.

Moon-splinter behind a tower.
What he heard: church bells

counting cormorants black
against the dawn,

bleat of a hungry goat, roar
of a plane pressed into air.

In his pocket, stones.
A piece of blue tile.

What she remembers: his palm
on the nape of her neck,

her fingers on his cock,
red ache like magma welling

from the earth's core.
What we share with the other side,

take in, mix, can't hold:
tears, juices, lava

of our loneliness, cells shed
into each other's hands.

JILLY DYBKA

Lost Things

Some things are just lost for good. That idea
after dinner. The cat you had at ten.
Gone, all gone away, raindrops in the sea.
As time unravels, the lost things sweeten
with simplicity, heighten with yearning,
or are quickly forgotten. Sometimes the lost
whisper wisdom—a belated warning:
please do not take this for granted. The cost
is a warm lover dressing at sunrise,
goldfinches carefully tending their song.
The cost is a multitude of goodbyes
spent for each surprising, certain leaving.

LYNNELL EDWARDS

The Farmer's Daughter; or Persephone's Return

On first return, she is *hey boys* and *whatcha doin*
and buckets of fresh milk sent from the big house
where her father leans in the doorway, watching under
the porch light as her swinging form disappears
into the stable of darkness. The low murmur
of beasts tells him she has arrived where the Hardt boys
wait for what they've been promised. Dumb as cattle,
they stand to greet her, tip their caps, and smile
in wide appreciation for the gift,
the farmer's hospitality they will receive.
At this late hour they will have all, including
you, Miss. You sure have grown up pretty.
And in between the fumblings of *let*
me help you with that and *when you were little*
and *just like your momma* the great barn door slides shut
and bales of hay are rearranged and this
is not the rapture she has dreamed, the day
when the fine-boned boy sings his words and they
escape to the city.
                                But there is laughter sure,
the cackle of a joke turned bad. She hears
the lifting wings of owls above their lofts;
the tied mare stamping in her stall. The bucket
spills but does not fill desire's dull thirst
rising in their throats. And she thinks
of calling to her father scratching out
accounts, waiting at the kitchen table,
water in a silver cup at his right hand.
But she remembers orchards that must be
burdened with their fruit, brown tobacco
hanging down in hands, rows of corn
rattling in the fields. She will endure
these sacrificial months of warmth and green,
the bargain hard, unfairly struck.

MOIRA EGAN

Questions Midway

Nel mezzo del cammin di nostra vita
—*Dante*

A man asks terrible questions
of me: why I, who might have done
anything, wear this life I've kept on

like a shiny rayon second-hand dress,
worn not for beauty, but effect, whose roses
bloom a Pepto-Bismol effervesce.

Why have I never had a job up to my intellect?
The sky cracked open today, circumspect
no more, and I'd left home without protection.

Can we go outside and play in the rain?
How can a letter hold so much pain
that the reader re-reads and weeps again?

Driving home a little lit last night
(God protects drunks and Irish girls, right?)
this thought sideswiped me at a stoplight:

I don't believe that love can last forever.
If I had to choose between safety and danger,
Gentle Reader, can you guess the answer?

Most nights I like the bed empty,
my arms a startled parenthesis.
(But should a spinster be this greedy?)

Will I always want to wake up alone?
Tonight, awakened by the shrill of the phone,
mistaking the twilight for the dawn,

I want a voice I've never heard
to speak in a language that has no word
for sadness. When will I learn?

SUSAN ELBE

Drought, 1937

All summer the sky a saffron tent of grit.
They say it's worse in Oklahoma.

I should have known this morning
when I saw two heifers licking oak bark.

Tonight, counting stars inside a ring around the moon,
I know it's true—in three days,
thank God, rain.

I'm 67, looking back because that's what happens
when the years pile up
like shut-eyed kittens mewling in a burlap sack.

An August night just like this one,
I went out alone
and waded through the winter wheat

as if that field was ocean and I could cross
its blonde waves to a different life.

What I wanted, to go under,
my brain slammed by a fist of gold.

My first-born, dead six months.
The barn, a struck and smoldered ruin.
Trouble with the well.

My chest thudded with an animal
who (I should have known)
paced back and forth

inside my ribcage, freed by the hand
of moonlight lifting up the yard latch.

I should have known
the winter I was 17—four night-blue crows
on the snowy fence rail. Bad luck.

Instead, I thought *how beautiful they are,*
the way these years transform,

become all sooty-voiced and magpie,
their clever thieving, me reflected
in the cooled lava of their eyes.

MENDI OBADIKE

Essay

Hi Lesley,

Thanks for asking me to write the comment on race on the Women's Poetry List. I'm really inundated and have recently made myself sick from saying yes too many times, so, though I was about to propose a date in the future by which I could possibly do this, I think I should just say no. I also have to say I'd have mixed feelings about doing it in any case. The first reason is because when I wrote my last message about "The Dinner Party" I promised myself that those words would be my last in that conversation. I did not want to get entangled in one of those neverending conversations that have been wearing out black women in predominantly white women's circles for longer than I've been alive. Also, although it's nice to be thought of, especially when it comes to my writing, I wonder how often my name would come up to discuss something other than race in this community. Maybe someone else—Julie Enszer, Yerra Sugarman, or Marilyn Hacker—could say something useful about race on the list. It occurs to me that I've just written a paragraph about race and the list. Feel free to use this one.

Best,
Mendi

JULIE R. ENSZER

Reparations

I.
Forty years ago, I would have been his secretary
not his boss, says a white woman
who works with my wife.
Yes, my wife responds,
And I would have been your maid.

II.
We were promised forty acres and a mule.
Where are my forty acres?
Where is my mule?

III.
When I meet white people
with the same last name as my wife,
I bait them.
My wife has the same last name,
I say. Inevitably, they respond,
Oh, we must be related.
Yes, I say. Your family owned her family.
They always fall silent. They always walk away.

IV.
We built this country.
We picked cotton, tobacco.
We harvested sugar cane.
We worked the land; we built the roads.
This country made money because of slaves.
This country was built on the backs of slaves.

V.
When the conversation turns
to reparations,
someone always says,
I never owned slaves,
nor did my parents or even my grandparents.
Why should I pay reparations?
People fall silent.

There is truth in that statement.
I wait through the discomfort.
Then, I say,
If not you, then who?

NANCY ESPOSITO

Snake Charmer

But I can see you're not stunned
enough, and it's the devil's work I see
you're accusing me. You're seeing
my arms and legs branch off
me like I was crisp as my snakes
and muscular as rage. You're dying
to inquire why a lady wants to risk
her limbs if it's got nothing
to do with divinity like I should be that
tree down in Eden folding its leaves
in prayer to keep from getting its fruits
swiped. Now when I was a copper-headed
little girl and always got put
in red to match, I'd swing out
back at the haunch of the old live
oak and press my toes into the fig
vine against Granddaddy's work
shed who called me the apple
of his eye and laughed about me going
to be the bad one in the bunch. That made sense
to me 'bout as much as snakes being God's
way of punishing generosity like a birth
-day minus the cake and presents. Especially
since the first time I handled
one like it was giving itself
wrapped up to me and waiting
to get opened. Just a tiny garter
snake, but I knew that I was knowing
what to do. It was like that
for such a long time I was almost sorry
there weren't going to be any more
secrets. And then like I'd been struck
by a poison dart, it landed on me
that those others were the gifts
saved for last. Not that I'd be drawn by anything
evil, but the way I was seeing
it, what's got danger lying
inside's got a subtlety going on. Maybe

the slip knot of meanness or something
elastic as the heart, something tender
and also tough with being
scared to wobble it out. But those ones
don't lie out on your back
lawn and slither across your raised
eyebrows like they were a satin
bow come untied and streaming
like a comet's tail in a once in your life
-time's miracle. A surprise
party is what it was, the first one
that beaded around the big rock
like it was his glassed in front
parlor, a rattler done up
in all his bangles dancing for my warm
blood. And then it was over
and I could've spread a picnic
blanket and invited him for a sandwich
and berries. Later and fast as dust
devils the hooded cobra
spitting at me like he'd just learned
the alphabet and corals like party
favors, all yellow, black,
and red. I can see I'm nuts
in your eyes, but I'd like to set you
at your ease as I've got no mind
to belly out of here hanging
my head. I suppose
you might say I've come
to cherish what nobody else allows
and feel right at home with it, unlikely
as it is to you like this snake
you see threaded 'round my calf
like a sheer stocking slipping into a shoe.

KATE EVANS

Middle Age

The dog got skinny overnight so we gave her cheese,
gravy on big scoops of dry food, cookies without
making her sit. We're lesbians in our forties
and we're dieting, who would have thought

it necessary. But we want to fly on our bikes
like the children we don't have, to wear our pants
with the ease of men. There have been too many nights
of wine, of another portion. We think about cancer,

that maybe the dog is sick. She's getting fatter but
when I run my hand along her back the bones jut
at new angles and she flinches in tender spots.
Still, she seems more content, sleeps a lot

and is given to snoring. Eating less, we wake early,
do laundry before dawn, drink coffee in bed to the pulse
of the dryer and read fat books. I had a skinny
husband, once. He didn't care about food, my pleasure

baffled him. I was supposed to be on a diet, like his
mother, but I'd eat hero sandwiches in my car and bags
of cookies when he was at work. Once I ordered ice-
cream and he marveled, watching me eat what should have

been restricted. It seems like I've lived two lives.
Maybe the dog didn't get skinny, just old overnight.
They live faster than us so it's like a time lapse,
what we must look like to rocks, tortoises, a cat

on her ninth life. Two of our cats dwindled so slowly
we didn't notice their bones until too late. Miraculously,
that doesn't seem to be so with the dog. She was just hungry,
it seems, and old. And us—we're still a little bit young.

DINA RIPSMAN EYLON

Tragic Figures

We are tragic figures dancing in a circle.
A gloomy thread passes through us
unnoticed, not understood.
The One who made us so similar to each other
sits on His throne
and ridicules our flaws.
And His entourage, cherubs of fire, chants hallelujah
for His spectacular creation:
"How great are Your deeds, Lord!"
And the flavor of human agonies
breathes out of their pure lips.
And I wonder if He knows
my personal, pathetic story.
A story that haunts me
on moldy nights
and dreary mornings.
A story in which I play
the main character
in a B-movie,
that even Hollywood
rejected
ex post factum.

MARCIA FALK

After Astounding Evil, the Promise of More to Come

Sister Dolores says she believes that good will triumph.
I believe only in the necessities of evolution; hence
this may be the beginning of the end.

But why must it be so personal?
Could we not live coolly in an ice age
unaware that the glaciers will soon split
and part and heave us to the sea?
What about a meteor? Something sudden and huge
and instantly obliterating?
Not this unabating terror that we inhabit,
our jaws clenched, our necks twisted and stiff
from turning to see behind our backs, night and day.

Perhaps we will evolve, if there is time (which it seems there is not),
into a many-eyed, many-eared creature,
exquisitely sensed to danger, yet endowed with a great courage,
the kind we know now only through denial.

Or perhaps we will devolve, each of us, back to our infancies
when our imaginations were small, our fears simple and few:
Hunger. Cold. Wet.
That she will not be there when we need her.
Her largeness, that powerful presence
so able to leave at any moment,
our fingers so tiny, so weak, so completely unable to hold on.

ANNIE FINCH

Letter for Emily Dickinson

When I cut words you never may have said
into fresh patterns, pierced in place with pins,
ready to hold them down with my own thread,
they change and twist sometimes, their color spins
loose, and your spider generosity
lends them from language that will never be
free of you after all. My sampler reads,
"called back." It says, "she scribbled out these screeds."
It calls, "she left this trace, and now we start"—
in stitched directions that follow the leads
I take from you, as you take me apart.

You wrote some of your lines while baking bread,
propping a sheet of paper by the bins
of salt and flour, so if your kneading led
to words, you'd tether them as if in thin
black loops on paper. When they sang to be free,
you captured those quick birds relentlessly
and kept a slow, sure mercy in your deeds,
leaving them room to peck and hunt their seeds
in the white cages your vast iron art
had made by moving books, and lives, and creeds.
I take from you as you take me apart.

Margaret Rockwell Finch

The Seventeenth Day of May

Grow maples in me this grow-maple day.
I lie in the long chair and wait your coming.
Spin from branches heavy with fruit of leaves
My sudden seeds, my one-wings, turning, turning!

Leap in the wind that understands the life:
Land on my leg and do not slide:
Catch in the ready furrows of my hair—I say
I have no pride.

For in me all the broad and murmuring branches
Wait but to hear it spoken.
The porch, the chair, the gutter will not take you.
But I am open.

Heads of life, stretched to the shape of flight
Plunge to my upturned palm and with good reason:
My earth, my rain, my sun, my shade will grow you.

Let your season bring me into season.

ANN FISHER-WIRTH

Blue Window

In that shadowy time before sorrow—
that twilight, October in Berkeley, the early 60's,

when I walked home along Euclid from Mrs. Runkle's
where I'd played Schumann's *"Traumerei"*

so beautifully, for once, I'd made her cry—
Before the missile crisis, when I sat on the bed in fear and exaltation

and thought of Anne Frank—while on the TV downstairs,
Soviet ships inched closer to Cuba—and wondered,

when they come to get me, when I hide beneath my desk,
my head in my hands, and the walls shake,

will I have told the world
how I love this life I am forced to lose?

Before Christian, my neighbor, drank developing fluid
and his death at Alta Bates took 48 hours, the poison dissolving his stomach,

and his father the beautiful philanderer told my mother,
"The divorce caused it," just failing to add, wringing

his elegant crooked fingers, "He did it for grief of me"—
before Ronnie, my neighbor, took acid and flew out a window,

and Jackie, my neighbor, drove 90 miles an hour into a stone wall
at prep school in Massachusetts, and Kwaasi, my neighbor,

talked to God and carved his arms and died at Napa,
the boys who lived around me lost, all dead by nineteen—

and before I had ever bled yet, ever got high, or
loved a boy, or played at kisses through Kleenex with Mary Lou—

In that time before my father lay in bed
all one year's end, the vast flower of his death blossoming,

and wrote, in a tiny crabbed hand, in the datebook I found years later,
"Had to increase the dosage today. Ann and Jink allowance"—

in that Christian Science household no one spoke,
to this day no one has ever said to me, "It was brain cancer,"

but last winter my husband got drunk in his rare blind fury,
ran weeping into the room and pounded the bed over and over,

shouting, "Don't you understand yet?
In the war they treated men for lice with lindane,

poured it over their heads,
they did it to your father, and now the fuckers tell us

lindane eats your brain." —In that time, that twilight,
when I walked slowly home along Euclid,

how I wanted to belong to the family I saw
through the blue, wisteria-covered window, to be their girl,

enter their garlicky dinnertime kitchen,
later, to sit on a high attic bed, legs crossed tailor-fashion,

and pick dreamily at white chenille—
I wondered, why not be anyone, go anywhere?

when light dies around the oak leaves
and white, ragged moths come out to beat against the streetlight,

why not knock at the door and say "I am yours. I am here"?

BARBARA FLAHERTY

Dark Raven

Upon the death of my mother

Today the hare hides beneath
the fallen tree. Deep leaves
linger on the bare blades
of grass, fingers faded made

cold, cawing like a warning,
a chill come hard like mourning.
A daughter hides inside
tearless cries as if she had died.

That blackbird heard. How many
memories blur into any
sense—sound of blue black bird
found, eyed high, heard, can stir,

can touch my hair tangled in
the root of you. Old tree, broken
branch of my branch. A small twig
is croaking a click clicking

click down in broken throated
sounds. Seed of your soil, spouted
flower and fruit of your ground,
no tears found, river underground

dried, died. Only click click sounds
in the nave of my voice pound
like heart beats pulsing in a cave.
A dark raven prayed today.

KATHLEEN FLENNIKEN

It's Not You, It's Me

Nature abhors a vacuum
but God loves a good vacuuming.

The garden was strewn with petals
and those whimsical helicopter seeds
so God created woman and watched
as Eve unwound the cord, plugged it
into the slot between good and evil
and tidied the footpaths
while all the animals sat there, dumb,
and when she was done

somebody got out the apple juice and spilled
somebody opened a box of crackers
somebody trimmed his nails without a thought
for collecting them in his palm

and after however many days of consecutive Eden
Eve said I gotta get outta here and she did
and the cord snaked after her.

LESLEY WHEELER

Essay

Most wompos know each other only as disembodied text on glowing screens. And yet this listserv is, in a way, premised on words' embodiment. By joining it, we're asserting not that we are women or poets, but that sex and gender matter where poetry is concerned. How do they matter, though? Do sex and gender shape our alliances, our use of poetic structures, our language itself? Is there something womanly or feminist in how we, female and male, behave as poets? Our conversations about politics and culture often focus on women's experiences, but not always—and many so-called women's experiences are not universal among us, from pregnancy to poverty or assault. We talk about sex and gender, and we don't talk about them, and both the words and the silences suggest their importance to us. Our sexed and sexual bodies haunt these posts even though the medium occludes our physical selves. It seems to me that we welcome this haunting, that we're all fascinated by it.

Race is another aspect of embodiment we talk and don't talk about on Wom-po. I recently searched the archives for the word "race," trying to get a historical sense of how racial and ethnic identity have shaped the list. I found that "appropriation" and "writing the other" have interested wompos at least since 1999. Wom-po has hosted heated, racially charged exchanges on Amiri Baraka, Ward Churchill, and Judy Chicago, as well as celebrations of women poets of color from Phillis Wheatley to Reetika Vazirani. Our membership becomes more diverse all the time, but our posts don't convey agreement that race matters where poetry is concerned. Race certainly haunts Wom-po, but we don't claim those ghosts so eagerly, their histories and afflictions.

CHERRYL FLOYD-MILLER

Otherness

I am in exile. Like everybody else, I live in a world that is given to me . . . But it is not my native home.
—*Paul Goodman,* Speaking and Language: Defence of Poetry, *1971*

A woman I know well has stolen my face.
She answers for me when someone asks my profession:
Writer, she says, then readies our body for the certain assault.

She makes small talk with my family
about the births and deaths of old neighbors and friends
and sidesteps the cancer that licks at my mother's brain,

malignancy that waits for my own breast or bones or lungs.
The woman has died for me a thousand times.
tends the pocks and scars that come from simple breathing.

When I am in the company of black poets, she holds
my tongue. Does not protest against the suitable way
to be black enough ... (write black enough poems).

My children adore her. She tells them stories
about how they came to be, gives them James Brown
over a plate of dirty rice, peach chutney and fried fish.

But there are days my son detects me (a front
can lie; a back always tells). He walks around the back of me
to find the face. Somewhere in the contour

of practiced muscle and grin, he discovers the brittle pupils,
cups the raised cheekbones, pulls me eye-to-his-eye,
asks the face: *Mommy, are you there?*

RUTH E. FOLEY

Triolet for Eric

After a while, we gathered in the rain.
When someone dug his hole, we let him down,
then quieted. Cold words cannot explain—
after a while, we gathered in the rain
and scrubbed our consciences. There were no stains
on us, no blood to trickle to the ground
after a while. We gathered in the rain
when someone dug his hole. We let him down.

AUDREY FRIEDMAN

The Morgan Health Center

I used to line up my dolls and prop them
against the wall, floppies alongside jointless
plastic bodies. Today I visit my friend, Eileen.
The elevator comes to her floor, steel door

slides open, and a whole new row of dolls faces me:
a few with skin as gray as their sparse hair,
three slumped over like a tired display of Raggedy
Anns with flat painted eyes fixed on one invisible

point. Others wear tubes or masks.
They face the elevator doors,
waiting for the Malekh Hamoves,
the death angel himself, to roll them

into the lift where there are two identical
buttons, H for Heaven or H for Hell.

SUZANNE FRISCHKORN

Mermaid

I still don't know how I washed up on shore,
      drunk from the storm, a third of me stuck
in mud. I used to sing this wild melody
like an Aeolian harp about a moment
      beneath red granite cliffs on the coast
of Aberdeenshire and a fisherman who combs
my dark hair to high gloss. That's so far west now.
Before those creatures with spliced tails freed me.
To teach me to kneel.
To teach me to spin.

HELEN FROST

First Deep Breath

All the angels crane their necks to see
who came, who opens her eyes tonight,
who takes her first deep breath of winter air.

It's Althea. Rosy finch, singing in the tree
outside, brings the first rays of her first day's light.
Brand new, the child is bundled with her mother in the rocking chair.

Her brother stands beside her. He touches her hair,
lets her curl her fingers round his thumb. He might
stand beside her on her last day, or she by him

on his, that hour and this one making right
of any wrongs between them. Strangers, friends, we
who stand at this periphery, see our own angers dim.
(What earthly good could come of them?)
Whose voice is that, entering this blessing, blessing me?

GLORIA FRYM

Medicate Specific

I am a soldier in the war and I am a person. Who left persons behind. I drink to medicate the specific. I find a vein and mine it to medicate the specific. All goes well except the specific. I have been commanded, I am afraid, I will kill, this is against my nature, so I must obey the order and remain lonely in my specific anti-desire. I do not wish to maim others; however, I was promised certain things, such as. When the band plays I forget. I go along, I hold myself erect, I enter the body of another country and I am ready. But I am scared. *This hour I tell things in confidence / I might not tell everybody, but I will tell you.* Like water, I have been everywhere I am needed. I wish to be needed. I wish to be a part of the human race, though I am asked to do things that seem in- and un-human. *We are all animals, though we behave worse than them.* I have to ignore this aspect of the current conflict. I am therefore I am. I was told, I was promised, I showed up. In order to do what I do, I medicate myself. How else could I do it. How else could I live among those who do what I do not really wish to do or be. You don't know me, you would never know me, I am unknowable, unseen, your servant, your loyalty, your surrogate. I carry the mutation of war in me. I deliver. War is born dead. I nurse it. I kill for it, defending what I deliver. Please understand. I am an ordinary. I am a person. I is I is I is and will be. Sweet Mary, who bore Jesus, who bore our savior. Help me now. Dear You at Home: Your photographs, in my pocket, do not marry anyone else, while I'm gone. Do not forsake me. I carry you with me. The thought of you enables me to go on. This has been written a million times and a million times women have written or not written back. No deceit just fatigue. I wear those too, camouflage. The forest, I am to resemble it, I am to deforest it, I am to be it, I am to be you in your stead. However, I know you do not want my service, you would rather I not be here, and I too would rather not. I signed up, I said Yes, it did not subtract from my love of you. Sweet You, whoever. Please forgive me, I will kill and I will kill again and it will be legal, it will be the "enemy," it will disable, destroy, shock, decivilize, I did not choose the specific consequences, but I do medicate the specific, with wine with pill with needle with anything to shut out the wound of the wounding. No history will forgive me, no history will absolve me, no history cares for me, do you care for me, do you love me. Say yes, say yes, say yes.

DIANE GAGE

Reading Anne Sexton

Amid the dull whine of leafblowers
by which this block sets its ordinary clock
a drama occurs. My neighbor Leon
is felled by a stroke. His Avon lady
wife Marcy dresses up to walk up
the hill to the hospital. Meanwhile,

I sit here in the insulation called
not-my-turn and contemplate
Anne's similes and metaphors: Snow
White's "cheeks as fragile as cigarette
paper," dwarves "little hot dogs."
I take Marcy some zucchini soup,

a rising to another's emergency
against the day that I'm the emergency,
the one straining at the tearing bonds
of my most recent cocoon, shivering
forth fragile, stained, bedraggled,
into some strange unimaginable land.

Or will it have leafblowers? Creatures
who show themselves as my familiars
by resembling hot dogs and cigarettes?
I think only nothing is unimaginable,
yet I know there are those who claim to have
imagined it, beyond the usefulness of zero,

as a kind of place that is of course,
paradoxically, no place. My neighbor
has already become a kind of place
where Leon used to be, but so far
his absence is not nothing.
So far memory's imagination serves.

JEANNINE HALL GAILEY

Female Comic Book Superheroes

are always fighting evil in a thong,
pulsing techno soundtrack in the background
as their tiny ankles thwack

against the bulk of male thugs.
With names like Buffy, Elektra, or Storm
they excel in code decryption, Egyptology, and pyrotechnics.

They pout when tortured, but always escape just in time,
still impeccable in lip gloss and pointy-toed boots,
to rescue male partners, love interests, or fathers.

Impossible chests burst out of tight leather jackets,
from which they extract the hidden scroll or antidote,
tousled hair covering one eye.

They return to their day jobs as forensic pathologists,
wearing their hair up, donning dainty glasses.
Of all the goddesses, these pneumatic heroines most

resemble Artemis, with her miniskirts and crossbow,
or Freya, with her giant gray cats.
Each has seen this apocalypse before.

See her perfect three-point landing on top of the chariot,
riding the silver moon into the horizon,
city crumbling around her heels.

ALICIA ZAVALA GALVÁN

Untitled

Schools' out.
Yet this morning he is up early.
Wanders slow
on the holiday-silenced
downtown sidewalks.
His eyes and head are slanted downward
until a small slice of bright color stops his step.

The colors start at the ground
become brighter, bolder,
increasing, rising.
His eyes and mouth open wider
as he sees a second, third and fourth floor
of a grand old building.

The kaleidoscope vision continues up
into the morning sky.

JENNIFER J. GANDEL

A Toilet

Four porcelain frogs belonged on the shelf. A child would dress them in doll clothes, if such things would fit. A child did dance them across the toilet, also porcelain, also cold but white like egg shells and goat's milk. They were a family—two big, two small—with one little god-hand to guide and drop them, on accident, to a linoleum floor. No one ever said be careful with the statues. No one said anything. But with every chipped web or fractured eye another spank; wet hand on bare ass: it echoes in small chambers. There is nothing felicitous here. Nothing patient like bubbles that rise from bath water, already cold.

LISHA ADELA GARCÍA

Snail

My *brujas* are here,
those ladies that pray over me
and massage my ankles and feet
to let the tired spirits out.
This is when I realize
I carry my home with me
like a snail,
a snail that likes the graveyard
too much. I am standing on a
headstone looking at myself.
My clothes cling to my body
in pockets turned outward
and inward, in pain or joy,
depending on how much life
I can contain at the moment.
I see a man haunting graves,
razor scars all over his body,
his neck, the rope burn of oblivion.
Perhaps this is why I like cemeteries
especially in Paris.
They have all those white
temples I can't take with me.
So many snail shells left on the ground.

ALICE GEORGE

The wingless aetheist remarks the number of birds

in literature and remembers Scarry's idea: we obsess
on birds and flowers because they're small,

so easily pulled into our skull, for we are limited
after all in our taste for beauty, so some fit

is required to trigger our lyrical praise.
And yes, yellow-throated warblers,

sprays of lilac do charge her with joy yet
the atheist remembers her college thrill at Sartre's

disgust with trees, the way he stood before nature
unsettled by nausea. The songs about birds bother

her most, the stress on 'wings' and 'little,' as if
we all wore heavy loads, such an urgent need for help,

as if those soft beasts with over-performing
hearts could enter us, could carry.

BERNADETTE GEYER

The Naming of Bones

"The sphenoid bone...somewhat resembles
a bat with its wings extended..."
—Gray's Anatomy, 1918

It was simple at first:

we named them as we broke
them—radius and ulna,
tibia and fibula—names
like celestial bodies.

We searched the sky
hoping to see
our phalanges and femurs
poised alongside Orion and Cassiopeia.

We bruised our bones
to make them stronger, pleased
with our ability to shape and mold
our bodies to our will.

When we began to name
the afflicted—*gimp, crip,*
the slow one—again,
we thought bruising
only made things stronger.

Experience taught us
the green twig may fracture
incompletely
but the damage
can never be undone.

ELLEN GOLDSTEIN

Meadowbrook Sapphics

Skipping class, we crossed over red-brick rubble,
razor grass, and chicory fields behind our school
to reach the stream where the tree-root banks sank
                down to the water.

It was ninth grade, you were the new girl. I took
you to see water spiraling over ledges,
falling, forming currents of sound, a steady
                curtain to hide us

from the others. We watched how the sunlight splintered,
fractured quiet pools with its glancing light that
slashed my gaze so all that I saw was your face
                shimmering slightly.

Then you touched me, all at once, hands against my
hair, the shocking taste of your mouth on mine like
sharpened light. And still how that small percussion
                echoes within me.

ANA DOINA

Essay

Every now and again someone posts on the Wom-po list the latest newspaper article, or an essay from a well-known literary magazine by some important cultural icon, heralding the death of poetry. Poetry is dead. Children don't read. The only public for poetry is poets themselves. Poems have never changed or in some important way influenced, affected, or afflicted the world. Well, since most of us on Wom-po are poets, we certainly have an opinion about the state of poetry and love to endlessly debate and dissect every sentence of such articles, bringing vigorous arguments against the presented opinions.

Whoever doesn't think of poetry as changing the world does not consider the world I know. Poetry has a part to play in the ethnogenesis of a group; it is still a repository for history and myth, a forger of national identities. Just think of all the national anthems and the eighteenth- and nineteenth-century poetry that inspired and inflamed the revolutionary ethos of that time, a time whose ideas and ideals are still part of our world. Every revolution had its poems.

In the totalitarian state of Romania under Ceausescu where I grew up and lived, poetry was a lifeline for many of us—from peasants to academics, it was a way of resisting the daily injustices the system visited upon us. It gave voice to our revolt; it allowed us to communicate "dangerous" opinions to one another in public by just reciting or mentioning a poem; it allowed us to fool the censors by employing the ciphered language and imagery poems gave us. Verses and poems were our resistance, our vindication, our oppressed selves mocking the censor in ways no one could punish. I wouldn't be who I am if not for poetry.

DAVID GRAHAM

Long Overdue Note to My College Professor
Who Broke Down and Cried One Morning in 1974
While Teaching Yeats

At long last I know what you mean.
That was no country for any man,
that classroom with its fluorescent rows
of groggy juniors equal in fear

and indifference. We were in
no one's arms but yours, and you split
open like a shell to reveal
the raw jelly inside. We froze,

thinking it was family woe,
maybe an old back injury
acting up, perhaps even fear
of tenure's blank guillotine.

Maybe so, maybe so. Now I
think it was us, our practiced slouch,
our gaze blank and pitiless as
the clock itching toward hour's end.

We weren't about to love Yeats
on your say-so. We were thinking
grades, thinking lunch, thinking firelight
playing upon a girlfriend's skin,

and we were thinking them so hard
we couldn't feel what you said
Yeats felt. So in piteous rage
at our held breaths, our cautious nods,

you wept. And we didn't know how
to be anything but polite
about it. You stammered, halted,
and stood bent over the lectern

in pain. We studied our notes. We
glanced at the swaying trees outside
while you cried silently into,
over, and about our silence.

NEILE GRAHAM

On Skye

Hard to know the right madness here—
Skye's hills have the twisted pine scent
of Montana, the air of Coyote's

bitter-bright games—but here the road
crosses the bridge where Macleod
said goodbye to his faery wife

and leads to the ruins of Trumpan Church
where Clan Macdonald was burned alive
by Clan Macleod. The crofts crumple

like abandoned ranches, houses and barns
folding in on themselves, stones falling
one by one. Here it was not hard weather

that emptied the fields but the Clearances:
the landlords and everywhere their sheep.
Stacks and hills and emptiness. Stones

rearing to the sky: churches and brochs
bending stone by stone nearer the grasses,
castles full of nettles and sheep, weeds

growing right to the sea, and everywhere,
on church walls, sea rocks, corners
of the castle windows, a strange green fern,

bright with brownish stems, everywhere
springing from the cracks in stone.
I dreamt a dog whose hair was these

ferns, thick, rich, alive. Looking at her
I saw how the stones love this land,
how the rain and wind and tides love stone,

how the grass does, how the woman who once lived
in the fallen croft shaped scones
from flour and sang while her children—

who grew to leave for the New World—
woke to the sure rhythm of her work
and the haunting lilt of a piper's tune

reeling in the righteous wind.
All this, with my fingers woven
into fronds on her back, moving from the cool

green growth to the warmth that rose
from her skin. And in the pause of flying home,
right at the Rockies' feet, there she is again:

standing stiff in the wind as my plane
touches down on the runway right by her.
A wolf on the tarmac, the blowing snow

swirling around her feet like fog,
like the cold and deep warmth
of her feral, human breath.

KATE GREENSTREET

Lives of the Saints

They have very long days, standing around.
A lot of chewing.
It always seems to be summer, the flies,
or else it rains.

Like us, they make the days
from the hours that are given.
They appreciate punctuality.
They show up on time. If you're late,
they look at you—a terrible look—
as if, for once, they're going to try to understand you.

They have a bony, hairy part on their face,
the top of their head would have horns.
They're really different from each other,
but they have a lot in common.

I could tell you so much about cows!
Their giant toenails. And how,
while still very young,
they begin to wait for something.
Soon, they seem to accept
it won't ever come. But they keep waiting.
What we imagine is their sadness
is this perfect, hopeless waiting.

I've watched a single cow
standing in a field a thousand times.

They have no respite, just the grass.
The mother acts detached,
almost indifferent to the calf
after it's born, but,
when it's taken away,
they begin to call each other.
They look for each other, with their voices,
and everybody knows
it's wrong.

It takes something like 345 squirts to get a gallon of milk.
You get a couple gallons a milking, it depends
on the cow. She needs to be milked twice a day,
morning and night, no matter what.
When a cow is moved
to a different field, the milk
changes flavor.
When they shit, it falls from a distance
and, in a cold barn, steam rises off it.
You can see the breath
come and go
through their immense
nostrils.

If you're a child when you see a calf born,
you always know
there's a place as big as you
inside a cow.

I think people don't love them more
because they don't do all that pet
pretending.
But when they're in their stanchion,
you can't resist laying a hand
flat on their side, even though

all you get back
is the rough switch of tail when you least
expect it. Did I mention
how they can shift
slightly, and push you—up against the hay bales,
when the barn gets full, and they don't notice.

SUSAN GRIMM

I, the Persona: Confessions

Balloon head. Antic galoot. Stick figure with triangle
for a dress. There's no scorn like the scorn

that can be heaped on this flighty I who's been
abandoned. Writer increases hair, decreases wit.

Not only was I there watching (third person
permeable), I was there vivid and lamenting (first

person persistent). Unreliable useful piece
of demonstration, lambasted because it's the I

and the I has now moved on. Writer and reader can be
clean in their glee; naked fool wearing Etruscan mask

gambols and improves, lambent in realization, sheep
shirred and shaped to be hung as sacrificial lamb.

EVE GRUBIN

Modesty

Does the head covering open
the interior eye?

*

The painter conceals the color—Eve emerging
from the hidden
part of Adam—behind black paint.

*

The willow, down-turned and silent, incites
the windows with its long leaves.

*

The clothed body as knowledge.

*

When love is gone
sexual pleasure detaches from the mouth
of the world.

*

The subway heaved forward

and the hand of the man I was with
jerked, from the quick motion, fell
to my waist

for less than one second lightly he touched
me as we lurched, our swoons lit

each tight light to a rupture
into the world beside this one.

*

The Torah is the body we clothe
and its laws are the body we kiss and hold
wrapping the soul
holding the soul of souls.

*

How is this longing a longing
for the one who clothes the naked? There is no
romance.

*

Why is the holy ark covered? As a woman
covers her body forever flowing and drawn.
When the eye sees inside the ark
God's presence is forgotten
when love is gone.

*

What I don't speak you will know.

*

Is the hidden more blessed than the revealed?

*

Why is the holy ark covered? As a woman
covers her body forever flowing and drawn.

SUSAN GUBERNAT

Hades

It took the coal man and all his sons
a long summer morning to back their truck
into the alley, slide the metal chutes
through the slit cellar windows, hooked wide
open, for once, and send tons of black clods
clattering into the bins. A single piece
of their coal was almost weightless, shiny
as a patent leather shoe, unstrapped,
dangling from a little girl's toe.
But the roar! As if the fires had escaped
without consuming the bowels of the house.
There they lay, glinting like an old man's dark
mouth when he remembers winter,
cold floors, how she couldn't deny him then.

CINDY WILLIAMS GUTIÉRREZ

A Lesson on Creation
from Sor Juana Inés to Novitiates

So in my case, it is not seemly
that I be viewed as feminine,
as I will never be a woman
who may as woman serve a man.
    —*Sor Juana Inés de la Cruz, 1648?-1695*

"Loves me, loves me not," poor Adam
Wonders: "Should I resist God's will?"
Eve does not demur or grapple.
Why can't Eve eschew the apple?
What still tempts us in the garden?

God arranged this futile marriage
Next to ripened fruits of knowledge.
Apples burst with sweeter juice
Than fig leaf over Adam's fruits.
Art or man?—Eve plucks with courage.

No more queens or cooks or nurses,
Clever women risk men's curses.
Still, the Muses birth—we who
Wed the Church (instead of men) to
Manifest irreverent verses.

Judith Arcana

Essay

Invited by Annie Finch and Judith Barrington, I signed on to the Wom-po list in May of 2004. I saw immediately that some women who post notes on the list are my age and older, but most are not. Many of these younger women became writers through the network of college writing programs that has prolifer-ated in the United States in the past twenty years, offering a source of information and attitude that is usefully counter to my own history. After teaching more than forty years, I got lucky; by chance and generosity, I received a pot of money—just enough to let me live as a writer, not a teacher-who-writes-when-she-can. I've moved writing into the center of my life. I've begun to create an image of myself as an old woman, writing. I'm burnishing that image, working and dreaming myself into my time among witches and spinners, magic queens and wise crones, imagining myself into a generative old woman who spends her days making art with words.

TAMI HAALAND

Reasons to Fly

If Icarus were forty he could balance
his course between sea and sun.

You see the bowl of flicker feathers,
the glorious underside of a cardinal,

and once you get over your fear
of heights, what could stop you?

You'll understand things that traverse the sky,
the meandering gnat, the hawk's claws.

Why not practice now, before spirit
floats over body, observing its static serenity?

You could see past sadness,
know the tangible interior of clouds.

Consider the cold fire of stars at your back,
the ground's contours and currents below.

It's what every restless ounce of you
has always wanted, the busy air.

MARILYN HACKER

Ghazal: In Summer

—for Mimi Khalvati

The air thickens, already more than half in summer.
At the corner café, girls in T-shirts laugh in summer.

The city streets, crowded with possibility
under spring rain, thin out, don't promise enough in summer.

That urge to write one's life instead of living it
makes sentences slip limply off-the-cuff in summer.

Slipped in a drawer under an expired passport,
curly-head in an orchard smiles for a photograph in summer.

Going downstairs early for bread: two winos snore on the landing,
« Can't they make do with sleeping in the rough in summer? »

Hard-case on the street, teacher out of class both harbor
a lowgrade fever and productive cough in summer.

Espresso winter, springtime of Juliénas:
black tea with honey's what I'll quaff in summer.

Despite my wall of books and Bach's geometries,
some scent wafts from the street to call my bluff in summer.

Not in a tank but a golf-cart rides the oligarch:
however, he does not dismiss his staff in summer.

Let them not, in Maryam's name or Marilyn's,
blot any cindered city off a graph in summer.

ANNE HAINES

Let X Equal . . .

Let the woman wake
from sleep, as she does each morning
of her life. Let her arm
reach out, drowsy, and brush
the bedroom curtains aside,
let her watch for five whole minutes
the cat washing herself
on the front lawn, the bird
pecking madly at damp earth,
the neighbor clutching the front of her robe
as she steps out the door
and stoops for her morning paper.

Let the sunlight be quiet
and warm across the lawn. Let the grass
be succulent and green.
Let the day unfold like a perfect
equation, every moment growing
toward some simple answer,
some singular integer.
Let the woman stand for the thesis,
the given, all the formulas that build
a body of knowledge. Let her waking
be the question, and the window
equal some visible understanding, the work
she is asked to show. Let the neighbor
and the curtains be variables, the light
and the lawn be the sum
of each other, the pure reciprocity of morning.
Let the woman's hand, opening
curtains, and the woman, rising,
be a new theorem, solid and given,
the beginning of an elegant
and irrefutable proof.

KENDRA HAMILTON

The Restless Dead

In the tiny brick ranch
you live in but we own
near the old colored hospital
and abandoned colored school
there are two fingers more of brandy
in a thin bell of crystal
and our easy camaraderie has frayed.

We've been talking about them,
about the question between us
that seems it's always been between us:
Who were these folk who made us?

The woman "Eliza" and child
"1,400.00" with a flourish beside the words,
nothing to divide them
from the five dollar pots one line above
the hundred dollar mule one line below
in an 1850 listing
for an old man's will.
The man James who bought her,
got three children on her,
replaced her, when she ran,
with the woman "colored" "housekeeper"
and child "mulatto" of the 1870 census.

You're shouting—won't let me speak.
Your words are the color of brandy.
There are trees in them, willows and oaks,
leaves shattering in a stiff wind,
charred bodies swinging from the limbs.
"To hell with that white man," you're shouting,
eyes dark and dilated.

I won't dispute you have the right.
But must it always be so?
Must our dead always divide us?

Again your rant, smashing my whys into your because:
"This is not a love story!"

Yes, I insist,
pouring two fingers more of brandy into the glass,
it is.

Are we not the wool of their weaving?
Is she not pieced tissues of my dreaming?
Is this not love's function—to fabricate?

Today a curl of parchment at the courthouse
shouted a country church,
a town called Scurry Springs,
Eliza . . .

Barefoot in ten acres of corn,
she is a mothersister as close
as the hoe in my hand.
When I am thirsty
she gives me to drink
well water tasting of clay in the cup.
When it is hot
she bends to the kerchief on my head
then stretches to the sun above us
citrine
ecstatic.

Where she goes I will follow.
Where Eliza goes I will ever follow,
singing,

as the ranks of the dead
close before and behind us.

MARYANNE HANNAN

To You Who Speak of Audre Lorde

You make me want to raise my hand and tell my story, tell how
if I'd met any of you alone, I too would retreat
because there are only one or two places, and all of them the same,
where I could be taken as a local.

But she dreamed a coming together, a working tomorrow,
and you swear she will not be buried alive with the liars,

so maybe you would understand
that even a white breast, lovely in its way,
saved by the blood of the Lamb and all that,
atrophies in time, with or without the blade.

LOIS MARIE HARROD

His Mouth

Those last six days
even the smile disappeared
and his mouth became the sink hole
I had been pushed back from as a child,
a weak spot where the earth gave way.

But the mouth did not give way.

It stretched itself
into the outline of a rotting pear,
a slack rubberband,
as if he were holding the left
side open for a last word
while the right lay too feeble to listen.

And all the while I could hear his voice
pleading from the speechless pulpit
cannot you wait with me one hour.

Of course, that too was understated
as his life had been. A man can live
without praise, and now he was
living without water. Three, four,
five, six days his gethsemane continued,
dying as he had dictated
without intervention.

Six days with his breath
so soiled my sister and I
held wet towels to our faces
when our mother was not watching.

I understood then how those
who died without odor
could be considered saints,
bodies incorruptible,
but not how my mother
could say she smelled
nothing at all.

MARY SENIOR HARWOOD

Healing from Inside Out

Was there ever any doubt
They would take a piece of you,
Leave a wound to heal from inside out?

The bone had festered, soft and foul.
From one pinprick infection grew.
Was there ever any doubt?

They packed the wound, we learned about
How skin could skim and form anew,
Leave a wound not healed from inside out.

They peeled away the skin and then we found
A truth once hidden, deep from view.
Was there ever any doubt

Our lives would change if we allowed
A whirlpool's waters washing through to
Leave a wound to heal from inside out?

We since have learned to live without;
Lessons learned from loss accrue.
There was never any doubt
The wound could heal from inside out.

FARIDEH HASSANZADEH-MOSTAFAVI

Isn't It Enough?

I gave up love
being satisfied with the quiet of shadows
and memories.

Time was past, lost,
moments exploded
by the rain of bombs.

At nightfall
I don't brush my dreams any more.
At nightfall
I don't care for the wandering sun any more.

At nightfall
I leave the frightened moon in the sky
to shelter under the ground.

I am neither a woman nor a poet any more.

Night by night
more and more,
I feel real.

Like the bloody sound of alarms,
Like the roaring anti-aircraft rounds,
Like the falling bombs and rockets,
which turn the ruins and ashes
into eternal reality;
I feel night by night more real
and old,

so old and real that in the mirror
I see nothing anymore
but an aisle of empty chairs.

Oh, isn't it enough?

What does a man need
more than a loaf of bread,
a quiet night
and an armful of bleak love,
for giving up and being satisfied
with the quiet of shadows
and memories?

JOYCE NOWER

Essay

The ocean of poetry is fed by many rivers, one of which has been the feminist movement. Only a handful of nineteenth-century American women poets survive in most anthologies. Women poets began to attain greater critical recognition and respect in the twentieth century, and their prominence grew dramatically as the century progressed. Much of this transformation is due to the Second Wave of the feminist movement, in the middle and late 1960s and throughout the 1970s, which supported and encouraged living women writers, and fostered the discovery and recovery of many who had been ignored or neglected.

But some rivers can dam up if they aren't constantly deepened and renewed. Today Wom-po is an engine of such deepening and renewal. While the First Wave of the movement in mid–nineteenth century set the scene for the development of our sense of internal authority, the Second Wave (and the Third Wave, depending on your age) has affirmed that authority, and the existence of Wom-po continues that affirmation. Subject matter once uniquely connected to the Second Wave—body imagery, female mythology, women's issues and concerns, and, above all, feminist consciousness—is extended and enriched by Wom-po poets and their discussions on our list. Furthermore, the rich sources of information that Wom-po members offer one another daily forge the connection between being a woman and a poet.

DOLORES HAYDEN

On the Hundred-Percent Corner

Academic couples improve their chances
in a tight job market if they are willing to try
a long-distance commute.

On the plane, I'm talking tough, like a pioneer.
I plat a town with the string, the stakes, the tents,
name unpaved streets Equality and Progress.

He wrestles a Conestoga. Oxen balk
and hex signs blaze like prairie stars. He steers
around old ruts, veers off the trail, heads back

on the inside curve of a creek he'll have to ford,
later. But watch, he'll raft that painted wagon,
provision us in Independence, push on.

I fly today, barter a Boston evening
for a sere late California afternoon,
charged to our joint account. Below me spin

alfalfa circles, green as the all-seeing eye
on the dollar. *Annuit coeptis:* God
Smiles on Our Undertakings. I am aware

grit desert shifts beneath those leafy clocks.
Look down: commercial blocks, wide open sky,
Loving, Utopia, and Roaring Springs.

Dry crossroads yawn at nowhere: Earth and Spur
and Matador, Happy, Goodnight, and Muleshoe,
risk-takers' towns we might have passed through then.

We claim both work and love. Our trail winds on,
arched like an oxbow, pioneers' old crosses
nailed and named, every mazy mile.

AVA LEAVELL HAYMON

Pose, Flammable

It was over for her. The fire,
when it came at last, a relief.
The pose was flammable as gauze,
a black rag skirt, the shawl
and broom. Her skin, like parchment
anyway, browned first in spots
then flashed into light and heat.

So silly, she thought to herself
as her eyes all at once gave up
their fierce attention, melted
the way water balloons burst in heat,
first the surface tension, then a rush
of steamy center: the pose a fraud
from the beginning. It bought me

time—time and children, this house,
the many meals, the craft. I let them
look at me however they chose—
priests, babies, old men gray as chalk.
Each comes away with a different story.
Only the children, chastened and generous,
have let me go.

ELOISE KLEIN HEALY

So the Teacher Jumped Up on the Desk

September 1961

So the teacher jumped up on the desk
in our Freshman English class, the front door
to the mind for us little less than middle
class Catholic girls at Immaculate Heart College, & our eyes
fixed on the professor, his split flying,
his jacket and tie flapping,
him waving a little black & white copy of this
Howl like it's a hymnal & he's got
religion, he's got the juju chant & rattle
of a million dead rosaries sent electrical
shock to revive & turn themselves into the
knuckle joints & knee bones of the living—
Let's dance it all started to say, let's
shake this thing, this hour, this book, this life
which is not going to be the one you registered
for—NO, you are not going to return to the
parish & iron the altar clothes. NO, you are not
going to carpool, learn golf, play bridge
on Tuesdays or join the Catholic Daughters
of America, you are NOT going to make
Jello molds & tat doilies. You are about to
smoke a lot of dope & waste the weekends
drinking gallons of Gallo Hearty Burgundy
shirtless on the patio & you won't be alone.
The Beatles are coming, the Beatles are coming &
you are getting a booster shot for anti-war proclivities,
you are getting so amped that language
will not rest a four-cylinder low-mileage
car in your garage but turn into a nitro-burning
dragster in your guts—peeling, wheeling, weaving
from lane to lane before abandoning the pavement
altogether, airborne without a parachute.
You are ready for *flame out flame out.*
The sky opening like a mouth & wrapping its lips

around your paganized shoeless feet says
inhale this impetus to flee your former self,
ditch all your classes & go who knows where
or cares

ALLISON ADELLE HEDGE COKE

Ghosts

When all the doghair, squirreltail, foxtail,
porcupine, buffalo, pony grasses run
impression strummed,
along slopes, gradient rise—

When Mullein presses low,
red willow limbs quiver, whirlwinds shiver,
release silver-spotted skippers,
monarchs,   white butterflies
take to wing, to firmament—

lifting miracle commotion,
phenomena now we.

In translucency of leaves,
overcast sun, rolling,
lightening, shadowing   breadth of green—

In this acuity, this keenness
insight pronounces utterances
not unlike prophecy.

For those who heed, prefigure, perceive.
For those who distinguish
modern from manifest,
in everything all familiar.

We will have beckoned you to return to us,
return our skeletal remains to shelter here,
return our longing.

Then, in quiet whispering,
momentary stillness reveals.

LIZ HENRY

Kissing Nadine in the Rain

The holy moment of transfiguration wetleaf thunder
Me swinging competent off my bike
completely soaked
& knowing the moment full is or will be lost
in time but by its holiness
will merge with all others,

Her warm at the sliding glass door
under the wooden walkway
under the labyrinth steps and blue rails of the 21st Street Co-op
warm & dry leaning up to the wet wood with a knowing look
kissing me as if I were about to leave for war
when in fact I was just coming home from work
to her thin arms & spider arms
thin from some past abortion & three months
of some kind of egyptian dysentery,

Once I heard that she described me:
"Kissing her is like falling into a sea of pillows"
and on hearing this my lower lip felt cautiously for the top one
looking for that mythical sea
and in the deep green thunderflash
could that be me, my bike spokes clicking
and pecan trees dropping
their fern fronds, their arm branches
at the arrival of noon's nightfall
green twilight of thunder it was the carnival moment
just before the kiss when her coarse black
waving hair and extreme pallor
lit up in the rain's warm dim light
leaning against the doorframe legs crossed casual and body bow-bent slim
not speaking though I can still hear her hoarse crow voice possibly sultry with Africa,

I am home from the wars, mother,
and take you in my arms knowing
you won't mind my clothes are wet
and everything broken can be fixed and all hunger fed,

Nadine standing tall as Grahn's Woman Talking to Death
standing strong and fragile on the bridge holding up her hand "Stop!"
aware of Israel and white South Africa and Birmingham Alabama and all injustice
and the divided city of Austin with highway 35 splitting the university from the east side,
Standing on the bridge at the edge of life
making the bridge her back like a diplomat to the unjust judge
as if in her knowledge of the world's imperfect love
she would protect and gently forgive my relative innocence
her strong and resistant life an elegy and apologia for all betrayals
since her own death like any of us could come at any time
and since we contained death embarrassed and naked between our lips
    meeting searching
for the mythical ocean and the thunderhead
of our important kiss a moment found in the vast lost unjust world,

O my child-wife with starved arms outstretched I would protect you,
thinking of how I thought you my first real friend
and because of the husky sincerity of your voice
I didn't look back,
At that point wiser than I am now I'd seize any day's offering
though I can throw myself back in time because of that moment
before kissing you in the rain and coming home to you,
it is unfair to make you the subject of my informed scrutiny,
since only today I bothered to think about what I didn't ask
but was content to assume or never know if you're a woman still living your life
though you are nearly forgotten in my stories
because at the time I was nearly insane with the intensity of memory
so that none of my loved ones now knows your name,
though I did run into you years later with your hair cut dyke short
screaming hoarse and deep "Liz Hen-e-ry!" from the parade's crowd
as I rollerskated naked down Market Street
overcome suddenly with love again for you and our past
and everything golden in the San Francisco sun and me overcome
by the guilt of having left you I don't remember how but I'm sure badly,

She, also a turncoat with her voice an informer on the run
having cooperated with the law to get out of jail by turning in her source
her voice still leading her to follow the Dead though no longer dealing
(It's clear that because you knew you weren't in jail
you were free on a vast great plain of freedom and should still be so free)
The knowledge of guilt infused through her thin bones
Possibly the responsibility of being born
who she was there in South Africa but also with so many dead before her
that not only having been born
but bearing the seed of survival in a big family nearly destroyed
all grandparents most certainly long ago starved ash in maybe Hungary
compromising her voice and her continued living
And me loving just the way she said "Birmingham Alabama"
gloom-friend holding the city's whole history with love
as if having lived there entailed a certain civic duty to enjoy life's dark history,

As if she were always inventing new ways to stay alive,
always ready to learn a new trade, handy with her hands and working hard
so that it seemed no Depression could ever overcome her handiness!
Anything—anything was possible,
such as, Here I am, I'll make the most of it,
as if her whole life and all our lives were a desert island where she was
inventing and creating everything necessary for the continuation of life
And coming up to her walking my sturdy bike having worked all day
and then ridden healthy home under my own steam
I felt my own self sufficiency and hers
would find all corners of use and beauty & use them and see them,
and so I seized the temptation to stay with you, impossible apocalypso,
though I know I'm destined to be the only survivor,

Village girl long-limbed and clean against the wet wood panels waiting,

Camp whore lounging in the doorway
with an eye out for the return of Odysseus
and the offer of a golden lotus,

Pale stick-girl in dull green straddling
the gun's huge cannon of some Israeli tank as if to say ride em cowgirl
a mysterious photograph unexplained of maybe being in the army
that you knew I thought of as a dirty army with full sympathy
for my fellow students and protesters in Palestinian checkered scarves
and other dirty wars and people who have been disappeared
but riding that tank squinting thin into the sun with joy
and now into the Texas thunderlight under the massy anvil, the cloud-wind anvil
casting its mossy penumbra over the Austin hills, my kibbutznik, my beloved and me
filled up with light incredible happiness from the rain-ocean;
I sent up a buoy to mark the spot for my own future grief
        already contained in my happiness
the way girls are born already containing all their ovaries' eggs fully developed
and the light blessing us until I saw every molecule
of our love in the moment
that was temporary beyond the nature of time
because you loved me forever
but as a wanderer alone
I could only look forward
to the moment of coming home
so I loved only forever

R. Joyce Heon

High Flying

Leave your purpling rooms.
Release your fragments from all bonds.
Bannered into ether,
become pastel shards of bliss.

Surpass the sun
tumbling a lemonade wind.
With eyes of infinity,
bypass the orbit of a dark hole.

Relax the quizzical eyebrow.
Kite every question
into the reverse of itself.

The answer spirals from
the creature of the liquid tongue
with four lips that never meet.
All vowels lionize euphoria:

> *Hail! I, Ohi-oh*
> *you Oah-who?*
> *align clear color*
> *unclothe wonder*
> *allelu-yeah*
> *yo-yo, yo-yo, yo-yo, yo*
> *hilarious, glorious, rock us*
> *gregarious   us, us, us!*

My needle drops to full
as you exit my frame,
escape the confines
of my checkerboard heart.

I, the whirling pie chart
of hair ribbons untied.

Inspired by Vasily Kandinsky's *Untitled Abstract,* 1936, Worcester Art Museum Permanent Collection.

ANNE HIGGINS

The Daruma Doll

You paint the first eye when you make the wish.
You paint the second when the wish comes true.

O Good Luck Doll, the shrapnel in the snow
will stay in Kosovo throughout July.
God is coming up from the inside.
I wish my first eye perfect vision.

A grey footprint marks my first eye's core,
a grey cat sitting center in the field.

The third charm added when I was confirmed.
My secret brother showed up, just in time,
the one flushed down the toilet by mistake
with all the blood of my mother's tears.

To fall seven times,
to rise eight times,
life starts from now.

ERIN SHANNON HOLLOWELL

Practice

The morning that I dedicate myself
to looking at the world more closely,
I wake to find everything covered by fog.

The nearest cherry tree still holds
hard fists of green fruit. Its neighbor,
five feet further away, turns in tatters.

Spruce trees become towering shadows,
brooding on a vague gray horizon
only twenty paces beyond the back door.

Somewhere a dog lifts his voice
to solitary song, anonymous,
reduced to long lone vowels.

In the kitchen, the coffee rattles and hisses
before the empty white cup. The plate
awaits the toast.

JEAN ANAPORTE-EASTON

Essay

One day, weeping to my former mentor, Judith Johnson, about how isolated from any poetry community I was in my new city, I found Wom-po. The members—male as well as female—a startling and then inspiring fact (how many places do men seek out the intellectual company of women?)—are generous. I have a folder of discussions and commentaries, including large pieces like Lesley Wheeler's book proposal on voice complete with bibliography and Jeffrey Levine's discussion of the "art of the manuscript." After ten years of sending out books, then chapbooks, feeling as though I were blindfolded, I understand.

The best thing about Wom-po, however, is that, in seeking discussions of craft, I was thrown back on individual truth—the intersection between form and content. On one occasion a poet I admired was being ridiculed for his new, freer (read *looser* for his critics) verse; even his sartorial style came up for scrutiny. Support for this view accumulated until I could no longer bear it. When I replied, filled with doubt about my own ability to judge and about this poet I thought I admired, a whole other segment of the Wom-po community surfaced, like the vase or facing profiles. Craft this time was associated with who you are, where your balance point is, what your gut tells you. What else is creativity, right? But accepting, believing, acting on it is something else. One of the great gifts of Wom-po for me has been the women who have described the struggle to grant themselves permission to do their own kind of creative work, conventions and traditions be damned.

ANN HOSTETLER

Resisting Geometry

The first time I saw my father defeated
he was leaving the only parent-teacher conference
he ever had concerning my academic failure,
his black raincoat drooping over one arm.
Settling his other arm over my shoulder,
he walked me to the car, told me about
his sixth-grade failure to master fractions.

How could I explain to him
it was the axioms themselves
I objected to, knowing that, like his whims,
I had to take them on faith.
Tested against experience
they appeared to be correct—
no two points could occupy the same space
at the same time; lines perfectly parallel
will never intersect; a straight line
is the shortest distance between two points.
But such self-evidence troubled me.

Imagining exceptions, I felt called
to test the axioms, to wage a battle
against givens, resisting at the root.
When the boys circled Mr. Oelkers
at the blackboard, arguing logic,
I sat at the back of the room
drawing shapes that defied these laws.

It was only in the spring, sprawled out
in front of the stereo, listening to James Taylor
and embroidering the margins of my geometry book
with blue ball-point pen, that I discovered
what was at stake for me was the axiomatic quality
of reasoning itself, the ways in which our assumptions
construct reality, become paradigms
that organize our vision.

I realized that no one else took geometry
as seriously as I did—at least no one
who was failing, that is—and that
in order to get on with life
I would have to get beyond axioms,
memorize theorems, prove hypotheses.

This was not art, where my doodles
might have some eccentric meaning.
This was a game with rules
and if I put aside my distrust of logic
long enough, I could learn to play.
But there was no longer time
to be good at it, only time to garner
a hard-won D.

When the final report came home
I tried to explain my triumph to my father—
my passing as an act of will—
that at the last minute
I had mastered something more
than grades reflected. As I began
to speak a shadow settled over his face.
Even at fourteen I saw that he was weighing
how much he could take on faith.

LOUISA HOWEROW

Forewarned

At fifteen, I might have ignored the boy
from the Arab quarter who sold fresh figs,
tear-shapes in soft gold skin, small enough

to fit a young girl's palm. I might have
heeded my mother's warning
how Eve, eyes open to her nakedness,

wore an apron of fig leaves. But
the close of summer sent me back
to eat from the boy's hand,

sink teeth into sweet, pink pulp, seeds
blushed red. At dusk, outside the garden gate,
our mouths flowered, reclaimed grace.

BETTE LYNCH HUSTED

Tending Adobe

A woman from the city called it dirt.
"That's all it is, New Mexico." She stared
through polished glass: old trailers in thin skirts,

bare yards; adobe in this light reflecting red
and pinks of sunset, yellowed shades of gold—
earth sprouting skyward in a mystery shared

with water, sun and straw. Some secrets told
cannot be heard. Once, I listened hard
at sunrise where the Posi ruins held

design in scooped handfuls, black-lightninged shards
that fit against my cheekbone, and felt again
that plaza at Chimayo: weed-grown rooms unbarred

to vision. Yet I'd heard voices—families unseen
inside those north side doors, a world I almost knew
with each intake of August breath. We tend

our lives with words, hands shape black lines that do
not tell our story. What's left us? Strangers' lies
and melted walls. A kiva hole. Those Abiquiu

teenagers singing a capella. Rap from high
tuned radios. Babies in hot cars. Red earth
and straw and water, vigas holding up the sky.

KARLA HUSTON

Monuments

I see them everywhere, small tributes
to those whose last breaths
were taken along these roads.

Crosses and bundles of silk flowers,
stuffed bears, small photos, and glittering
streamers grow alongside the weeds.

So many memorials: the shoulder seems
too small to hold it all.
Some lean under the weight of their grief.

The silver chain hangs around my neck:
his hands were the last to touch it.
It's just long enough to drop between

my breasts. At first it was cold and foreign,
but I let it warm, let the sliver of it
rise and fall, mark this empty space.

LUISA IGLORIA

Orchises

—for Myrna

Bolus of moss and inconsequential matter
  smuggled by voyagers from hothouse
    Edens on the rim of the known world,

from rainforests in South America and
  islands in the Ring of Fire; from continents which,
    on old maps, are colored dark as the outer

lips of furled-away petals, peopled with
  fantastic beasts and Gorgon's heads. Whole books
    have been devoted to them—antlered herbaria,

specimens resembling butterfly wings; ladies' waxed
  pink slippers, their sticky throats and sex pondered
    by painters unafraid to look

origin in the eye. They send their velvet
  pennants like flares or wounds into this life,
    taunting with sketchy promises: musk,

flash fire, a dusting of pollen. From his throne
  in the underworld, Orcus numbers their heads,
    lipsticked and edible across surfaces of torched

sugar. I could live alone, suspended between air and water,
  my roots parted merely by gravel. I might nestle, velvet
    as a cod-piece between thigh and groin, speckle

the bedspread with magenta. But darling,
  unwrap me like a birthday present. Whip
    my seeds into melted cream. Fragrant

pheromone, ruby rump, exquisite
  sideshow, I'll share your vivid four-poster, look under
    your caul for a little tongue to suck with pleasure.

JUDY JENSEN

Past Perfect

For Art Tatum whose grave is marked only with 'Someone to Watch over Me'

Why? As if you'd ever give it up,
easily. Others may negotiate
by rote the melancholic but,
underneath your fingertips, an onyx night
facets into deeply glinting sapphire.
Calculated as an ivory silk gardenia, chords
spill like riffled whiskies
but it's the single notes that chinkle—
sly against flirtatious crystal.
This is where
your secrets lie, in the tension
between the assiduously tender
absolution and the hard-struck
conviction that you have,
in fact, walked unassisted
off the edge of rooftops and sauntered on,
whistling.

LIESL JOBSON

Vocal Warm-Up at the Co-Op

So what you been up to young lady?
Niks, Oom.
Is that right?
Ja, Oom.
How's your ma?

She's home from the hospital but she never sleeps,
so she wakes me in the middle of the night saying,
Fern, you must audition for the lead role in the opera,
they want a lyrical soprano for the role of Lucia,
you'd be perfect, and Pa comes to put her back to bed,
he tells her, no Nellie, there's no opera anymore,
the State Theatre is finished doing opera,
they only do 'Phantom' now and she clucks her tongue,
shakes her head, yet next night it's the same
and in the morning when we wake up she's boiling
three pots of bones doing vocal warm ups and Pa
rolls his eyes and goes to fix a hole in the garage roof,
or so he says, but there's not really a hole, not one
you can see, while Ma's grilling the corn black
she sings "Bel-la Si-gno-o-o-o-o-o-rah!"
with perfect pitch, gouging holes out the back
of cucumbers with the potato peeler, to let
the air in, she says, like when she's frothing
up egg white with the beater till it's stiff
and she's drenched in perspiration, air creates
overtones from the nasal cavity, but the new pills
Doctor Bezuidenhout gave her don't really work,
so Pa has hidden the razors, all the belts and the sharp
knives, which makes it tricky to cook, not that one
cooks with belts, but you know what I mean, Oom?

What would your ma like today?
Four bottles of Tylenol.
Is that right?
Ja, Oom.
That'll be eighty bucks.
Dankie, Oom.
Anything else?
Nee, Oom, dankie, Oom.

JUDITH E. JOHNSON

Sestina for William Bronk (Genoa, 1980)

Dear friend, isn't it equally likely that the opening,
though the curtain never rose, displayed every set,
action, character, just as they unfolded? When the lights
blasted on behind the shuddering of the curtain
and you saw that dense fabric as gauze, what brilliant deals
you made between what you'd hoped and what you felt.

Even now, while in another country all you might have felt
waits in suspension, the play has had a clear opening,
a first line in a language you don't know but will remember. Certain deals—
can you spot them?—exchange light for shadow in those sets
we've constructed behind the material of the curtain.
Already a shift in the air and in the grid of lights

has dimmed you. You're gone, Bill Matthews, too, but a blaze lights
the other side. What crazy joy, past Genoa, as the barrier fades into a mesh, unfelt
except as hypothesis. The pulse of strobes over the invisible curtain
has stilled. Again we order wine: Matthews, Simic, you, and i, opening
rare vintages from the dark side. Didn't we always know that those painted sets
were really the pit of this theater where we spin and make deals?

While you dance no known step to no known music, they're working out deals—
critics, actors—in that white blaze, according to their own lights,
and not one term of their equation is yours. Look again: your mind has set
out every detail. Through the fourth wall, you can see, unfelt,
cool, passionate observer, that other theater which opens
out like a mirror from the other side of the curtain,

and it can see you. There, in the play of desire, you curtain
off what you can see from the place where you've been seen making deals.
Long past touch, do you see the one who scans the counter-opening,
who measures your life as observer, whose careful gaze lights
your world? Dear friend, in this absolute, perfect attentiveness, i have felt
your mind plot me, have seen the force of desire set

you here for me to plot. How clearly each lens sets
darkness swooping behind the transparent curtain
in that dance with no pattern which enacts what we feel.
It is always enough and never enough, what desire deals
out from this fabric. Say that we demand more than fabrication: lights,
cries of gladness, even love. Though in fact no curtain has opened

here, we who remain applaud this opening, this triumph that sets
all unknowns ablaze. Even the curtain, when my dark lights
on yours, deals out charged particles whose force we feel.

Notes: This sestina has used as its textual sources two poems by William Bronk, "At the Theatre" and
"The Force of Desire," taking six words from "Theatre" for its end words, and a mix of language and
metaphor from both. William Matthews, Charles Simic, William Bronk and I were at a poetry
conference in Genoa in 1980.

ADRIANNE KALFOPOULOU

The Meal

You give me caviar on crackers,
I make you ginger chicken.
You bring me special chocolates,
I tell you of artichokes cooked in lemon.
You show me garlic melts in stir-fried broccoli,
I show you how to boil basmati.
You find a rare Merlot for Christmas,
I choose thick salmon slabs for dinner.
You speak of Guatemala coffee,
I offer "Tahini with some honey?"

You learn my tastes; I spiral
fingers down your face, teach me
how to pace my kisses
as we do this sifting of the right amounts
for mixing the spice of how
you touch my secret spine, salt the movement
we get caught in——a thing not always fed,
this coming back for more
is now my climb along your shore,
baste these knees and thighs in gourmet sweat,
lick the curves and crevices
of all that's on your plate,
swallow joy like champagne.

Margo Berdeshevsky

Essay

Yes, alien. Wearing grey make-up, doing the snake dance I'd learned and performed for the "Ramayana"—the Upper East Side NYC girls taunted me. Darted their fingers at me in the way I had made mine into a serpent's head—to beautifully dance. Much later, for nearly twenty winters, I lived on a Pacific island three thousand miles from a good bookstore. I invented myself as a poet there, under a billion quiet stars. Taught local children to make poems of stones and ancestors and rain. There was no community of poets. There was silence and its poetry. My Hawaiian lover reminded me that my culture of Western thought had stolen and prohibited his ancient language. That hurt, and was true. I read and made poems in my fellow thieves' tongue. I remembered that once, before the snake dance, I used to speak French. No one on my island spoke French but one renowned poet, a hermit, who raised exotic palms.

I became a hermit, raising myself. I had a computer. I mailed poems like sea-bottles to New York. Marie Ponsot, receiving them, gave me a treasured introduction to a new friend-to-be, and *voisine*: Marilyn Hacker smiled, *I love Paris and I live there, neighbor*. She said, *join Wom-po*.

A land of the argumentative, educated, poetic feminine; no horizon. I lurked. I moved like a bipolar arachnid, a leg at a time between my island and the virtual world and the page and Paris. I posted my Paris Notes. Wompos e-mailed: *Traveling to France, could we meet?*

Paris is stone and water too, in the middle of the global. Writers have always come here to be aliens, to make words. When it's dawn here, it's midnight yesterday where the Digest gets sent. I read it by candlelight, with my first coffee, often. The world is screen-sized, 500-plus souls. I think I might hear their poems. I think we are almost a collective mind, punctuated by fragmentation and ambition and love and anima. I think they might not jeer at my snake dance. I'm addicted to the morning hit of fragmented poetic community. Or as Yerra Sugarman just wrote of the prose poem today: "formal structural rebellion." (Which is maybe not a bad passport for an alien.)

216

JULIE KANE

Aldy Street

She still has nightmares of that third-story window
through which her mother leans to hang the laundry
with brown wooden clothespins on a pulley-fed line
between two tenement apartments in Boston.
One minute she's screaming in her mother's lap,
and the next, she's plummeting down to the sidewalk.

Her bean-thin father comes striding up the sidewalk
and her black-haired mother spies him from the window.
Reaching for a bottle of cologne, her mother slaps
two drops behind her ears, abandons the wet laundry,
and thinks about going to a jazz club in Boston.
They can get there and back on the MBTA line.

But what about the child? They have to realign
their priorities. The Italian widow across the walk
might sit with the infant for one night in Boston.
They look out the window to see her lighted window,
her clothesline of cone-bra and housedress laundry
against which a Back Bay wind begins to slap.

Later, the baby wakes with the croup. Her mother slaps
her on the back, but she can't breathe, so her father makes a beeline
for the tub, runs the hot water, and dangles her like laundry
over the steaming cauldron. *Put me down, let me walk,*
the baby's thinking. Through the fogged-up bathroom window,
snow falls on the popsicle laundry of Boston.

The dead do not always stay buried in Boston.
One weekday, hanging laundry, the child's mother slaps
her own mouth to see a ghost appearing out the window—
her husband, aged to sixty. She had fallen for the line
that his old man was dead, but there he was on the sidewalk,
dying of prostate cancer, a stick hung with laundry,

coming to see his grandchild, swaddled in laundry,
before being buried in the stony ground of Boston,
a latter-day wise man at the end of his walk.
"You lied to me," the child's mother cries as she slaps
her drunk husband, unable to walk a straight line,
though he claims he "worked late" as she paced by the window.

Airing her dirty laundry, her mother says, "I slapped
you so hard, once, in Boston, my hand left a line;
how I longed, as I walked you, to hurl you out that window."

JULIA SPICHER KASDORF

Poetry in America

The Barnes and Noble in Evansville, Indiana, mostly sells coffee
though the manager said ten or twelve showed up once for a local author.
One, besides my friend Laura, came for me. I thought of priests
who must pronounce the full Eucharist even if no one goes to mass,
thought Virginia Woolf and Oscar Wilde looked kind of pained
as Barnes and Noble posters, and facing fifteen empty folding chairs,
I suggested we all just go downstairs for coffee. I was hopeful—
I hate bookstore readings which pay nothing but constant interruptions:
Customer service on line eight. Does one keep reading in that case, or pause
to incorporate the line into her poem? "No way! I came to hear poetry!"
said a woman in walking shorts and sandals with socks. "I'm a poet, too.
Can't help the disease. It's either write or go mad." She had bangs
and plastic glasses like Ramona the Pest. "I'm Barbara. Don't write
much now, too busy working and labor organizing at the Whirlpool plant.
Come from Henderson, Kentucky, over the river. You hear of a white person
committing a crime in Henderson, that would be my relative.
But let's get going. I've got things to do yet tonight." So I got going.

Sometimes Barbara moaned as if she'd tasted something delicious or cried,
"Hey, that was a good one." People walking by eyed us the way
they look at preachers in bus stations. A woman and little girl sat in back.
The Mom held a book about women who love too much in front of her face
like a mask, the girl imitated with a Madeline storybook, but sometimes
she peeked at me, and they stayed almost to the end. Barbara took my book
from the stack waiting to be returned. "Wouldn't buy it if I didn't like the work,"
she said as I signed, then walked out with us. "You know, it's still 73 cents
to the dollar. No matter how much education you have, you're working harder
and making less than a white man. For women of color, it's worse.
And now all we get is backlash. Well, I'm a 50-year-old woman, and
they can kiss my ass." That spring, Barbara fasted for 19 days at the gates
of the governor's mansion because he'd turned Kentucky's community colleges
into trade schools. "Do you know what that means?" she jabbed me with her bird eyes.
"No history, no political science, no literature, no going on for a college degree
like I did, and you watch, it's coming to other states. Evil bastards will call it
job training, but it's just one more way to keep poor people down." Outside,
light mist was falling on cars in the parking lot, softening neon signs down the strip.
"Take care of yourself," she waved a blessing. "Where the hell is your umbrella?"

PRATIBHA KELAPURE

Annealing

Vase cracks at the moment of creation,
an innocent drop of water
glides on the flaming red neck.
Unhurried tolerant toil,
skilled slicing, fire burnishing, and the
final moment of creation goes awry.
The shards of tormented glass fly around,
rip retinas, and scar smiles.

At the threshold of adulthood,
years of loving, tender rearing
suddenly stolen by secret demons
silently loitering inside the mind, and the
final moment of creation goes awry.
Adolescence explodes,
goodbye, ultimate!
Crimson menacing shards of
eternal damnation remain lodged on
the foreheads of the survivors.

BRIDGET KELLEY-LOSSADA

In Morocco

—for Julie

Sunrise scrapes
the nape of my neck
like hummingbird beaks.
I know—
because I have eaten their eyes
and tasted dawn.

ROBIN KEMP

New Breast

—for Dr. Kathryn Walker Kemp, alive, well, and teaching history

Mama's got a new breast and she cries for the old one that her children never nursed and she cries for the new one that no one ever can and she cries for the scars that crisscross her breast and she cries for the skin of her new skinny belly where my brother and I came from now peering through the hole in her new breast with no nipple and she cries for the spiderwebs of blood threading beneath the skin of her new breast that does not feel anything but very hard

It is so hard she weeps and it is and I kneel at her feet and wrap my arms around her legs and hug them tight because she is afraid for anyone to touch her right side and her tears fall on my head and she says *I love you* and I say *I love you too we all do everybody does* and I say *you're going to be okay* and I say *you're not going to die* and I say *Daddy won't stop looking at you*

And she says *he has been so good he has emptied the drains the rubber tubes that have sprouted like parasitic vines that bloom rubber bulbs that fill with the pink sap of surgical drainage he empties them three times a day each into its own little cup and he holds each cup to the light and he judges where the mark falls and he does not judge and he dumps the serum into the toilet and he washes me like a baby he washes me so tenderly he is so good*

And I tell her she can go to Mardi Gras she can go to Bourbon Street she can stand on the balcony where she stood before she first gave birth and when the college boys scream SHOW YOUR TITS she can and they will all fall down and worship her great knockers and Daddy says he will go out and buy her a pair of tassels and she laughs and I say she probably would hit him with one of them

Black tassels hang from the corners of her degrees everything she gave her right tit for: the trophies of the triumph of her mind over Lamarque's miles of longhorn pastures and petrochemical plants, passports through marriage and motherhood and tears breaking her crisscrossed reflection peering back from the flooded dishwasher, through *get out of my study, I don't care if the house is on fire*, through battle-scarred bachelor master Ph.D. and the fear she's too late to get tenure, through her pointed letters politely demanding amnesty from dictators, never too late for true words, my Mama, the Amazon archer who lives forever

DIANE KENDIG

Marie Blanchard, 1914

Years later, she laughed about the steak
that came between her and Rivera
in the studio they shared in Paris,
how it weighed raw on the plate,
uncovered for days, a *naturaleza muerta*
that grew more *muerta* each day.
She'd put up with his visions
of man-eating spiders, his stare, too,
at bedposts and lamps; he'd thrown his shoe
at the light bulbs, broken the bathroom mirror
each day. Each day, she'd replace the mirror,
talk him through.
So the steak left to rot
did not symbolize their friendship.
For his part, it was not
a macho matter of cooking exactly.
He had rustled up feasts for many,
filled the table with Mexican dishes once
for Angelina, Apollinaire, and Modigliani.
But Diego would not fry a steak for one woman.
Two weeks passed. The meat, looking
slimy, then green, looked worse.
And Marie wouldn't ditch the mess, become
just one of the rest of his women, cooking,
cleaning, washing, and cooking more—
though most of his other women were painters.
Why, Angelina's work shrank to miniatures
while she fed his appetites,
the way Frida, two wives later in '32,
would drop her brush to walk to his scaffold
carrying a lunch basket covered
with napkins hand-embroidered, "I adore you."
Not Marie. Not her. She ignored the stench.
But the neighbors couldn't. The twentieth day
they sent the janitor who came and took
plate, steak, and stench away.

LILLIAN BAKER KENNEDY

Notions

When I was sixteen, I worked in notions.
The small spools of thread,
a color to match material of every dress,
lined up in rows. I knew where everything was.

What a salesperson I was for thread!
I carefully matched each one
to un-cut cotton folded on customers' arms.

Later, when we got an apartment, we hardly knew
that the candlesticks came from noisy, brick mills
with large looms that had to be fixed
by supervisors working in shifts.
Women waited while machines broke down.
Their commissions were docked by the passage of time.

Someone told me souls are threads
spread all across the universe,
like a pattern, a sphere of souls
that cross and re-cross oceans and continents.
Threads clipped like umbilical cords
or torn off between the teeth, a hasty impatience
to finish connecting or ripping out a seam.
I once lined a jacket, orange, in satin. The edges peeled.
There is no end to this poem, only a kind of unraveling
and unlit candles on empty spools.

LAURA KENNELLY

Helen with Insomnia at the Clavier

Paris was not the first. Did you think he was? How quaint.
There was Agamemnon, yes. His own brother. At my wedding
feast he fondled my breasts, laughed, called my husband a
lucky man. After a while resisting seemed more trouble than
it was worth.

He loved me. But he loved her, Clytemnestra, too. He said. I
think he loved power rich life more. But his was a nasty
family: ate each other. That he didn't carry me off was all
right.

It was less all right with Odysseus. No one
ever dreamed that when I walked long walks at
night I did not walk alone. No one ever saw
how we twined and tangled and became one,
startling night birds from the trees we sported
under. His stories, his laugh, his lips I could
have hung on forever.

But he was a hearth lover too. Stuck on status quo:
There she sat, always patiently waiting, lovely
Penelope. Slight smile on her perfect face—Oh,
I excited him more, but he's really a
coward—don't you know—it would have broken his
dear wife's heart and ruined his boy.

By the time Paris came, I was more than ready.
It's boring, you know, to be an old man's toy.
Of course I jumped: A foreign city, passionate
lover. (I never thought, then, to wonder why he
was so experienced, so knowing.) Yes, I went with him.

Yet now he wanders from me and
the battlefield, chasing women, fleeing
slaughter, crying "Mama"
till she sweeps him to safety in a golden mist.

And the only real man here is tied
to Andromache. I've seen the looks he gives me—
A man like that knows how to love his wife—
which (don't laugh) means
I can never have him,
but just once, I'd like to strip that plumed
helmet off his head, loosen the armor plate,
touch his skin and bring him to fevers,
feel his sweat dripping on
my body stretched beneath his—

And, yes, it's too bad about the war,
unfortunate really—
but Aphrodite, after all, is not Athena.
Love cannot be expected to think
about everything.

JUDITH KERMAN

One-Book Poet

Her bony face fades, knuckles
grow large and strange
amid the dusky rivers
of her hands, her gaze
a history without
old cities and great names.

The last of her denim overalls
went to the Goodwill years ago,
but she was thinking of
dirt roads when an uptown taxi
almost hit her
as she crossed Tenth Avenue.

She tracks each turn
of the market, but never invests.
Says it's a game for fools.

ANN FISHER-WIRTH

Essay

There's a joke in Oxford, Mississippi, where I have lived for 17 years, that if you turn over a rock you find a novelist. Sometimes that seems pretty much true. But Oxford—which claims William Faulkner, Barry Hannah, Larry Brown, Willie Morris, Tom Franklin, and used to claim John Grisham—has until recently run considerably thinner on poets. Sure, I was in a writing group, and sure, I taught workshops and seminars, but to those few of us poets here, poetry (and especially poetry written by women) felt eclipsed. As indeed it was, to the larger public. I went with Athena Kildegaard once to a talk given by two prominent Midwest editors who announced that the South had produced no women poets they could think of. Naturally, we felt a little subdued—though Athena promptly rattled off ten names.

And this is where Wom-po entered my life. Mairéad Byrne, who taught here for a year, first told me about it, and informed me in her utterly charming way that I'd be an idiot if I didn't seek a larger poetic community. She was right. I can't begin to list the doors that Wom-po has opened for me, can't begin to enumerate the conversations among various combinations of our nearly 500 members in which I've taken part, and from which I've learned. I just know so much more, now. It's not always fun and not always friendly. But then again, my family is not always fun and not always friendly. Yet I wouldn't change a hair on their heads. And I think of Wom-po as poetry family.

CLAIRE KEYES

Bridge to Savannah

Because the bridge we cross
driving south to Savannah
rises so high into great sweeps
of silver-looking steel—
and because I can see only the crest
and not the shore beyond—
I grip the wheel a little tighter,
touching a fear that surfaces
only in dreams: it's night
and I'm driving onto a bridge
into a strange city. Four lanes
compress into one, my car wedged
between trucks. My hands sweat,
the truck behind thundering so close
it could drive me over the edge.

It's madness to follow
a red dragon tail of lights
speeding towards a distance
that means pure terror
and I've forgotten
what others seem to know:
where they are,
where they want to be.

But I'm not asleep now
and can tell you about the bridge
tormenting the dreamer.
It's not the same as this bridge:
a luminous and graceful arc
of strength married to beauty
even as it recedes
in the rear-view mirror,
slipping lower and lower
down under the sky, connecting
near shore and far.

ATHENA KILDEGAARD

Aria

Mimi died once in our family room.
My mother opened her throat
not to sing but to keep the keen
back, protect her children
from her deepest regret.

Mimi died in the opera house
rigged out to sail across Sydney Harbor.
She died at the Palacio de Bellas Artes
where a dapper-suited man
sang along, his tears turned to melody.

Mimi died again in New Orleans.
Something burst against my ribs
afterwards, crossing the parking lot.
I swore it off. No more Bohemians
in their turreted poverty.

No more violins, their strings
the sinews of Rodolfo's heart.
No more gelida manina, it would kill me, too.
But that was a lie.
The way we lie sometimes

to cover up for what we know
will again break inside us—
not a breaking that leaves shards
or wounds, but breaking as the sun does
into darkness, as joy breaks from our tears.

SALLY ROSEN KINDRED

To Eve

Like you, I want things done in red.
Like you, I'm tired of being tested,
never said I could stand it,
never wanted to stand
within seven inches of my life.
What's temptation anyway? Don't say *Fruit*—
a red bulge like that
I could hide under my dress.
I'm tired of being told what I want,
told your story sets us
at the start. I'm greedy now to end it:

why don't we halve your apple
and set it in the sun
and watch it brown over like gauze
once bloodied? I want to rust. I want to watch
dawn corroded by falling rusty stars,
seven gold lampstands tarnish
the skies with blood-light,
and horses pound the red earth down—
currents of horses like giant red fractures
breaking the wet clay into grit.
Why don't we taste it?

I want our mouths covered over
in this, air finally denser than fruit,
the taste of blood and blessings withdrawn.
Won't that reassure us? Won't it be a sign
to find ourselves clotted in red ruin? And Eve,
sleep at last, that fruit we'd know how to crave,
the dreams dry, falling behind us,
the wrong world finally drained
to one color, that color itself drained down,
blood to rust, red to brown,
no longer the color of fire.

AMY KING

Cynthia McKinney Cast the Lone Dissenting Vote

—from a Georgia native

An equation enacts its splayed self,
soft organs delicate, exposed, intact.
A reader licks the stigmata of words
left out, quiets a redder rust stripping
her superhero down. The citizen pretends
the one unknown entity distressed.

Except the more I spoke her rejection aloud,
the more sense knocked us out—

Very well then, I contradict
myself: I am a Democrat opposed
to hand-to-hand death, a Republican
in the hierarchy of man over human,
an Independent bidding on noble killers,
those lean-to shacks of three-party wealth.

As for the personal
subjunctive,
I don't like pink—
it looks weak,
the way they
make it into soft things.

For the penance of politics, I've smeared
my fingerprints, my lungs itch,
and the sweat that numbs
won't appease our satellite feed tonight.

Just as one might consider the ways heaven
manifests, you walk into a field
where stands a flag with the number seven,
and you're hit in the neck
by small dimpled balls of age and sting.

Each golfer keeps track of his dollars for taxes,
traces lines on hook-and-worm truths,
the stench of bills leaving finger-safe harbors
with a small hope that one day
our vacant factories will exhale and collapse.

We bare teeth for the promise
of the sportsman within,
tongues crossed behind
our smiles, unhinged with terror in grief.

Baptismal justice is constantly sought,
conclusive truth a bargain unused,
that these things we feel
might be translated, that these fears
will turn into wooden crosses,
readied to balance and mount.

Likewise, we tend to leave the circle,
seeking the labyrinth in a mole's damp tunnels,
hoping all that's found will be lost again.

Just as the days of youth
are not yet upon me, I have seen my own buildings
in the distance and disregarded them.

I have laid my guns and children down.

Closer to calm each morning, I know,
like demon young women before me,
it is only a matter of streets
before I am lost enough
to meet my next life
in a New York City heat.
Beyond these tunneled grounds,
she cast her lone dissenting vote.

JANET R. KIRCHHEIMER

Dogs

"I came across something," my father tells me
as I'm driving him to cardiac rehab, "in my mind,"
as if his mind were a filing cabinet
or the dish in the hall where coins and keys are kept.
It was something an old man told him when he was a boy,
how the stones freeze in winter, but the dogs
who chase you don't, and two days later we're sitting
on the back porch on Rosh HaShanah afternoon,
and he tells me that the way of life
he grew up with in southern Germany
no longer exists and if he thinks about it too much
it will make him crazy and is not worth
the consequences, and I want to tell him that I can hear
the cantor singing in shul, and I can smell the raisin challahs
his mother baked for a sweet new year,
but it will not stop the dogs, so we just sit there
and watch the birds that have gathered at the feeder.

KAAREN KITCHELL

Hawk

For Samuel Farrand Kitchell
November 6, 1921—September 11, 2006

From his bed, he faces Camelback,
Mummy Mountain to the north.
The man of action cannot move.

9/11, eleven of us gather.
He looks like a hawk: the gentle curve of his nose,
silvery feathers on his head, his fierce strength.

Radiance fills the room. Our adoration
surrounds him. 11 pm, his breath stops,
his death the deep echo of his life.

Next morning a hawk lands in the paloverde
outside the window. He faces
my mother at breakfast.

I and three sisters watch.
He is brown and cream
and gold,

one wing awkward, as if he's just assumed
a new form. Eyes bright, composed,
he picks at the feathers on his breast,

gazes at mother, then swivels his head
and stares north, then south
toward my brother's welcoming home.

Then he lifts over the house to the east,
floats the cobalt air between Camelback and Mummy,
above the valley where he built his home.

Mother has never seen a hawk light
near the house before—
it could be a Swainson's, she says.

In the ancestral book, I read
that his family crest was a hawk, wings
raised, belled and jessed, on a field of blue

within a border of gold. A person who does not fear
to make his approach known
to either friend or foe.

How can you imagine his immense,
benevolent spirit unless you knew him as we did?
Yet we who knew him best did not know

until we saw him in the final room, in tennis white,
innocent as a boy, regal as a pharaoh,
and keened as if life itself had fled.

KATRINA KOSTRO

Recipe for Drizzling

Pick three dying daisies whose petals are still attached
Detach the petals and lay them
    on an olive green clay plate
Sprinkle powdered sugar over the daisy petals
    and tell them just because they have exceeded
    their time of living, they are not powerless
The goal is to lift up their self-esteem
Play old Bruce Springsteen; make it loud enough for them to hear
    so it's not as if he has died as well, but
    don't blast it, because the dead daisy petals are delicate
Have a cry
Collect your tears in a tall dark blue glass
Stop crying now
Sing along to a couple of Bruce lines, so the petals
    know you're listening too
Get an eye dropper
Dip it in the dark sea in the blue glass
Fill up the dropper
And drip a few tear-drops over the petals
    so it's as if they've been drizzled on
Turn off Bruce
The daisies will be angry
Tell them to treat others as they are treated
And it will start to drizzle outside

ANN NEUSER LEDERER

The Undifferentiated

They will clump together
and find each other, pulling hair.

They will climb all over,
like ants on the undersides of leaves,
sucking out juice.

They will poke grubby little fingers
into each other's eyes,
just to do it.

Sometimes they will rake their fingernails
along each other's skin,
like undisciplined day campers.

It is called "loss of contact inhibition,"
what those unruly cells are doing.
There are lists of other behaviors as well:
invading, escaping surveillance, diverting resources.
There is no end to what these naughty ones might do.

They should be spanked, then bathed,
then tucked back into little cots in rows.

DONNA J. GELAGOTIS LEE

Uncertain wavering

in your voice, when your arm
touches mine, as if we were poised
on the wind-struck branch.

Understand, there must be this
delicate maneuvering, like
a bird deciding direction,

pausing, then retreating. I
look at your throat, the
large apple of beginnings,

and hesitate to watch
you swallow. I know
the words will circle me

like O's, smoke signals
in clouds bursting with rain.
Hard to decide which

we would prefer. The quivering
of baring limbs, the last leaves
lithe. What can be determined

in the final minutes,
the breeze tilting the branch
downward, the branch leveling up?

SHARON LEITER

The Dream of Leaving

It was a life.
The waking and sleeping,
the slow train journeying
over the mountain, steaming
again and again into still,
pleasant stations
whose name-plates told us
we lived what
we'd never planned.

And endless brave
mornings when we'd go
again, only to learn
how space is curved
to the contours
of the Mobius fate
that returned us
at nightfall
to the old house,
the dream of leaving,
the hours that sucked us,
moth-like, into each other's
arms and eyes and mouths.

I cannot wrap
these fourteen years
going on fifteen
going on infinity
into a gala package
for God's eyes,
saying, *this we did,*
it wasn't enough, this is gone.
I cannot become
that camera
that snaps us in
terrible poses
for future museums
to sort and discard.

I'd rather stay
sunk with you here
in the great animal fate,
the tall grass around us,
the summer smells,
the orchestra of insects,

longing for where we are,
going wherever we go next.

AMY LEMMON

Karyotype

What would it look like,
I wondered, this map
of gene particles, counted
and crossed? As we waited,
I imagined a tidy grid
of lines and numbers,
stark spirals in red-green-blue,
anything but these tiny worms
photographed, magnified and ordered
in pairs except for the infamous
twenty-first: the error,
the glitch, the wrench
in your infant clockwork. Striped
and annelidic, the chromosomes
weren't even yours, just
a picture of someone
else's, someone else's child
who also had too much,
too many worms. I picture
the other parents seeing these
squirming for the first time   squinting hard
like we do now. You're here.
What do we make of it?

CAROL LEVIN

The Perfumer

Eyes shut ardent
lover he buries
his nose
in his palm
delicate with perfume.

Blind in childhood
his grandfather
kept him close
teaching him
how to smell
Grandpapa's empire
of perfume. Frangaponi,
patchouli, iris and palm.

Now he's the luminary
of fragrance, featured
in an interview.
Tall, short,
bald, blue eyed?
I'm awakened
by the music

of his French accent
on low volume.
The soufflé voice
follows me everywhere
and I follow it.
I close the door,

take off my dress,
turn out each light.
In the dark he teaches
how to strip habit
from my eyes, teaches
me to lace you
with nothing
but my scent.

ANNE-MARIE LEVINE

Four November 9ths

My family expected I would be born on Armistice Day,
November 11, and that would be one thing,
that would have been something to joke about
in those days. But I came into being two days earlier,
on November 9, in the evening, and that was another thing,
it was not a joke, and it was evidently not a thing
to be remembered or told,
because I was not made aware of the coincidence
of my birth until several months before my 50th birthday,
which coincided with, and was commemorated and announced as,
the 50th anniversary of Kristallnacht.
So there I was, and even more than that here I am,
quite surprised, not to mention still unprepared,
and quite unable to avoid thinking about both at once.
The reminders since then have been constant and grim.
Coincidence: the visible traces of invisible principles.

And now my friend Gottfried Wagner,
who since the day he discovered the date
has never forgotten my birthday,
has informed me that there are four November 9ths
in history, that it is a very big day in the history of Germany
in this century. There is even a book written,
it is called *The Four November 9ths*.
I can't read the book, it is written in German,
but I have done some research, and as far as I can tell

The first November 9 was 1918;
it was a revolution in which the Kaiser abdicated,
which culminated in the Proclamation of the Republic in Berlin
on November 9. The above-mentioned Armistice
between the Allies and Germany
followed on the 11th.

The second November 9 was 1923;
it was Hitler's abortive "Beer Hall Putsch"

against the Bavarian government in Munich.
Hitler, who was at first imprisoned, eventually emerged
as the undisputed leader of the radical right.

The third November 9 was, as you know, My November 9th,
Kristallnacht.

And on November 9, 1989, the Berlin Wall came down.

So there you are and here we are, on my birthday,
and all of this is to say what Gertrude Stein has already said,
what can I teach you about history——history teaches.

It is not a simple matter, the birthday, or the telling.

SHAYLA MOLLOHAN

Essay

I'm understanding now, that in order to thrive in whatever circumstances we may find ourselves, we must choose a personal way to be "in the world." Sometimes, by necessity, we have to get pretty darn creative to accomplish this! People living with all kinds of challenges do this every day. We don't always know who they are. I didn't know how I might make this happen when it became my turn.

Admittedly, I did momentarily hesitate to present this piece to the anthology, as it's been my experience that discussing physical disabilities occasionally makes some people uncomfortable; I didn't want that to be the case for our readers. I'm not embarrassed about being crippled at all, though for years I felt a little bit anxious when it was brought up to me face-to-face. The first time someone patted my chair, instead of me, I wanted to disappear. Yet, actually, it has been in this environment that I've learned to talk about the frightening, and sometimes funny, issues and feel at ease! What I love about electronic communities is that I'm just another good face and voice in the circle. No one sees the wheelchair, my voice software, or that I can't hold a pencil. They see "me." If I share my challenges, that's fine. If I choose not to for whatever reason, that's fine, too.

So how does one visit a friend, learn to write a cinquain, discuss women poets, share work, find mentors, laugh out loud, reach out to suffering children, protest wars, and invest these quick precious hours that we are given—and never leave bed? I'm maybe the luckiest woman I know. The Internet led me to writers, the Internet Writing Workshop, to Wom-po and the Wom-po workshop. And from this place and in this way, I enjoy in my daily life all the companionship, education, resources, and ordinary human connections available to any able-bodied person I know. My poetry and my spirit do thrive in this world and I am most grateful for it, my funny husband, my friends and family, and waking up to hot coffee every morning.

KAREN L. LEWIS

Even if

After Adrienne Rich

Even if the woman was raped 96 times instead of 97
  and she was found years later   laughing under a tree
  her body a defaced limb   of history
  she would have the power   of growth

Even if my mother didn't die
  and she was found walking   without aids   on a dirt road
  in Africa   her shoulders chanting a soft chorus   with sun

Even if I had a cure
      for grief

Even if my father could sleep   through the night
  and his dreams   were not cinéma vérité—
  he would put his money down   for pornography

Even if it were free

Even if my mouth did not attract flies
  and I could   not speak
  inhumane words :
  starvation, racism, fanaticism,
  relentless atrocities   indifference
  we might discover pieces
  of hate
  under our   fingernails

Even if beauty   didn't have an ulterior motive
  and you could love me   whoever you and I are
  it could be   something   temporary
  looking into each other
  eyes fixed and mutable

Barbara E. Lightner

Peg and the Ancient God Now Disappearing

There, on sun-pleased waters
   clear and clean
      as from the mountain-starting
streams all original feeding is,
             Peg takes paddle to kayak
    this good day.

Of these Ozark hills,
    shaped by ancient rock
           and springs that flow
     to the measure of these mountains,

Peg,
    big gold tooth,
        big strong woman,
           a kayak and a paddle,
             in the middle of her always start,
                goes;
   all the 65 years of her,
             this telltale day.

Squares her up a'heave
    of roistering waves
          rippling, running to flat and valley, vorticing,
     little tents of splash up and down,
       a play on the dazzle of
           sun-undulate waters.

To the picnicking point,
     the hot dog dads and the sunscreen moms,
the mewling babes, the raucous young,
        and Aunt Jeremy into her cups
     for the 5th happy time of this day,

Beyond the beer-bellied, gin-belting, summer,
    to the long lawns and high houses;
        down cove, around the rock beach and the
   harried, to smooth waters;

under the plank-ribbed bridge, rocks
        thumped down from above by
  the red rattletrap truck
in its still-going glory.

Over the old, broken old, bridge
  and downed pylons,
rich-mossed;
   unseen the cold, crystal flow
 of the returning spring-scattered waters,
Peg and kayak, surface baubles.

 Into a screech of heron,
     and foliates, reds and blues, to a spectrum
  of tatting in cups of downed trees;

     a plenitude: tree-borne, animal rife,
curl of ferns back to
   the richness of earth down-drawn water,
      tannin-brown,
   as old as the geography of ancient maps;

in the dapple of the sun,
    and the sudden holy hush of ancient gardens.

The old, old, turtles,
  their clawed feet slow-
 riding the give and take of their
   sun-hatched underwater
 Sabbath-
   holy home.

The snake, stock still
  in the sacred-centered water
   but for the head turning,
     eyes, elliptical, burning,
deep in the mystery of its holding,

where no thought intercedes
    the alleluia pulsing glory of this day.

—Until consciousness flicks,
    turns exhilaration at its heels,
      tears from the catch pin
        of the serpent
      riding on the water,
    this world   split asunder;

the hills, the sky, the trees,
  the ark-called and the springs,
one by one becoming,
      alterity, the ever-after meaning.
Peg keening of her loss,
     the ancient god now disappearing,
 turns the fragile kayak back
  onto the beer-bellied, gin-belting, summer
    carried on the surface of the water;

no heaven's arc but
 a glint of gold—
    our Peg,
      so merry of the waves—
    this good day
in one forever-after meaning.

FRANNIE LINDSAY

Walking an Old Woman into the Sea

She doesn't need her bathing cap
but she wants it on, the rubber peony
over one temple, the ear flaps up;

and the scratched yellow goggles
that won't get wet today
belong right here around her neck.

She can't hear the gulls' beady voices
yack over our sandwich crusts,

or the sea, out late again, tripping home
over its skirts;

and she frets about where I have left
her terrycloth jacket and watch.

But she knows by the popping
of stones and shell bits
under her flip-flops, and by my own

aged hands that grip the slack
elastic waist of her suit,

that this is a swim-day, no matter
how long the water
will have to wait.

JULIA LISELLA

Rosebush

See here where the earth swells,
where he knocked back the rosebush, punishment for its branches collapsing atop

the Saturn? See how we name our cars for planets? See how these cars don't
bring us closer to the sun? See how we can't fly yet? And see how the rosebush

sat in its aged roots, not as aged as the house it had leaned on for years,
but old enough to know it had come to its own starvation, flailing in the wind

on an angry night when my husband yelled to stop my anger, get the hell out, and I did
go grocery shopping and I did come back though I said I wouldn't

and that rosebush was just gone at his hands, but at its own self, too. Because
it couldn't stand up anymore. Attacking us each day with its useless thorns. Because

it couldn't protect what it did best. Each day I feel I am getting younger
in the awful way, not in the happy *Cosmo* way, but in the awful empathic way

born of remembering how hard it was to get to the age I am. See the moon
tonight? It is smaller now that we know there are many galaxies, and planets

with their own moons out there, their own dried up rivers, their own ice ages and
fossilized lives. See how I cannot bear to bear witness to the loss of our lovely

unwieldy rosebush that extended its growth too far and too long and too dangerously
into the other world of our driveway? See how I must look up at the moon and down at

my shoes, and away from my car, away from my children, my husband, my unwritten
books? See how those gentle brown stumps of life that will come back better than before

can't convince me that it's alright right now to be in my little middle-class
heaven? See the mistakes we've made being less than the boys and the girls in us

dreamed of becoming? See how I've made my problem yours,
the groundswell swaying me down to the ground, scared to nibble at the rose's

last leaves?

DIANE LOCKWARD

Losing the Blues

Stuck in traffic and lost
without you, I see it on a bumper sticker:
Wild women don't get the blues. Swerving

off the highway, I pull up to a neon
martini glass, order a shot of tequila. I suck
salt with a lemon wedge, slip

on a red satin dress, nail taps to my spikes, fasten
      castanets to my thumbs. I eat rare meat
         and all seven layers of a devil's food cake.

I hardly remember your name.

               Chartreuse
    flows through my veins. I'm every color on the palette
but blue. I'm so hot I'm cool. I spit
    in the street, and men swoon

when I do it. No more jazz for me, no rhythm
    and blues, no gospel, no country, no soul. I'm all
rock 'n' roll. I hang out

with gangsters, play the ponies, and encourage
    my urges. I'm no shade of blue—
        no sky, no periwinkle, sapphire, or indigo.

             I'll never again be royal for you.

          I'm cerise, vermilion, scarlet,
     ruby, crimson, fuchsia, magenta,
  and flame. I could burn
the hands off a man.

RACHEL LODEN

Miss October

If I have to be a playmate
In my time on earth
I want to be the girl
Of drifting leaves, cold cheeks

And passionate regrets.
I think Hef loves October best
Because although he cannot
Say so, he is *this* close

To death. December
In its stealth has hung
Long spikes of ice
Around his sagging ears, his

Sex. So in October
I'll be the centerfold of gay
Pretense, the girl who says
We're at our blondest

And most perilously beautiful
Right before we check out
Of the manse.
Soon all Hef's dreaming

Will be ash, his favorite pipe
And smoking jacket,
Last vial of Viagra
Safely under glass

At the Smithsonian.
When my shelf life here
Is done and all the damp
Boys stealing glimpses

At the newsstands
Are old men, I want them
To remember how many
Playmate-months

Are gone, how many rooms
Stand empty, shutters
Drawn, the last girls slipped
Away in bright October.

JUDY LONGLEY

We Knock upon Silence
for an Answering Music

Shining pearl, the night's one eye,
heavenly ghost, wings layered
with every blue hue, trailing
the sea dragon roaring below.
Framed by my balcony window,
your silver path beckons. Had I faith
enough my feet could glide
across waves until I rise, my arms
encircle your radiant sphere.
How many nights you were a whisper
of silk sliding across my bedroom floor,
the chime of a clock in the hall below.
I could join the measured pace
of your realm, the long magnetic
kiss that binds you in planetary time.
But earth is my home, the sand
that tingles my heels composed
of infinitesimal glittering moons.
Through the glass wall hangs
an eternal structure of sea, sky, moon
and my room reflected against it,
my head rising like its own moon
the mirror receives like a wafer.

BOBBI LURIE

And the Shoes Will Take Us There in Spite of the Circumference

Which world? I wonder as the therapist tells me my son
   will never be able to live within it
     Unless
Yes. I see the posed photos on her desk
   (*daughter? husband?*) she points to the chart
   which says my nine year old son is really five
She says my son's narrow interests (mathematics, Weird Al)
   will not allow him to enter
   the vast circumference of the universe
I stare into her double chin, down to the bunions on her feet
   pot belly, shirt tucked neat in her pants
She quotes Mel Levine who says *kids who are not well-rounded*
   cannot succeed
She sends me to a room where I pay $117 for the hour
A screaming infant reaches for her mother's glasses, throws
   them on the floor

Are you mad at me? my son asks as we walk out the door

I bend down, hold him so tight in my arms
So tight the green trees
So tight the blue and distant distant
Shape of my epiphany (were it half round, half yellow)
My son's small body, his heart pounds against my chest
   and this world
Of detritus and oblivious footnotes
How the fluid gold floats
How sound fills
Space and captures the tiniest beyond
Particles, waves
Mass of sunlight wrapped around our legs
Our hands

GLENNA LUSCHEI

Essay

When I went online to ask Wom-po members for poems to read at a memorial, rich answers streamed back to me. This response opened up new possibilities in my own poetry. Since my request to Wom-po I have been practicing the elegy form, realizing I can insert humor into a tragic situation as obituary writers do into their essays.

When my dear friend and mentor of forty years died, his family pleaded with me to fulfill his last wish: to scatter his ashes at Delphi. This task, which seems formidable to me, became my challenge in poetry. In a previous poem, before "Kestrel" (the poem published here), the poet confesses:

> *I told you everything. When you lost hearing*
> *aids we sifted through vacuum bags, swept*
> *clippings at the barber shop. Not the furnace?*
> *We found them in your mahogany*
> *bed stand. How can I find you?...*
>
> *This year I promise: your ashes to Delphi.*
> *Speak to me through the Oracle.*
> *I know they deserve better than the plastic*
> *bag next to my biking helmet.*

In "Kestrel," I get laughs when I read the last stanzas about tasting his ashes. I am grateful to Wom-po responses for making me see the potentials of wit in all poetry.

GLENNA LUSCHEI

Kestrel

Dammit! I couldn't send you a Val-
entine this year; I drove you . . . I mean
your ashes to Yosemite.

When I saw you in your mask
I swerved into the fence post
but you perched again and

again, kestrel beside crow on the high
tension wire, everywhere along the Grapevine.
In the Lodge, too, the Kachina figure

of the kestrel said endurance.
The turtle on your garment said energy
from underground. In your codicil

you requested Delphi, the navel of the world.
Sure, I would chew those laurel
leaves for you, shimmy down the crevice

and screech my prophecy, "You'll fry in Hell
for leaving me!" Fat lot of good that would do.
So I hike . . . unsteady on the ice to

Bridal Veil Falls, throw a fist full of you
into the mist. My nostrils catch grit
flying back. Not bad.

Kestrel's message from underground:
Endurance. I couldn't get rid
of you if I tried.

Be Mine.

CATHERINE MACDONALD

Grace

In this raw corner of a no-rank town, rusting
swing sets wobble under the weight of fierce

children. Thunderstorm torrents ride pin-straight
alleys down the backsides of backyards. My brothers

pee on the alley storm-grates when they think
no one is looking. This is my footpath

to Grace. Seventh house on the left. An air
conditioner—the only one for blocks—

sweats and sighs in the jalousied
window as August simmers. Grace

is abandoned. A monkey balances
on her bare right shoulder. It simpers

and shrieks, grips her dull blonde hair
with an infant's avid hands—it's a gift

from her ex, an airman late of Saigon.
Outside her door frothy mimosas

waft scent over the dying lawn as Grace ties
one on. *Don't bother her,* my mother scolds,

She's a drunk. But I knock anyway, every
day. Exhilarated by the monkey's cry

and the air conditioner's cold invitation,
I face Grace on the front stoop. As roaring

jets rope the morning sky, Grace
raises her glass to invite me inside.

SHAWN MAEDER

The Needle

In my tiny hands the needle pokes at the cloth,
waits underneath, and emerges hesitantly.
One half of one stitch.

I envied my mother's needle
gliding horizontally across the surface,
making two holes to my one,
each pair a dash of color
in lavender, lilac or vine.

With age, I no longer hear
the popping sound of the needle
as it pierces the stretched muslin
or the long sigh of the silk
pulled through.

So, I did not hear the surgeon's needle
jab in search of cells.
Only saw the blood red flash
drop into the nurse's gloved hand.

MARIE-ELIZABETH MALI

Walking in Winter

Walking in winter, breath
stinging, I pass

a small waterfall
emerging from under

the frozen lake-top,
flowing beneath the road

to cascade downhill
on the other side.

Icicles hang from rocks,
weeping, gleaming

in afternoon's fading light.
For all my love of winter trees

stripped to reveal gritty twisting,
I hate the cold, the stiffness,

the way my eyes run
when exposed to wind.

If only authenticity didn't require
so much dying.

CHARLOTTE MANDEL

Still Life

Transfixed within the scrolled frame of marriage—
Glossy, still as a Flemish *nature mort*—
You are the basket's woven lines,

I the overripe purpling grapes. What is marriage
without realism, plain detail, the more
examined the more discretely outlined?

Gleam seizes shadow, motionless. Marriage
of canvas, oil and turpentine. One more
scrape of the palette's umber and aniline's

blue thin menace. I animated marriage
cartoons as a child, bright crayon, not a mor-
bid thought in view. Polka dot curtains lined

window frames with daisies: picture marriage
as bungalow tilting, blue skies evermore,
uplifted arms diaper-pinning the line.

Watercolors risk salt: over marriage
tides flow. Initials carved in sycamore
erode the jackknife wriggle of their lines.

A playhouse, yet a serious marriage.
Undeclared we knew the stakes, how much more
asked of us. Anniversaries fall in line—

patina thickens—varnish conceals—marriages
shiver apart—ours strains its well-mixed mor-
tar—surfaces enhanced by spider line.

Who sees us defines us by this marriage.
Hand in hand, smile/click. To viewers, a maud-
lin sentiment. To ourselves, still, life line.

CHARLOTTE MANDEL

Essay

"A girl has to get married by eighteen," instructed my mother, "after that she loses her looks." Saved, I made the deadline—in part by observing that "if you can't say anything nice, don't say anything at all." These were dicta for adolescent girls in the 1940s. And so I bought a ruffled apron, and so I stayed mute, oblivious to my need to say words that lived for truth and might, therefore, not be nice at all. Result was a housewife's isolation of mind and repression of feeling.

In midlife, poetry opened inner and outer connections to language and idea. Starting late, however, without the benefits of an MFA network, and despite eventually publishing six books of poetry, I still felt isolated from a world of colleagues. Enter Wom-po where a keyboard links arms of women of my generation with those of my daughter's. When several Wom-po members held up a sign at my reading at the Dodge Festival in New Jersey, I felt greeted as at a reunion—a "marriage" now of "true minds."

ARGIE MANOLIS

Dancing the Men's Dances

In memory of Thea Katina

The record's black grooves spin
like a storm beneath the needle.
She's shouting out the steps—
toes in, toes out, tap forward, tap back—
stomping her feet harder than she needs to.

My ankles ache with the weight of every
turn. I'm learning the song by heart,
each chord, each word, each screech
of the bouzouki's strings. It's like
my yiayia's hands, this music,
like a brushstroke waterfall over
a long, narrow landscape of black.

At twelve, I've forgotten how my yiayia
pinned up each section of hair to look like a queen.
I've forgotten my mother, who is dying
just like her, in the same makeshift sickroom
on the same first floor. I've forgotten
my mother's hand clasped in mine, two birds
settled into their nests, how we sometimes
hum this song together. I've forgotten my father's
hand on my shoulder, pushing me hard.

I'm getting it. My aunt Katina
throws her head back, laughs at the ceiling.
She's pulling us along, gasping for air,
but she doesn't stop. She's singing the words
off key, and I think, after this, she'll touch
my chin and turn my face away from all
the suffering. She'll stop my father's rage,

his fierce love, his everything and nothing.
She'll bring my mother back from the place
between living and dying, and my grandmother,
with the wave of her hand.

At twelve, I believe she has this power.
Something about her hair in her face,
her scratchy voice, her bulging knees,
her eyes—how they grow wet effortlessly,
never close all the way, even in exhaustion.

"When I was little, girls weren't allowed
to learn this dance," she shouts, and I
watch her feet—the gold shoes she bought
especially for dancing. My arm's
linked with hers, hand to shoulder,
and I dig my fingers in, tighter,
as if the whole world
depends upon this lesson.

LOUISE MATHIAS

Desert Flux

Here is a lesson in discard. After the fire
Bird "A" continues to hover

on her scientific twig (on the shadow
of twig-)

Bird "B" is flying in circles. Ruptured hoop
of the sun's corona. What led

you here? The wrecking moon;
the vast,

tight passage of impasse. Light that is bridal,
& in the end, a nuisance.

How to fathom

the sequence of the body; its trial
& veil.

JANET McCANN

Answering Machine

A poem to open a reading

I call my house, it's empty
and my own voice responds,
painfully hesitant, saying I'm
unavailable. I can hear
gaps in the apology, the whirring
tape, a stammer, a repetition,
an indrawn breath, then finally
and blessedly, the beep.

And I had redone that three times,
the first inaudible, the second
grammatically incorrect, and then
this one. I listen to the tape
recording silence, an expectant
hum, and I hang up.

If it was all that hard
just to express absence,
then how can I begin
to tell you that I'm here?

WANDA McCOLLAR

Oh, Radio

A hunker of bony knees
as chin rest,
her "almost red" hair streams
from crown to sock tops.
With grape jelly glissando
on wonder white bread,
she's consumed by airwaves,
"Jack Armstrong,
the A-l-l-l American Boy!"
She reaches out, and turns the dial.

Spent waves hiss along the
shore teasing her dancing feet.
Twirling, arms outstretched,
skimming the wet flat sand,
hair flying, swept in a medley
of gull and Beatle cries,
she is lifted up by airwaves,
skyward to Lucy,
and feathered dreams.
She reaches out, and turns the dial.

Distant lightning crackles
on the airwaves, pocking
those murmuring meaningless
voices, endlessly talking.
She pushes back her hair,
gray and damp,
looks out on the still, flat land,
and the blackbirds looking back,
and sighs, "Where are you now,
all American boy?"

GWYN MCVAY

In the Dirt

The miracle is not one of us is saved.
—Jane Miller, "Submission"

Children in underwear,
deformed the same:

a girl of eight,
grinning, hair clamped

with two barrettes—
one florid good hand

and one stump
with a bit of thumb;

a boy of thirteen,
his young penis

filling the thin
cloth of his briefs,

one arm like a cock-
stump at his side;

kids, photographed
for evidence, their homes

plotted in a radius
from the site—

The apple is hot
but the two babushkas

feed it to their cow,
who blinks her white eyes

and gives hot milk.
It is in the dirt

their sneakers stand on,
these women who moved back.

It is said "to love
is to love the most feared

on this red earth."
In the home for retarded

teenagers, Zoshka hangs
an elbow over the head

of her bed and grins:
"I love America.

I will go there and be president."

SUSAN MEYERS

Awaiting My Brother's Pathology Report,
My Husband and I Take to the River

Laughing gulls laugh, and laugh, what they do best.
Hilarious, I guess, the afternoon sun.
They can barely contain themselves. A pageant
of cedar, Chinese tallow, more cedar.
                                        I'm half sick
of all this beauty. Grapevines thread
the bank's bramble. An osprey repeats its pitiful call—
odd, its small cry.

                    Blue stands at the bow
and whips his line past a bumble bee droning
from rod to unused rod propped up against the seat.
Fish crows talk their low crow talk.
                                    The bee buzzes
so near my head (almost touching my nape) I cringe
and break out in goose bumps.

                                Here's the hope:
a dried-up vine clings to whatever it can.
Still there, a wrecked boat and motor,
half submerged, left to rust. A stand of sumac,
that determined weed.
                        Dead stumps dot the water.
We have come here to ease through something green
and growing.

                    Is that a bullfrog, or alligator,
bellowing low? Out here the birds are kind
with their remarks, pickerelweed thrives
                                        in clumps.
Full to crested over, what does the river care?
A frog jumps from the bank in its long, perfect arc.
Blue switches bait. Above us, a grackle
fusses and flits from limb to limb.

    —for Gene

ANN E. MICHAEL

Stabled

Now horses, living upon the land, eat grass and drink water.
When happy, they twine their necks and run together, when angry,
they turn their backs to one another and kick. This is what horses know.
…They have learned now, from their capable hearts, how to be outlaws.
—from Chuang Tzu: Horses' Hoofs

I run down the meadow's slope
tramp at water's edge

       hair streaming behind me. The long tail—

Ask, if you want me:
I might kick   I might run
restless

I know my territory, stay
in the familiar valley, hollow
           small sway
           of my back.

I don't need the big house, I need
wide field, melodious scrim of trees.

But add a yoke and a moon-shaped plate on the forehead,
and horses know boundaries and limits, they know
       they are enslaved…

I buck and kick
beat down
the stall door   I bite the tether
           when the door is strengthened
I crib
and huff   I close my teeth
           on flesh
flail
twist   yet,

taught to buckle under the bit,
rein in the killing-blow.
I strain with the yoke smooth and unyielding
on my neck. I learn gentling.

Because my heart is capable,
because the law has made me outlaw,
   —I domesticate my fury.

PEGGY MILLER

Aedes albopictus

Getting Things in Context

There is a lot of blending of what's going on
in the universe before a tiny bit makes it
to this insignificant pocket. If ours were the only gravity

I'd be amazingly heavy, heavy as boulders.
Asteroids. You too. But as it is I am lightened,
I'd like to think, or balanced, by all the gravities

pulling me back out into the universe.
Those fat 400 billion stars in the Milky Way
to begin with. I'd be colder without their heat,

this globe quieter without the echo of the Big Bang,
and the thunder I can't hear from all those worlds
makes loud the silence that wakes me in the night.

Fading threads of my voice accompany
the murmur of a calf in Banff or Burma.
The sparkle of my uncountable cells is the least

mimic of a cosmos filled with cataclysmic fire, motion,
explosions, even gamma rays, which would make
toast of me if I ventured too close. I'm average.

The average of hot and cold, dark and light, energy,
rock and vacuum, and probably you are too.
A tangle of elements come halfway

across the galaxy for ingredients. Dressed with senses
that track a small mosquito or taste a brief moment
among all the immensity of time and space.

mosquito

275

SHAYLA MOLLOHAN

Desert Lyrics, I

1.
In the aftermath of
blooming in the high desert

I am sunblinded,
mirage of miles disclosed
by these scars in starlight
where sandmiles led nowhere
where bared skin blistered
where the road ended blunt
where love went black

beneath the shadow of
her wingspread.

2.
Deserts look smaller on maps
and pink as a murderer's tongue.
I'm part of her food chain now,
felon from the belly of the crow.

Up from cholla nest, twigs and feathers,
I ride, a thorn upon her sheeny head
where ravens stalk into sand devils,
lift like smoke into high cumuli.

From mesa, to moon, and back,
past scrub-brush, red-blooming cacti,
where scorpions tuck tail
where she swallows them down.

3.
Nothing is really lost in the desert—
fangs weather longer than the serpent,
needles bleed a sweet poison for days,
tarantulas turn brittle, hollowed out
by predators, by wren and raven akin.

There is healing in the yellow grass.
Cloud, wind, sun, downpour, at once,
bringers of food, bearers of destruction:

> sage rustles in quiet night
> coyote sways in afternoon heat
> vulture watches from the rocks
> side-winder coils beneath cholla nest
> wings flutter danger in their birdsleep.

4.
Oasis to oasis,
desert and desire survive:

> it is sand-flood-sand-flood
> it is bottomless, recreated
> it is beneath my skin
> it is in the aslope of an eye
> it is a lovely sore nipple
> it is the blooming flamingsword
> it is a crow's dried talon.

Sometimes the mystery
makes me cry beneath the white sun.
Mural etched with a bloody thorn.

JUDITH H. MONTGOMERY

Sonata for Tide and Light

I am trying to dismiss the moon: cool archer who plucks
the tides of blood, the brain's fluxing blues—

trying to deny the surge that keys the five
hundred thousand bubbles moored above my womb.

How I yearn for anchor, for the certainty of tideless life—
to be raised beyond the tug of surf,

to be the skiff in drydock, or the hundred-
year-old pine fixed at noon above highwater mark.

But I live subject to the plum reticule that nets up
bubbles one by pearly one. To fluctuating

whim that bellies or denies a second heart
within. That waters me. Or drives me dry. This night

I long for constancy, for shadowless sun—for body
less tuned to blood so I might steal away

to the private slip where peaches yield ripe
to the thumb, and lilies mellow blooms in even light.

Yet I ride bound to Diana's glinting bow, brightened
and shadowed as she whorls the white sail

of her gown to onyx, as she turns from bowl
to scimitar to night. The mirror shines only backed

with blacking—I must embrace the play between
the silver sheen and carbon smear, the cup

of day melting to the saucer of the dark.
The ebony glaze that gleams inside this skin of light.

ANNY BALLARDINI

Essay

As the editor of the Poets' Corner, or better, as the curator of the Corner, I am always looking for good poets to include in my virtual gathering. The Poets' Corner is a page of Fieralingue, a site supported by the Pedagogical Institute here in Bolzano, Italy. Like Wom-po, this site helps spread poetry and poetry talk around the globe. Many are the subscribers to the Wom-po list I've featured on the Corner, starting with Annie Finch (founder and moderator of Wom-po), and including Diane Lockward (on Wom-po, our Lady of the Gazette), Rebecca Seiferle, who advised me to join the list, and others whom I esteem highly. I am so grateful that these wompos accepted my invitation to appear on the Poets' Corner—their presence is enlightening.

ELLEN MOODY

Now hope has died

Now hope has died:
what once upon a time
made me eager, bold.
But I grieve the less,
since I have understood
no one is constant;
nothing endures.

Hope has now died.

Once upon a time
hope's deceit melted me, and I held on.
Now my pain is a game to her;
when she's driven me to tears,
she abandons me,
worn out from love and desire;
she continually tempts me with dying:
a tenacious, strong passion,
which perseveres yet more strongly.

Hope has now died.

I hoped, and fed myself with sweet fire;
I shall not hope any more,
only cry, my soul wrenched with longing,
I call everywhere on death,
seek succour for my grief,
since my heart is without hope
whom I once turned to
as sweet refuge.

Now hope is dead.

While I had her as guide,
every evil seemed light;
without her I am bewildered, bleak,
the least thing is too much;
long anxiety and brief pleasure

are all I've known until now:
my only reward has been
to be a slave.

Now hope has died.

Gentle, sweet, soft hope,
—ah—fled from me—
why didn't she take with her
this burnt heart, my weary life?
I am so frightened,
of hope wholly deprived,
not living, yet alive
at length I have no hope.

Hope has now died.

A translation of a ballata by Veronica Gambara: *"Or passata è la speranza"*.

D.O. Moore

Splitting Oaks

I'd like to speak in arrows. These would be the seventeen Cabeza de Vaca described. He was always admiring Indian arrows delivered into the core of a tree, splitting the *roble*.

What is the heart of the matter, I would ask Cabeza. And where does yours fit in? My heart is full of pins, he'd say, that keep it sewn together. But after something's sewn, you take the pins out. Not this time, Cabeza'd say.

Cabeza de Vaca had the heart of an adventurer. You might call his boyhood "picaresque." What can be had in the New World, he'd often ask his mother. She'd send him to confession.

Cabeza de Vaca's first name is Alvar. Accent on the "A." He never wrote what *los indios* called him during the six years they kept him their slave. It must have been something nice, though, because he stayed on with them three more years once freed.

What is the function of the pericardium? I'd like to ask Cabeza de Vaca this very question. What is the role of the pericardium? Is it a raincoat for the heart?

I know you are talking, but I don't understand what you're saying. Los indios didn't speak to Cabeza in Spanish. It was something else.

My heart is made of Lincoln Logs and words not in the dictionary. Cabeza has taken his heart apart, remade it many times since. I haven't found where he describes the how-to's: connectors, roof pieces, glue.

Cabeza de Vaca wrote and wrote about his shipwreck adventure when he returned. He was happy to see his Spain again, but he never did include all the words he learned while he was away.

Cabeza will agree an oak is motionless, even when I remind him that the heart is a muscle. He has never revealed in his pages if the heart of the *roble* is quick water over sticks, hasn't said how to get there, or what you can see when you do.

LouAnn Shepard Muhm

Waitress

They speak to you
in Spanish
to be funny
or in response to
your dark hair and eyes
and you answer in French
so they know
this is no ordinary
restaurant
but you laugh along
because they *are* funny
on vacation with their compadres
and they love the food
the drink
and you who bring it to them
and remember from last summer
a lime not a lemon
in their iced tea
or no salt on the margarita,
and for every one who asks
for your number
or comments on your dress
there are two who ask
what you are reading
or whether you have published
lately
and you are there with *your* compadres
dancing out an incredible ballet
of hot plates and crushed ice
until you go home
where your husband says
you smell like quesadillas
and he likes it
and your children
to whom checks mean nothing
squeal

as you empty your pockets
of all the gleaming coins
that they can count.

AIMEE NEZHUKUMATATHIL

Last Aerogramme to You, with Lizard

Kovalam, India

I found a bat today—its belly full of bloody mosquitoes.
If I squint, the shoreline of coconut trees becomes green star
lights strung across a patio. On the other side of this window

you and our dog sleep on packed bright earth. Follow
the leggy cats in this village, some curled up in bars
tucked up in tea and smoke. Newspapers here report callow

boys sneaking into nearby huts with machetes—all for easy dough
to finger in the sweaty pockets of their jeans. Can you smell the cigars
in this place? I sit on one of the boys' spinning chairs—some fellow

still warms me and it's not you, not even a nicked photo
of us ankle-deep in a lake I swore was full of snakes. The sandbar
sinks lower when I try to walk across, so I spread my toes

for extra balance. I have followed you for years, sent jumbo-
sized letters smudged and slicked down, but this I *swear*
is the last aerogramme to you. Now even my saliva glows

in the dark. Cats pool near the bed but I know there is one gecko
left to thrill my sleep. I know it won't bite, but the bizarre
way it skitters a loop around my wrist—exploring each elbow—
makes me weep for you. My cheek is wet. A lizard makes it so.

JOYCE NOWER

Maybe the Rocks Did Soften in the Sun

Maybe the rocks did soften in the sun,
trees bow, dogs sprawl on the green tongue of the lawn.
I know I hid in the high leaves of the apple,

listening as the notes flowed out the piano's mouth,
the sole stirring, and took me to a cave
where I heard the echo of myself bounce

from wall to wall, the reverberations plunging
into the mysterious heart where harmonized
with cicadas the self settled and sang.

Ghosts of childhood flit through the leafing trees.
If we look back, we change, but not to stone:
this poem the severed head that keeps on singing.

Mendi Lewis Obadike

Strut

New Orleans, night

Our last night in town, my friend is just from her mother
When the elevator catches her made-up face unawares.
Wrapped in myself, I miss the down-turned eyes,
But manage to plead, *Come with us,* and she does.

Ours is a party of strangers, as tightly
Bound by lack as by what we hold
Between us. Who knows what could be
Ailing another? Alone as we are,

We make our way through the blacker part
Of the city in a pack. We wear the night
And one another as a perfect skin. This city converts
Our words into whatever magic we need.

We're on the catwalk. This side of Congo Square,
Men buzz, but not to us. Here, they reach
And call to each other as if old friends: *Work,
Sweetness.* This is to the brothers who walk

Among us, who keep aloof but nonetheless, flock
Here. Right now they flank her, my sad friend,
Noting her strut. A few steps behind, I am
Watching them raise the veil of sorrow from her eyes

And send it to the stars. She likes it when they talk
To her in third person: *The girl is fly.* One lifts
Her hand above her head to twirl her. *Hair / shoes,*
Someone whispers. *Skin / hair,* someone whispers back.

ANNE BRITTING OLESON

Looking Back Up the Hospital Drive

They do not come easily to me, these words
like glass in my mouth, cutting until
I taste blood:

the blood whispering through the chambers
of an enlarged heart, failing
the old woman at the upstairs window.

Is she real, or an old reflection, standing
with an upraised hand, waving
or patting hair into place?

This place with the barred windows, gray
in stone, in hair, in face, in clothing,
all color wasting away,

washed away like the ink on a letter
left to suffer the laundry, forgotten
in a pocket, words never sent, never read.

ALICIA OSTRIKER

Everywoman Her Own Theology

I am nailing them up to the cathedral door
Like Martin Luther. Actually, no,
I don't want to resemble that *Schmutzkopf*
(See Erik Erikson and N.O. Brown
On the Refortner's anal aberrations,
Not to mention his hatred of Jews and peasants),
So I am thumbtacking these ninety-five
Theses to the bulletin board in my kitchen.

My proposals, or should I say requirements,
Include at least one image of a god,
Virile, beard optional, one of a goddess,
Nubile, breast size approximating mine,
One divine baby, one lion, one lamb,
All nude as figs, all dancing wildly,
All shining. Reproducible
In marble, metal, in fact any material.

Ethically, I am looking for
An absolute endorsement of loving-kindness.
No loopholes except maybe mosquitoes.
Virtue and sin will henceforth be discouraged,
Along with suffering and martyrdom.
There will be no concept of infidels;
Consequently the faithful must entertain
Themselves some other way than killing infidels.

And so forth and so on. I understand
This piece of paper is going to be
Spattered with wine one night at a party
And covered over with newer pieces of paper.
That is how it goes with bulletin boards.
Nevertheless it will be there.
Like an invitation, like a chalk pentangle,
It will emanate certain occult vibrations.

If something sacred wants to swoop from the universe
Through a ceiling, and materialize,
Folding its silver wings
In a kitchen, and bump its chest against mine,
My paper will tell this being where to find me.

CHRISTINA PACOSZ

Summer Is Fraying

Squirrel nests are falling down
Fourth of July has been here and gone
Summer is waning
Though swallows still chortle as they dance through the air
And robins strut on stunted lawns
The drought drags on

Squirrels pair off
On the back porch rail
To groom each other
Before their rut
It is the season
Though summer is fraying

My thoughts stray to her, to him
Each of those four gone
The family pentacle broken now
Leaving me alone
On the lone prairie
Too exhausted to howl at the moon

And the war drags on
The bloody war drags on
And spreads
Around the world
Like an awful fleet of ships
A terrible wind filling their sails

SHIN YU PAI

it does a body good

the

food   pyramid

was not   **3 - 5**   built

by   **servings in a day**   M.D.s

or   nutrition experts   but   the agricultural industry

HOOD®ed promotions
from the dairy farmers
of America

build strong teeth
&
bones,
grow
lactose
intolerance

flatulence
&   the runs

GOT MILK?

(of magnesia)

CHERYL PALLANT

A Declaration of Independence

Who holds these truths to be self-evident, that to shun
or welcome are equal, give or take a sum, give or take
a man bedding woman or a headstrong woman stroked by
the sun. Who held them once as sacred and undeniable,
let them grow beyond the first field, a declaration
that stunned a race mentioning blame. Abused powers
abolish the need to polish silver. Light and transient
causes shall not undue long established powers, forks
on the left, knives on the right. Experience hath shown
itself inexperienced and prone to intestinal distress,
disposed to suffer insufferably. When a train or ship
empties its excesses into a pot, boiling or simmering
can test patience or make the cook despotic. It is our
right to throw, to govern, or usurp the first taste. To
prove this, let facts be submitted to a candid world.
Might this candied world be absinthe or mint.

Who refuses the wholesome
has utterly neglected
large districts
with manly firmness
the laws of naturalization.

Who obstructs
has refused for a long time
erecting a multitude
sent hither to harass our people,
and eat out their substance
for quartering large bodies of armed troops.

Protect, cut off, impose, deprive
at once an example for introducing the same.
Plunder, ravage, burn, destroy
excited domestic insurrections.
Bring on the merciless
destruction of all ages, sexes, and conditions
in every stage petitioned for redress in the most humble terms,
for rectitude in the name
ought to be totally dissolved
as free and independent
to each other our fortunes.

SUSAN FIRGHIL PARK

Prayer

Today I feel like invoking
the wild goddess, the bad mad
one most mythology books discuss
with a touch of
polite distaste, all skulls and blood
and primitive death. I'd love
to get my fingers in
her mud, help her
crack bones and tear up
body parts to throw into
her foul stew. Let me

crouch with her on a stony
cave floor, watch her pour her
black, fetid brew into the mouths
of unsuspecting, sleeping souls.
       Let her
lead me underground
into the surety of darkness, that

great darkness
that folds around you

like no blanket you could ever find
as a child.

KELLI RUSSELL AGODON

Essay

By joining Wom-po, my poetry-town became larger. Where there were just one or two bookstores, there are now hundreds, where there were just a few poets passing by each other, there are now women standing side by side. I open my e-mail to find conversations that stretch from Seattle to England and down to New Zealand. At anytime, I can add to the exchange or just listen. My poetry-town has grown into a community of voices across the planet, each of us a unique person, yet all joined together by words.

CYNTHIA PARKER-OHENE

Weather Report

boots mean mud from the kilmarnock shore buck-eyed oyster trout, and salty blue crabs
carried in under uncle william's red slicker from his fishing boat appear on steamy plates
of colored-made food in a 1921 white stucco house with 3 missing steps and a parked
horse drawn carriage driven illegally by the colored owner in a colored enclave near
lancaster county virginia the land they lived on thought to be barren by previous owners
was deeded to william kelly.   but moisture from her bark appeared several grandchildren
beyond   the white stucco with 3 missing steps sits under a drapery of willow wisps and
pink cottonwoods follow a pollen path of papillon beadings scattered petals and yucca
casts   sometimes sun   wife of moon spreads fodder to feed for 9 fortnights at a time.
its dawn and dewy   earth's heartbeat wakes us.

ELISE PASCHEN

Engagement

The king is murdered and his daughter, Mis, goes mad,
growing fur and killer claws, escaping into the woods.
She is tamed by Dubh Ruis, a harp player. Marrying her,
he becomes king.
—Irish legend

Don't touch me, don't come near. I'll shred
your flesh from bone. Don't even stare.

I can smell you from here. You don't
reek like the hunters who tailed me,

all salt and sod. You smack of hay.
Show me what you're hiding. The strings

trap a sun's glint. Sounds like leaf-play
at night beneath a tree. Here's where

I lay me down – inside this notch.
Play it for me and let me play.

★

What's in your mouth? You swallow hard.
It's coming back. A waking whiff –

out on the flagstones in the courtyard,
through the doorways, the gates.

I feel I'm coming home. It's like
a hearth. I never get enough.

★

Nights I still rave. The beast is out.
Your arms around me pin it down.

*

Your collar's tight. But look. My fingers
have grown shells now, not claws. Stop tying

that cloth across my skin. I need
the air, these woods. Keep here. Let's stay

above moss, beneath leaf. Help me
shake down rowans, rub our flesh red.

You've stripped away the fur, and, after
months of those deer-fat baths, I'm bare.

LYNN PATMALNEE

A Screw

taped inside a man's
birthday card makes him
laugh, but not like the lei
he got last year.

A screw in a Ferris wheel
bears the creaky weight
of romance, rust
and too much cotton candy.

A screw falls to the ground
in silence . . .
then a scream.

A screw forgotten
in a back pocket
clangs endlessly in the dryer,
a dinner bell rung by a woman
standing in an empty yard.

Rolling around the bottom
of a dead man's toolbox,
a screw sounds like
loneliness.

Clasped tightly as a rosary,
a screw leaves an imprint
like a flower
in a woman's hand.

MOLLY PEACOCK

The Flaw

The best thing about a hand-made pattern
is the flaw.
Sooner or later in your hand-loomed rug,
among the squares and flattened triangles,
a little red nub will soar above a blue field,
or a purple cross will sneak in between
the neat ochre teeth of the border.
The flaw we live by, the wrong bit of floss
that wreathes among the uniform strands
and, because it does not match,
makes a red bird fly,
turns that blue field into sky.
It is almost, after long silence, a word
spoken aloud, a hand saying through the flaw,
I'm alive, discovered by your eye.

CAROL PETERS

Investment

—after Lyn Hejinian

By turning away
    she's not rejecting him.
It's familiar, cumulative, but temporary,
    yet in its summarily remote
    calculation fond—
The bed
    shudders,
Panic shimmers,
The preferred option is
    to wait
    and see.
She compounds disfavor by
    forecasting a next
    time,
She asks to be held
    even as she declines to
    capitulate.
It is that castle keep,
    that interest, that exposure, those
    hours per week, that inequality,
    that transience, that misalignment.
All things missing or withheld
    bring returns.

KATHA POLLITT

The Expulsion

Adam was happy— now he had someone to blame
for everything: shipwrecks, Troy,
the gray face in the mirror.

Eve was happy— now he would always need her.
She walked on boldly, swaying her beautiful hips.

The serpent admired his emerald coat,
the Angel burst into flames
(he'd never approved of them, and he was right).

Even God was secretly pleased: Let
History begin!

The dog had no regrets, trotting by Adam's side
self-importantly, glad to be rid

of the lion, the toad, the basilisk, the white-footed mouse,
who were also happy and forgot their names immediately.

Only the Tree of Knowledge stood forlorn,
its small hard bitter crabapples

glinting high up, in a twilight of black leaves:
how pleasant it had been, how unexpected

to have been, however briefly,
the center of attention.

CATI PORTER

Pomegranate, Juiced

He tells me, "squeeze it, like this," hands it to me,
cupping with my fingers, squeezing with my hand.

This squeezing into dew drinkable from the red cup
of itself, the leathery orb hand-like,

is like I'm squeezing his hand. I juice rubied knuckles
and tension's released. He hands me a knife

to "pierce it, right there." With it I tease the skin,
open a little wound. "Put your mouth there—No. Give me your hand."

He shows me how to make it flow. I draw it in.
"Good?" he asks. I nod, not answering simply

about the fruit, about its juice. About the wanting.
About wanting his hands to me.

REN POWELL

A Matter of Course

First I saw the kitten, tiny and red,
then saw, in her movements, the cat.
Then the blue eye, larger than the gray one,

the blind one
the deformity of the skull
the infection.

But I saw it all too late: as I bent to pet her,
carefully. And I did it in front of my son.

Knowing it was too late to change direction,
knowing she would follow in a wide circle around us both,

I saw beyond the instant we stood at the corner:
The truck that would come around and catch her under its
wheels. We don't need death today, not today, not today. And
she would scurry off to die—

    and it happens like that
    she goes on her way, and at first
    you think she's all right.

    And, if the bladder happens to be empty,
    she can even survive a half-ton of metal on her back
for an instant.

KRISTIN PREVALLET

The Mother Maker

An older poet talks about making:
the maker creates
meaning out of the sources at hand
he says.

I made a meaning
and named her Sophie.
And she makes meaning
out of an elephant named Elmer
and a snowman named Egg.

And all the animals make a meaning
called play and this is what
making is all about.

To the older poet
I said
the child makes a world
of her own design
just as a mother
makes a child
out of hers—

And from this attention
to the source
comes meaning.

I learned all this
from an older poet
but I always knew it
to be true:
within myself
come the sources
out of which the world
makes.

SINA QUEYRAS

A Lilac Begins to Leaf

Last night the memory of her mother walked out into the parking lot of the *Long Rail Tavern* at precisely five minutes to twelve. Where her tears fell, tiny puffs of dust. X-ray her now you will see her mother filing her nails. Her heart flickers off and on, random as a cat's paw. She will not fall to pieces here, she says. Though at least if she did, she could now put herself together again. She remembers a superhero made of boulders. He could assemble and reassemble. She could get bigger, she thinks. There might be room for two. And in her mind a lilac begins to leaf.

ELLEN RACHLIN

Night Swim

Swim out; trust buoyancy,
although what holds also falls
through the fingers.
Nothing separates
the smoky meeting place
of sea and sky.

Lair of water, hollow:
does kicking make
the drowning think they swim?

BEVERLY RAINBOLT

The Text Is Dead—Long Live the Text

Words mill around in crowded chaos.
Language and *technology* square off, push up
their sleeves and walk the boundaries of their turf.

Chicken and *Little* pair off, capitalize
on everyone's fears and run around yelling:
"The margins are falling! . . . margins are falling!"

Scrabble pieces clatter about the board
trying to land on the red Triple Word Score
squares in bold effort to prove the edge worth more.

Magnetic Poetry Kits may have the idea,
words bonding in ways that cover
their backs, but leave their discourse

exposed to random acts of composition,
their meaning determined by how they fall.
If *sumptuous* lands next to *dead*

can the heart handle it—put it off
to chance or to the symbolism of an
older order that could explain the way

things change so quickly.

ATHENA KILDEGAARD

Essay

I am not a lurker. I'm a listener.

There are only a handful of wompos I know in the flesh. They would not likely describe me as a lurker, a wallflower, a listener. Among friends I'm a talker, gregarious.

But at the computer, in the quiet of my study, with no eyes to look into, no hand's gestures to follow, I find myself most comfortable listening.

When the topic arose of mother-poets and the balance required, I imagined all those Wom-po mother-poets sitting up in the dark—as I did now fifteen years ago—their first child suckling at their breast, moonlight pouring through the transom, crickets purring outside, a line or image rising up like breast milk, since making is making no matter if it's metaphor or matter.

When the subject arose of women in the nineteenth century giving poetry readings, suddenly all these named but faceless wompos stood before me, watches pinned to the lace at their bosom, hat pins catching the light, all of them reading. Never mind that it's the twenty-first century. In the listening place, time stands still.

When the discussion turned to ordering a manuscript, all my Wom-po compatriots were in a long room, a room with light pouring down on to us from windows open to the sky, and there we all were in a row, our poems spread around us, each of us trying poems with poems, some of us stretching our legs, wandering down the row, leaning over the shoulders of others pointing, "How about that one with this one, that one there, no there."

I listen from my study in the basement of a house in a neighborhood on the edge of a town with a population of 5000 if you count the student body at the public liberal arts college here. More poetry talk happens in my study in one week than in six months in this little town—I'm sure of it. And what talk it is—talk enough for the most devoted listener.

D'ARCY RANDALL

Wrong Window

Weeks after I'd moved in they still arrived,
long-limbed roses I could not keep alive,
bottles of champagne I also killed.
I found her everywhere—bright bows
in drawers, the hairs that coiled
like worms across the tile.
Then late one night, the clacks
that plastic boot heels make
on concrete broke my sleep,
then stopped below my open window.
A cry for "Donna, Donna," curled
across the sill, lingered in the room
like smoke. I woke into another's dream—
my ivory curtains heaved and blew,
ready for somebody's angel.
Not for me. I gazed
out upon him anyway; my single
spotlight pared his shoulder's curves,
splashed through his hair, pooled in his face
already drowned with longing.
I've been told you never try
to wake a sleepwalker or someone deep in love,
but I, the skinny-one with cropped-off hair,
leaned to scream out, "Donna's gone!
She doesn't live here anymore!"
The night was naked black. The banished form
slipped water-like away. I turned around
and found her scent
ghosting through the room, and there,
on its silver pedestal,
my tilted mirror watched for her in vain.

ELIZABETH REES

Talia

In Hebrew, God's dew

Five days old, she already feels the burden
of her body, born with all the eggs she will
ever shed, eggs that will fall like the moon,
and she wakes with a mouth full of tears,
shaking her fist, singing sharply,
a shard of beach glass against stone.

And just when she is most difficult to calm,
an agéd smile creeps across her mouth.
She will keep her secrets. She listens
for every sound, as if each could explain
the mystery of birth, that record of tears,
the tears that stars weep

and turn to beads, the gems of morning.
Inside every tear a hundred eggs sloughed,
inside every egg a hundred wishes growing.
And every month may teach her mercy.
Talia, wise, already
a woman waiting inside.

MARTHA RHODES

Low Ceiling'd

I woke up pink and smiling on my birthday.
I was the birthday girl!

But my family frowned me into a corner.
I could not stand up. All day
They ate my cake in front of me.
I was no longer pink.
I was a blue boy!

I was their blue, puny, birthday boy.

SUSAN RICH

For Sale

Xhosa women in clothes too light
for the weather have brought wild flowers
and sit sloped along the Claremont road.
I see her through rolled windows,

watch her, watch me, to decide if I'll pay.
It's South Africa, after all, after apartheid;
but we're still idling here, my car to her curb,
my automatic locks, to her inadequate wage.

MOIRA RICHARDS

Doing my bit agin domestic violence

The women wait in a corridor of the magistrate's court. Mostly alone, sometimes a friend, kids.

I see them one after the other in the small room with three chairs, a desk, box of tissues. Listen to each same story. Sometimes she lifts her skirt, rolls a sleeve, shows me her hurting. I explain the law, help her file for protection, invite the next woman in.

But I am an accountant—unable to leave other women behind when I go home—lie awake and count tears. I fear I will come to hate my father, brothers, my lover, my sons ... everyman.

I have not the skills to continue this volunteer work.

      first violets smearing her make-up on

MARGARET RICKETTS

The Mountain, the Mayfly

Say no one knows the date or the
Hour, but actually that's only true

about those creatures who
refuse to kill themselves and

who don't have an execution
date set, which Black Mountain

does. This taints the past, the day
we went to Merton's monastery

and I was so entranced by the yellow
gingko leaves sheltering the ground. I

despise the way the mountain's demise
alters the way I look at my friends, who are
small and mortal, who grasp this no better than I,

but if you added all of us together
one of us might understand   this.

Not everything in this earth
can be pulled and teased apart.   The separations,

the gaps in this life don't matter
much to me, not when

nothing much in my life has pointed away
from this tenacious, sticky web of connection,
so swiftly being yanked apart.

EVE RIFKAH

Solomon

I bare my head, O Lord. Rend my clothes, cover my upper lip
I cry Unclean, Unclean

banished from wife and sons O Lord, from the children I taught
yet I am not alone. Surely, O Lord, you did not mean
leper and leper shall not dwell together?

I can no longer tie the tefillin with my own hands.
O Lord, even lepers can pray, can sing praises unto You.

the wool of my tallis I kiss, but there is no Torah here
to touch cloth to holy skin I touch my books that I may not forget.
You cast us out
but did not deny us the holy words.
If I do not remember thee, let my tongue cleave to the roof of my mouth

in this desert, on this island, O Lord
on this desert island, I raise my voice to You.
I will sing praises unto my God while I have any being.

in my defilement, heart sore, skin white
already a ghost,
Sh'ma Israel, hear me O Lord, in my ugliness,
I cry unto thee, Thou art my refuge.
I exalt Your glory.

Solomon Goodman, 64, was born in Russia, and came to the United States with his wife and 2 children in 1898. He lived in the North End of Boston where he taught Hebrew until diagnosed with leprosy. Goodman was sent to the Penikese Island Leper Hospital, March 27, 1909. He died at the Penikese Island Leper Colony on August, 16, 1916, at age 71 and is buried on the island.

KIM ROBERTS

Fowler and Wells' Phrenological Cabinet

Walt Whitman made regular visits
        He loved to touch the white porcelain head,
marked off in sections: Appetite, Grief,
Acquisitiveness. Like a butcher's chart

mapping the choicest meats.
        Whitman knew the body's limits,
and how the mind, a grid
of memory and fear, narrows the range

even further. He hated limits,
        prudence, high manners,
but he loved a good system
and wanted to learn this one's

steady answers. Why wouldn't
        what's inside show up on the skin?
The bumps of the head,
small ones like hiccups,

large ones that span three or four
categories, elongated heads, ones
        that come to a point. His categories
would need new names:

Voluptuousness wears an open collar,
        Indolence takes the shape
of a cardboard butterfly perched
on his finger. Adhesiveness wants a walk

on the dark docks, a ferry ride across the river.
        And Sublimity roars like a leaf.
His home in Camden,
where I touched his rubber galoshes,

once overflowed with stacks of paper,
        a chaos, a fire hazard.
He wouldn't let the hired woman touch it.
Whitman claimed an internal logic

even to Disorder; he loved
        a good system. In the prison
across the street from his house, men line the windows.
Women on the sidewalk dance, arms above their heads,

hold a pose like Cleopatra, then change.
        I thought at first: performance art?
Then realized they were spelling
with their bodies, forming O

and L and P in the air.
        The body's news comes slowly.
Whitman knew about longing,
he nursed dying Civil War soldiers,

knew the stink of rotting flesh,
        of pus staining a bandage yellow,
the angel face we wear when we're asleep.
He was large in Sympathy.

He knew something of fate
        and its strange journey through the grey
thickets of Infelicity and Melancholia,
the temperaments that form in the womb.

ALEIDA RODRÍGUEZ

Apple

Just as an object may move in three perpendicular directions, . . .
so an object may participate in three perpendicular futures.
—*Alan Lightman,* Einstein's Dreams

I have not written a new poem
in two years, servant to illness and death.
I have voided my dreams and waking hours
with the drugs of distraction and tedium,
antidotes to hope.
Nevertheless, every day paths branch before me
that I do not take, staying indoors,
avoiding the sun's glare and my own failings.
But accidents happen anyway: my life
calls me away, and on the road
temptation blooms, though I barely recognize it,
retired as I am from longing.
No use pursuing—it's cauterized
shut as youth.
But a ghostly part of me rises,
puts on its smoky coat
and departs through my mouth.
I return home with a sense
of having given up
a child for adoption.
For years I'll calculate its age,
conjure up its face—now, then now.
If I had not left my house,
I may never have understood
how the impossible instructs us,
tangible and sweet
as the apple I am savoring,
or as the never path I almost followed,
no less real for its impossibility.

Tara Betts

Essay

I was introduced to the Wom-po LISTSERV by Marilyn Nelson in 2003 and was pleased to meet Annie Finch shortly thereafter. I had expressed my interest in a woman's writing community and had been seeking that on an academic level as I was preparing to enter graduate school. Prior to that, I founded, volunteered, studied, and performed at many organizations in Chicago and Eugene, Oregon, which were devoted to the empowerment of women writers. I was privileged to meet many wonderful women with stories as outlandish as my own, but I also wanted to meet women who wrestled with ideas with an intellectual rigor of the same intensity as mine. Sometimes, my path re-converged with the women I'd met in the various places I'd worked, and so many times I found myself being considered an example. I've never considered myself a model, especially at such a modest point in my writing career, but I did and still want to grow into that role.

I needed support from experienced women from various backgrounds, and in some ways, this electronic community has provided that, connecting me with new groups of women and rekindling bonds with familiar names and faces. Allison Joseph smiles at me from her occasional notes about her classes, French poetic forms, and her overall joy. Wendy Carlisle and I found each other after a long separation after our first meeting at Flight of the Mind in Eugene. Marilyn Hacker astounds me with her brilliance. I smile when Mendi Obadike offers some salient point that I haven't considered. I mourn and remember our sisters lost—like Reetika Vazirani or Octavia Butler. The consideration of Foremothers has perked my interest in digging deeper into the work of other poets, spurred me to remember the ones that I love, like June Jordan, or led me to find the unexpected new poet. Wom-po is an opening of arms, a firm hand on the shoulder. It supports my sojourn into myself and into poetry, and offers a possible welcome into a larger world of women who influence the world with a craft that sings.

Lois Roma-Deeley

Throwing a Chair through the Hospital Window

We didn't have any money not even for milk much less insurance when my cousin said *why don't you buy some from the school at least it's cheap* and I could not say one more time that we do not do not have any money or that I borrow cigarettes from strangers and fake putting quarters in the tin can labeled *donations* for coffee which is always brewing on the brown Formica table at the student union because I want to kill my own hunger and get by with the one meal and leave most of dinner for the kids though they did not go hungry but my son's pants were always too short and the kids in the fourth grade called him Floods now I can barely stand to write this and want to shoot myself in the head for having lived such a life how can anyone live such a life? why wasn't I smarter? my husband tried the best he could he tried selling things no one wants or needs finally then he hired himself out as a day laborer and he and my brother caught bricks and we were grateful to be able to buy chop meat and cereal and apples but the canary someone gave to my daughter *did* die only because *I* couldn't buy it food until Friday which was payday and it was just that the bird couldn't wait until the weekend and then I was going to go the store and even now people can't believe I couldn't afford bird seed and I tell you there was one day when I saw how a person could be *just that far away* from living on the streets if a few more things go wrong though I could always sell my wedding rings before that happened then my father who was a salesman got lung cancer and got fired at 57 because his *bosses couldn't carry him any longer* and I didn't know how to take care of everyone but I was going to school no matter what and I'm not sure I want to continue telling you this story because people like me aren't supposed to have stories like this and I can hear you say *why weren't you smarter? so why didn't you figure it out sooner?* but then my three-year-old broke her arm and she was my baby my baby my baby do you under-stand what that means? it means you lie down in the street and let a car run over you if you have to in order to protect your child but we didn't we didn't have any insurance and when we took her to the hospital my husband passed out after he said... *how you doing baby?* and then I could not could not stop crying and they sent the young social worker to the room where I was rocking back and forth and crying and this guy shows me his own arm which had been broken 20 years ago as if to show me how it was all going to be all right but I would not stop crying because I thought w*hen they find out I have no insurance they will not take care of my baby* and I should have insurance but I don't I don't some day I will but right now I don't so I gave them my old Blue Cross card and I thought to myself that when they find out the card is no good they will tell me *no we won't take care of your baby* then I thought I will pick up this waiting room chair and I swear by Almighty God I will throw this cheap little piece of shit through that plate glass window and they will think that I am insane and they will take care of my little girl because crazy people get listened to that much I learned from my mother.

RACHEL ROSE

Sheets

It has all gone according to plan,
mine, made when I was ten. My mother divorced the man
who came to take the place of my father.

Every time we left in her cold car
I held my breath, hoping we'd go so far
we couldn't go home: *Please mum; I can make you happy*

but by the time she left I'd long since moved out West
and learned to love him more, or her less.
Now she comes to visit me alone, stays for a week,

hides the pots in unexpected places, cooks with too much fat.
He comes for a single night, hangs up his coat and hat
and picks up his step-grandson. His face has softened with defeat,

as has her own. Each in turn asks me for news of the other,
and I tell them the parts that hurt—devious daughter—
the parts that prove they were right to part,

but finally my intentions are pure. I do not tell them how
between her visit and his I went down
with my son on one arm, clean sheets on the other, intending

to change the bed, but the smell of roses from the lotion my mother wears
drifted like a rainstorm up the stairs
and I turned around, lugging clean sheets and my oblivious baby,

leaving the bed just as it was, awaiting his arrival:
her scent of roses a reproachful perfume, a rival
for his dream-time, a thorn—

or perhaps the scent became the dream itself: bouquet
of ivory wedding roses dried upon a shelf.

CYNTHIA ROTH

The Sound of Love Failing

It is not the kthump of a large book closing,
or of air pushed fast by nausea up the eustachian tubes.
More like the clink of Judas' bloodmoney
or a parent's backhand crack across a child's face,
echo of curled body rolling against one wall
then another. It is in the whine of trees cleared off
the backyard forest you thought your father owned.
Those chainsaws sent you out to the wood across the highway
climbing strange trees until you could smell only the blood
in your hair, skin of your fingers, ammonia halo
of sound conducted in spiral time to the cries
of Mary Godwin's babies when she died.

The sound returned in the slammed door of a seventies two-door,
hard like the heavy look your first husband threw you
after that metal and right before you left him.
And later in the low hum of humiliation
behind eyes that could not comprehend
why your new lover would fly you both to New York in his jet
for a quiet weekend, then call you *not Jewish enough*
in Yiddish slang for lingering outside a cathedral.
Every slammed screen door in this world knows it by heart.
The land mines and missiles treatied away
come back through the black market, the plowed and dozed earth,
threatening suburban sleep, whispering *Munich*.

HELEN RUGGIERI

Jazz on a Summer Afternoon
—Newport Jazz Festival, 1958

Gerry Mulligan is playing—
the audience watches through cat's eye
glasses, shades, man, crew cuts,
pretty women in the half light
glazed with August, jazz
in all their indications.

Anita O'Day is singing "Sweet Georgia Brown"
perfectly pitched into the folding chairs
from the column of her black sheath;
she releases from her reedy throat
each pitch the band must mock
each note a scatty inspiration.

If I'm born again, I'll have
that voice, the strength of a B flat
clarinet, the upper reaches of a saxophone.
She could not have been invented without
a perfect metal music to
match herself against.

In the aisles couples begin to dance
the intricate jitterbug of cool
and my muscles tense for each
spin and turn, remembering those moves
as if they were tattooed, indelible.

The body's memory, balance tied
to unarticulated longings—
to be rich, to be smart, to be there,
the empty aisle, ours, splendidly
lit for evening, as we move as we must
under the capering moths.

I want that music with me everywhere,
my feet sliding and pivoting,
my voice pitched out across the front
in tune with everything.

C. J. SAGE

Sonnet for Carryhouse and Keeper

I met a man who'd kept a snail as pet
beneath a cold stone house which held no wife;
too dank it was for even cats to thrive.
Inside an old fish tank his snail friend slept.

The man's round back was proof he'd not forget
to spend good time in keeping things alive
between his care-filled self and his shelled bride.
All day he'd curve around her as she crept

among the leafy shadows of his hands;
he'd trace her pearl-string trails with his fingers,
his breath would set small clouds into her glass.

The day he set her free she took one half
a day to slip into good-bye; she lingered
in the lovegrass, like the lovelorn, said this man.

CIN SALACH

Ripe

Everywhere I look, grown-ups are eating
babies—mothers munching on chubby necks,

fathers on fat little feet, sucking in
buttery baby skin as if it were summer's

last cob of sweet corn, tired teeth aching
for more. Oh the taste of fresh baby—

there is nothing like it—except of course
for the smell. Voluptuous innocence,

coil of cuddle-up-ness curled in our arms
ready to dip in powder and consume.

Even my own mouth waters! What is it
that makes us want to bite this flesh wholly

as if it were the first apple, as if
after one swallow, we'd know everything.

METTA SÁMA

Fluid, fecund, forget me not

Yes. The moon metaphors you. A pulse of
Yes. The moon metamorphoses you. A push of
Yes. The moon metathesizes you. A pucker of
Yes. The moon meteorites you. A puddle of
Yes. The moon. Metonym. You. Pukka.
You. A punch. A meta-. A muse. The yes.
You. A metallic puff. The powdered mood. Yes.

RATI SAXENA

In the Swamps of Alzheimer

Her trembling feet
move forward into the future
She slips suddenly, falls into
the past, starts chuckling
Look! trees are talking to me
She starts chatting
with branches, leaves
of the neem tree
in the courtyard of grandfather's house
I pull her back with force
from the heights of coconut trees
She gets irritated
runs towards
grand-uncle's store room
starts searching
for all the addresses
whose ink was wiped away.

I am pulling her
she is becoming a little girl
again and again
Mother in the swamps of
Alzheimer

*

It is my turn
I shall comb your hair now
You are pulling my hair she says
apply a lot of oil

Putting fingers in the
gray thin hair
the daughter is thinking
the little girl has grown up
and old mother has changed into
a little girl

✳

These days she is upset
because of quarreling memories
Whatever happens now
wiped away by
a crowd of memories coming
from behind

She is forgetting
the meaning of relevant words
entering forcefully
stories, which were sleeping
sometimes climbing in the
kitchen basket.

✳

After wetting bed
she tries to hide with pillow
looks carefully
smiles like opening bud
even after getting scolding
naughtiness swims
at the corner of her lips

Oh! Is this mother
or a careless little girl

✳

These days
everyone talks to her
chair, table or box
Dogs, lion and leopard
come to her room
without any fear
She plays with houseflies

dances with ants
Mother has become friend
to everyone
who cannot be seen by
we intelligent

Like a flying kite
she is slipping from our hands
mother
in the swamp of Alzheimer

ADA JILL SCHNEIDER

Waiting for You

Your plane isn't due till six-nineteen.
It's only two o'clock but I'm prepared,
hair washed, legs shaved, make-up on,
jumping and clean as a Lubavitcher
fresh from the *mikvah*.
How could it be that I want you,
want you so much after all these years!

Remember Fort Benning, Georgia?
Me holed up reading all week
at the Shady Pines Motel,
washing my hair, doing my nails,
waiting and waiting. Then
two sweet hours together
at Friday night service with sandwiches.
Weekend leave, you in fatigues
and combat boots, walking backwards,
waving goodbye across the field,
falling into a ditch,
coming up smiling.

When you come home each evening,
I feel I've come home too.
Our parents fled from the same
little town in Poland. We would've
been slaughtered if we lived there.
One day the *chevra kadisha*
will cleanse my dead body,
wash my hair, wrap me in a clean
white shroud of seven layers,
preparing me to meet God.
But, heresy of all heresies, my love,
I will be preparing to meet you.

PENELOPE SCAMBLY SCHOTT

April, Again

The most brutal movie I ever saw
was time-lapse film of fruit in a dish,
all that tender ripeness caving in
on itself: the collapse of *is* into *was*.

When I glimpse my face in a mirror,
I remember a chipped colander
mounded with yellow cherries,
some rotting and some just dried.

Remarkable, all remarkable,
like this loose pebble in my palm,
its sparkle of mica, speck of lichen
thinking of nothing but *cling, cling*.

My fists are clusters of blossoms,
and inside them, the stone knuckles
with whatever of flesh will adhere,
adhering. Yes, I am old enough

to discuss April with a certain
earned authority: how pale petals
on the cherry tree guess nothing
about the hard pit.

MARGARET PETERS SCHWED

Penelope

The years are little to me
Less than you think
And the waiting

The waiting too is good—centuries
Even millennia
Are a night with few stars.

Like every stone
Turned by chafing seas
I neither fail in hope nor hope.

Tears were my reason
Dreams my waking
While the palace filled with stale suitors

Wanting a great king's end.
He'd stalled their story too
Their hope of greatness.

What better way remained for them
Than to presume: devour his stores
Humiliate the would-be heir

And have the wife?
Short of rape, however,
Nothing could be done.

Reputation (theirs)
Compelled the decency, they called it,
Of securing my assent.

And so I stretched the love game's
Filament.
I sought no other way.

The weaving and unweaving
I am famous for
Amused me

As almost nothing could.
Not one of those who wanted
Penelope

Deserved the woman I was then
But I am far greater now.
Time makes a masterpiece of grief.

Let it be said
I was never the fool—
I could sort dreams from waking

Gods from delusion
My husband from the rest.
Do you not think

I heard the women? *Bitch*, they tittered
When I called
As if fidelity were fit for dogs.

The palace whispers
As the armor rotted on the walls—
Did I not hear them?

And when my son despised me
Even then did I not hear?
Had there been another way

I'd have taken it
But my destiny came like a god
To me.

I stopped time
That's why they hated me.
No bridegroom took a bride

The girls turned whores and spied
To break me from my purpose.
But I was truly wed;

My man of pain and I
We made one
Great suffering.

Fools, if you can, understand—
From such as we had
There's no deliverance.

MOIRA RICHARDS

Essay

Wom-po and one of its offshoots, Ana Doina's Wom-po workshop critique list, lift me out of the small country on the southernmost tip of Africa where I live. These two online communities bring me experience of an upside-down world of poetry in which international lit mags name their issues backwards after the seasons, and poems long for a March spring. Here, I catch glimpses of what it must be like to write in countries that have a single official language, in which cultural identities are self-effacing, countries that are situated on the other side of post-colonialism. So much to stretch my mind even before the discussions of poems and poetesses begin—armchair travel at its most enticing. :-)

ELAINE SEXTON

Public Transportation

She is perfectly ordinary, a cashmere scarf
snugly wrapped around her neck. She is
a middle age that is crisp, appealing in New York.
She is a brain surgeon or a designer of blowdryers.
I know this because I am in her skin this morning
riding the bus, happy to be not young, happy to be
thrilled that it is cold and I have a warm hat on.
Everyone is someone other than you think
under her skin. The driver does not have
a peanut butter and jelly sandwich in his metal
lunchbox. He has caviar left over from New Year's
and a love note from his mistress, whom he just left
on the corner of Sixth Avenue and 14th Street.
When she steps off his bus to take over the wheel
of the crosstown No. 8, she knows she is anything
but ordinary. She climbs under the safety bar
and straps the belt on over her seat. She lets
the old lady who is rich but looks poor take her time
getting on. She lets the mugger who looks like
a parish priest help her. She waits as we sit, quiet
in our private, gorgeous lives.

DEEMA K. SHEHABI

Lights across the Dead Sea

Where were we
if not at the beginning?
The wind ambled
off the salt water,
the distance fractured
our gaze without a blink,
and the moon rushed
into the dark rouge of the hills.
Imagine, I said, *if those hills
were still ours.*
But you had already counted
the bone bites
of a lost country,
opened each page
of those wounds to full glow.

The calm was too far off
to be remembered—
All around us: leftover
stones, look-alike
orchards full of lemons
and guavas,
white bolts of bandaged
children—
morning still trembling
on their lips,
their grassy lashes glaring
across makeshift coffins:
why do we carry
those children in the blur

of the moon's afterglow?
*But at least they lived
and fought on their land,* I said
recalling our last return—

was it the last?
when my mother soured
the soldier's eyes
with her talk of blood
and the laws of its searing.
Then she loosened
her forehead and said:
Look closely and you will still
see the etch of sweet sap
that comes from loving your land.

But you crimped your breath
and held it in your mouth,
your eyes embering darkly.
Listen, I told you,
this affection is not a failure,
while the lights across the Dead Sea
unsheathed
but betrayed nothing.

EVIE SHOCKLEY

possibilities of poetry, upon her death

ars poetica, rough ship, drag
        me from world to brutal word,
                mental passage. (write.) be
a wail of a sound, surfacing
        to fountain dark water found
                in valleys of shadow of breath.
i will brook no evil, for
        thou art not gone, gwen,
                and poems made of tears
evaporate. when the drops
        dry, scrape gray lines of salt
                and dreams from brown faces.
(rite.) melt like a verb into
        this rich white earth of paper.
                grow an oeuvre from a need.

—for gwendolyn brooks (1917—2000)

PEGGY SHUMAKER

Walker Lake

The sow bear ripped
down the boat tarp,
scraped black fur

into twisted wingnuts,
that bear
eased her itch and disappeared.

And still she stayed near,
while we hiked
uphill to fill our jug,

the spring covered over
with autumn's leavings.
We skimmed clear

frosted growth floating,
sank our jerrycans,
felt them pull deeper.

The surface healed
around wrists
stiff with cold.

Bubbles shook free
from river weeds, rose up,
tumbled downstream.

The still place returned
to reflection. Birch
startled us with gold

so loud our bodies
flared like fireweed
gone to seed.

Twilight
put its slant
on the afternoon—

four loons
swam near
our seaplane,

nudging this
strange relative
who would not speak.

The moon had eaten itself
down to the rind,
and in that sliver,

that lingering
of autumn, stars borrowed
the voices of loons.

SHOSHAUNA SHY

Detour to Devil's Rock

Tidy and definitive
the karate chop
like flicking off a switch,
neck under bone.
That much I could picture

as I folded her sweater
into dove-soft wings,
washed and pressed the pleats
of her Bridge-luncheon dresses,
remembered the scent
of her lilac patience—

till the photographs were passed
and the faces of the jury
showed me there was more

than the coroner admitted,
that it wasn't as quick
as the flap of a cardinal
nor did she fall gently like a leaf
from a maple,

that kickboxing happened,
did not happen last.

MARTHA SILANO

Harborview

By the roots of my hair some god got hold of me
—Sylvia Plath

By the roots of my hair, by the reinforced elastic
of my floral Bravado bra, by the fraying strands

of my blue-checked briefs, some god's gotten hold of me,
some god's squeezed hard the spit-up rag of my soul, rung me

like the little girl who rang our doorbell on Halloween, took
our M&Ms *is your baby okay? Why did they take him away?*

Some god's got me thinking my milk's poison, unfit
for a hungry child, some god's got me pacing,

set me flying like the black felt bats dangling
in the hall, some god so that now I can't trust my best friend's

healing hands, the Phad Thai she's spooning beside the rice (ditto
to the meds the doctors say will help me sleep) *Poison poison!*

as if the god who's got hold of me doesn't want me
well, doesn't want my rapid-fire brain to slow,

wants this ride for as long as it lasts, wants to take it
to its over-Niagara-in-a-barrel end, which is where

this god is taking me, one rung at a time, one ambulance,
one EMT strapping me in, throwing me off this earth,

cuz I've not only killed my son but a heap of others too.
Some god's got me by my shiny golden locks, by my milk-

leaking breasts, got me in this hospital, wisps like white scarves
circling my head, wisps the voices of men *back to bed you whore!*

Some god till I'm believing I've been shot, guts dribbling out,
till I'm sure I've ridden all over town in a spaceship, sure

I'm dead, a ghost, a smoldering corpse, though not before I'm holding up
a shaking wall, urging the others to help me (a plane about to land

on our heads), though soon enough thrown down by two night nurses,
strapped to a bed, though for weeks the flowers my in-laws sent

charred at the tips (having been to hell and back), clang of pots,
hissing shower, the two blue pills my roommate left in the sink,

all signals of doom, though some god got hold of me,
shook and shook me long and hard, she also brought me back.

ELLEN McGRATH SMITH

The Rain Can Say

The rain can say a thousand things once you let your body into it,
forget the social seal that keeps you dry and undisheveled. Today,

the rain's as warm as the mud; waterbeds accept the slap
of naked, road-worn bodies in motels. Your hair at first was rain,

and then excretion in the age of relics, then was shaped
by civil tongues into perruques of character. Your skin

is a theater of call and response, of open palms and rivulets,
and bones are flagpoles marking territories you don't have

to fight to keep on moving through. In this sloughing light—
the mountains are the unassuming land inhaling once before

it breathes out soothing darkness in a concave giving-in.
I don't care how much acid rides this rain, how I might catch

my death in it. I used to care, when all I heard
were bullets lodged as facts inside my brain.

Baptism is no guarantee you'll never drown.

ELIZABETH SMUCKER

East of Mending

When I can sit without a headache and all
the lights stay off, I know I will find you.

A skinless avocado, I am left out and turning
brown. He is full of bravado, says I love to watch you

grow. But I was born pregnant
and it is winter now.

Glass splinters in the dark.
Moonlight trickles across the softwood floor.

We sliced lumber like vegetables once.
I am a distracted soul-kisser.

Out of the bathroom mildew has grown
a tree, ripe and ready

to consume. If I love you, it is only that
I'm thirsty.

I have enormous taste buds
and I want to go home.

HEIDI LYNN STAPLES

The Sun Quite Bride

o yes, i have strummed love
flung lit spin and shout, bright clasped rain
yes, my favor friend a true-love
and none day we'll be fright as lain.

o once up in a spree, eyes met a true-love
i grasped him if i may
behold beheld become opposite of grave
o met was a whole nude day.

he spelt with me attention, fold me up
and dawn, he's how i burnt thru speak
my fond, o before wife looked so grave
now he of he'll not let life sleep.

he as a rave of grave,
he as a lep of sleep,
and of lep of his lips,
of lips kiss of kissing seek.

not of seek sick, of lips
slip up. yes, it's us strong
has an always, o lisp of lips,
i of you as the dock is longing.

yes, once up in a spree, we of green
a bout, hour's reelings, wind and a walk
we risked, lit as quiet a seen.
he said, let's grow flower a little stalk,

lover this way, he all lit me love,
and i remember it too with this very decay;
he said, let's grow flowers here, love
together till our days away.

ROSEMARY STARACE

Kind Thoughts

All my girls grew up to be weeds.
There's the tall one strolling through grass,

she skirts the trees and flirts with sun.
And the one who never leaves the yard,

she studies the bees with her sharp blue eyes.
And the one named *rose*—they tried to offer her bouquets.

She roams along the seashore and the forest's edge,
spending her petals on the chance to be enough.

WENDY VARDAMAN

Essay

Will your daughters become strong, professional women because you don't expose them to pink? Few topics on Wom-po have stirred as much passionate response during the short time I've belonged to the list as the one that exploded over this seemingly innocuous color. Reading the posts on pink and its associations—Cinderella, Barbies, stickers—I was surprised by the emotional and political connotations it carries for so many of us and disturbed by the way the word pink got tossed back and forth as if it were some uniform, monolithic entity, when a moment's reflection serves to demonstrate this obvious fact: pink is not one color.

I quit a university teaching position twelve years ago and simultaneously reconnected with my own creative desires: to write poetry, to sew, to paint my house. Color, like exercise, gives me a lift, so I have it everywhere and in unlikely combinations. Pink, in multiple manifestations, happens to be a favorite: sockeye-salmon swirled with orange in the dining room; fuchsia patterned with purple and yellow in the kitchen; twelve different pinks in the towels, rug, and shower curtain of a small bathroom. I stand by my choices, professionally and decoratively, but I find that women, not men, will sometimes say surprising and rude things to me, such as "What do you do all day?" or "Someone else must have chosen these colors."

The flap about pink—whether it's good or bad—whether or not we should allow our daughters to wear it or to get pink stickers at doctors' offices—seems to me to be at the heart of what women, sadly, still do to other women, trying to impose our own ideas about what's normal on each other, although we ought to know better. Sometimes I think the true test of tolerance, not to mention imagination—and maybe they are the same thing—is how we react to aesthetic choices that differ from our own. Isn't that one of the reasons women's writing suffered for so long? Not that women didn't want to write or didn't write, but that what they wrote wasn't considered good, publishable, or worth reading.

Pink isn't the problem: we don't need to banish it on principle. We do need to widen our minds, to accept that just as we write in ways that reflect different backgrounds, choices, aesthetics, so we make decisions both about our lives and about the colors of our kitchens and bedrooms.

FRANCINE STERLE

Untitled (rear view of nude)

(Man Ray)

Neither the lascivious rump of a monkey
nor the flashy buttocks of a baboon.
No suggestion of the crimson vulva,
the showy, red-lipped rear.
No hint of a bald, fringed anus
erupting like a boil or a soft piece of fruit.
No licentious distraction here. No
sexual signaling in this chaste,
inverted heart, this pear-shaped
derrière. In the erotic
S of the body, her flesh is idle,
tranquil as a pillow. Her thoughts
are elsewhere. Given such nonchalance,
who cares about the relationship
between plane and protuberance?
Naked man is a mollusc, Lacan wrote,
but he never saw this milkwhite bottom,
this silken pair of thighs.
There's grace in her well-rounded flesh
as if, as Apollinaire once said,
an angel had puffed out its cheeks.
This is an adored, triumphant,
spiritualized backside. Not so much
a body part as a potent, untouchable idea.
The vertical cleft separating the buttocks,
two ample, harmonious halves, becomes
a bridge. One takes comfort in this
opulent bottom which does not bother—
like hands or lips or eyes—with emotion
but simply expresses its tender presence
as if it were a cloud or a shell or a scroll.
I am the celestial sphere. *I* am divinity
expressed in the exquisite curves of the world.

DIANA STOKES

choreography

a riddle, when does an empty container overflow?

when it holds a single breath. mist in a common-clay bowl

like the palm that cradles blessed dust

before her day of rest

YERRA SUGARMAN

To Miklós Radnóti

(Radnóti, a Hungarian poet of Jewish birth, was killed in
1944 during a forced march from a labor camp, and buried in a
mass grave. In 1946, his body was exhumed; in his coat pocket,
his widow found a notebook containing his last poems.)

My mind throws its crumbs into the night's stopped river.
This is its ceremony to cast off sin, to become pure,
What we Jews call *Tashlich,* an emptying of pockets.
Night's dark darkened by the museum of human ash, its lights switched off.

The stars' corollas stammer and, muzzled by clouds, vanish.
A spot of blood throbs under God's moony thumbnail.
I would like you to know our foundations for burning flesh have not yet been razed.
I pay their victims homage by day's inebriated bright.

But understand, I still love the glass scent given off by groves of lemon.
I gladly feel the olive trees' arthritic branches pulsing in my knees.
And despite everything, I participate in the crime of music.
My body still an instrument, strums its many forms of abandonment.

(Although I ask you whether what's truly ephemeral can be abandoned.)
My lips, after passion, scrape like leaves along pavement, incoherent, tarrying . . .
Yes, my mind flings crusts into the night's taut river.
And I see by the moon's weak lamp, it's as flat as the bottom of a pot.

The night so motionless, it seems an inertia devised by angels or devils,
Who pull on it from both ends.
The night's surface like a trampoline, resistant, rubber.
And so, my sins fly back at me.

They splash my face like spindrift, leaving river on my lips.
They reenter me through my eyes and teeth,
As my mind rears up, a wild horse.
For I understand, you were murdered by hands like mine.

And I understand I am helpless, a reveler at the table of the void,
A pilgrim who's journeyed only to discover herself.
And I'm ashamed to speak you or read the poems you shine on my skin.
And the sky does not kindly let me empty my pockets.

KATHLEEN SULLIVAN

Sonnet to Mrs. Dalloway

Mrs. Dalloway said she would buy the flowers. . .
—*Virginia Woolf*

Mrs. Dalloway said she would buy the flowers
and stepped into the dew-rinsed morning air.
The bloom of June's fresh beauty overpowers
her smooth composure, her British savoir-faire.

Oh what a lark, oh what a plunge! This life
of fifty years, her own green spring of girl-
ish hopes, unblemished once by time and strife,
vanished, like violets in fall, like unstrung pearls.

Be brave! Do not lose heart by what men say
about how pale your face, how like the moth-
thin wing your skin. Remember, Mrs. Dalloway,
the swing and tramp and trudge, the swill and froth

of certain hours. And though your beauty fades—
there are flowers in the shop and parties to be made!

Amanda Surkont

Why Clarence Married Effie

'told his folks it was
the white sop gravy
with its little bits
of salted pork browned
just right the color so even
he knew she had stood
right there, never moving
waiting and watching and
turning each little piece
until it was done as good
and as right as his mama's

BARBARA A. TAYLOR

A Sonnet for My Botox Baby

Jana, dear, you are my Botox Baby.
I love the way your skin stays smooth. No lines
of laughter or sorrow that one can see
in your shining unpuckered skin so fine.
You never frown nor raise your voice to me,
and when I seek your help you always come.
My mood you raise and I am filled with glee
giving and taking in our shared freedom.
When dawn light slants into my bedroom I
look at your glistening face and must smile.
Last night our lovemaking caused me to cry.
I wanted our breakup to be in style.
And this morning, after all that's happened
Jana, you show no emotion. The end.

Audio version on line at http://batsword.tripod.com/id63.htm.

PATRICIA BRODY

Essay

Through the list I have been blessed to join a sisterhood, seven of us, who now call ourselves the Sonnet Sisters. Kathrine Varnes began coordinating groups of women to collaborate specifically on writing sonnet crowns. Our group became so enamoured of the work and each other we couldn't stop after one round, and ended up with a Triple Crown of Sonnets, full of sex, slush, and rock 'n' roll, called "What Lips." I do not mean drugs—exactly. I mean iambic pentameter with the occasional free fall into dactyls, or worse.

I do not know how I ever lived without my Sisters. We have become a truly independent, self-contained female community functioning not only as sister poets but nurses, lawyers, and psychotherapists. We are straight, lesbian, single, married, parents, childless, breastfeeding, breasts, uh, lifted to the sky— never dried out. (And we're not talking "white ink" here.) Long Live Sisterhood!!

MARILYN L. TAYLOR

Reading the Obituaries

Now the Barbaras have begun to die,
trailing their older sisters to the grave,
the Helens, Margies, Nans—who said goodbye
just days ago, it seems, taking their leave
a step or two behind the hooded girls
who bloomed and withered with the century—
the Dorotheas, Eleanors and Pearls
now swaying on the edge of memory.
Soon, soon, the scythe will sweep for Jeanne
and Angela, Patricia and Diane—
pause, and return for Karen and Christine
while Susan spends a sleepless night again.
     Ah, Debra, how can you be growing old?
     Jennifer, Michelle, your hands are cold.

DIANE THIEL

Lost in Translation

My childhood was filled with untranslatable points
of view—the way the child came under the wheels,
Das Kind kam unter die Räder.

When the child was run over,
it was her fault. Did it have something to do
with the order of things? Children

are disorder—they run under wheels
like lizards. Even the signs on the trains
as we traveled through my father's country

reminded us how much was
expressly *verboten,*
how much our tongues divide us.

What was not my mother's cup of tea
was not my father's beer.
Das ist nicht mein Bier, he'd always say.

Traveling into each new lexicon
is to inhabit a new country,
map its pathways into the mind.

Every language a labyrinth, weaving
more than words, but a cultural Psyche,
sorting the grains in the syntax.

In Russia, they lock the doors
not to let thieves in,
while America keeps thieves out.

In Colombia I learned that fear
doesn't ride on a burro—*El miedo
no anda en burro.* Fear hath wings

and the reason given for so many things

is por sus pistolas—for your pistols
(just because).

Pushing through a thick net of language
all my life, trying to find some way out
from under the wheels

Always on the shore of another culture
even in this ancient bond—marriage
searching for the words I'd need

to make my way in that new country,
only to be told that there simply is
no word in Greek for privacy.

Only secrecy. Or loneliness.

ANN TOWNSEND

Her Black Shoe

First the notes left
on her door's bulletin board,

then the trip-ups, nudges,
random stepping into her field

of privacy. He kept bumping
into her. He liked her eyes,

their American friendliness.
From Nowhere, U.S.A., he found

a home in her face.
Then it came to pass: she wandered

home from a dance,
there but not there, her mind fixed

on the pleasant flux and buzz
of her blood, awash with wine.

He swam into her sight
like an element of plot

a reader knows in advance
and turns from in despair.

He brought forth the next day's
dawn, the scraped hollow

in the road where they both stopped,
for a time. It was her eyes,

staring out of newsprint, already
yellowed, crisp, ready to be

tossed like trash, and the detail
of a shoe left behind

that he lingered over, with coffee,
for the days to come.   •

ELIZABETH TREADWELL

Dalva or Delphine

So we can smoke candy cigarettes in the foreground, exquisite replicas, landscape of feminine docent. *The heavy dress of history*, Heid E. Erdrich calls it. Kate Lilley says only, *unlimited emotions need chemical assistance / to achieve a plateau of friendliness*. Imagine my collar is straight, tits pert, shoes interesting, zipper astray. My hair flips perfectly and I am most thin, uncreased in the mirrors flanking the garment aisles I proceed down to *the central of europe*, where there are bugs writhing cooped inside plastic formation along with the frightful imitation. Then just as suddenly, your organdy prickly. But on this journey, I have a sense of freedom. So we can smoke candy cigarettes in the foreground.

December, 2005

PATRICIA VALDATA

Matryoshka

—for J. S., the Lathe-Meister

She came from an apple, like Eve.
Voluptuous as a neolithic Venus,
she wears the wood grain like a shawl.

Hollow where her womb should be,
she hid in the heart of the wood,
a Russian doll lurking inside another.

Imagine her: a piece of scrap, before
the rot, the termites, and the man
turned her into a Mother Goddess.

DIANE VANCE

Rehoboth

How lonely shallow water is; spun clouds
cleave the air, everything light and full
with light. The sea is like the first time
your lover lied and you said nothing.
Light washes everything pale
until there is no horizon and the world is a jar
of opaque glass. Now it hurts your eyes
to stand in the shallows thinking how it was
you used to float in weed and brine listening
to the interior you loved in spite of its breaking
noise. Ankle-deep in sand you are thinking yourself
emptied as the suitcase under your unmade bed.
You could stand like this all day
watching the gritty world smooth into night.
Vacant as the sky that holds the clouds you are
wondering how it is the moon hollows you
and leaves you full.

WENDY VARDAMAN

An Old Woman's Pants

Waist-gathered together and thickened there,
where blessed elastic yields to accommodate
wide possibilities, accordionate
fast and feast, atop this inverted pear:

I hesitate in folds above a pointless
pocket, whose purpose, neither decorative nor
functional, eludes me and raises a moral
dilemma regarding aesthetics, charity and blindness.

This particular blue pair of pants—their new glass
fabric finish worn and washed away—
lie considerately flat, in profile, careful to stay
as still and quiet as unwatered, just-cut grass,

waiting under the iron, which scarcely alters
what they were, part pressed and filled with her.

MARGARET RICKETTS

Essay

During my six years as lurker/occasional poster, Wom-po has meant many things—seventeen new ways to read Oliver and Olds, good publishing tips, and requests for reading materials that comprise some of the most fascinating book lists I've ever seen in my life.

Wom-po makes my in-box very warm and lively, a damn good thing, because that same in-box contains news of a lot of horrors like the pitiful shrinking of civil liberties in this country—something I never imagined and can barely tolerate. In such a climate, I am afraid that many people will simply stop writing and publishing. The Wom-po people, however, still write, publish, and associate with known dissidents and heretics. Without access to a community like this, I would not be able to go on writing.

KATHRINE VARNES

The Bra Burners

You know those little blow torches chefs use to caramelize the sugar
on your *creme brulée*? That's how you know a professional,

one who loves the stench of smoldering Lycra, knows just when to give it another blast.
It takes a steady hand to singe the little bow first, experience

to understand to start the straps early and back off any foam padding,
patience to get the underwires charred to just the right smoky black

that even Georgia O'Keeffe wouldn't mind painting.
It's expensive, as a habit, and I suggest for your first time to offer a bra with bulky seams,

bad lace, elastic beginning to sag. That way, the snap of release
from the hooks will feel right; no regrets as you pull your elbow through one loop,

then the whole contraption out through your other sleeve. Look at it—dangling
between your pinched thumb and finger. How truly awkward

it is without you. How gangly and wrong.
The performance burners are another thing, not just about providing a service.

I've seen them use hibachis, fondue pots, gas ranges, a pack of cigarettes,
fry daddies, hot-wired electrolysis machines, crossed jumper cables, curling irons,

kilns, vanilla-scented candles, university-owned Bunsen burners, a shot of brandy
flambé, magnifying glasses on a sunny day, even easy-bake ovens.

You might mistake a few as amateurs at first, pulling out a big red box
of kitchen matches like cub scouts building their first fire.

But when Janice leaves the bra on and presses the pink hot match tip to the satiny cup,
you settle into your metal folding chair, the sweat on the back of your thighs,

and watch the transformation, the delicate pointillism revealing a flower, the figure
of a real woman, your mesmerized face.

PRAMILA VENKATESWARAN

Rules of Contact

The great poet looks slowly through my poems,
his silhouette matching the angles around him,
bookcases, staircase, wooden porch, old siding.

His wife, on her knees in the dirt, pulling weeds,
glances up briefly. The heat is rising
and the plants around her appear wilted.

You have the line, I don't know how, but you do,
he pronounces. Not knowing if I should thank him,
I stand silent. I'm taking her upstairs, he announces

to his wife and without waiting for her reply,
he climbs the stairs and I follow him to his library,
large, covered wall to wall with books, a plush
rug on the floor, a desk by the window.

We enter an ante room buzzing with machines.
He prints out a list of publishers, hands it to me
with Send them your poems. He looks wizened,

dwarfed further by the tall shelves, high ceilings
and his young wife still on her knees in the sun.
Instead of thanking him, I wonder why
he told his wife he was taking me upstairs.

I find myself outside the black gate,
driving on the road lacing the Sound,
his dream for my poems balled in my fist.

LYNN WAGNER

Loomed Potholder

—for Jeannie, for Anna

That a child could have made this
and you're not and did speaks volumes
to the art and knack of living.

Homely thing. What we've lost
and haven't a name for lies hidden in America
thick with excess but lukewarm

to our tongues. Today, we have forgotten
what to do with our hands. Can only count on
can openers and take-away.

You belong to the wooden spoon,
the casserole, the cast iron frying pan.
Safe in a small house filled

with fresh bread. There, lived
my grandmother, who braided
rag rugs for the bathrooms.

Soft square, good ground.
Crazy thing we didn't know
we needed.

GALE RENEE WALDEN

Dead Poets' Houses

I don't know exactly how it came up in the conversation,
But a woman I didn't really know, next to a man I didn't really know,
Suddenly said, "I love poets' houses, but I hate
How they pin the dresses to the wall."
The comment wasn't any more unusual than anything
Anyone else had said that day and I would have let it go
But the ubiquity of dresses on the walls in poets' houses
Bothered her so much that she repeated her disdain,
Causing me to question how it was that I had never seen
A dress on any of the many walls in any of the many houses
Where at least one person thought a poet lived.
I started to question my powers of observation
And also to consider whether the absence of a dress
On my own walls signified lack of literary ambition
Or whether an embroidered shawl counted.
I got that far down the wrong road in my mind
Before I thought about a brick sidewalk in Amherst
Leading up to a house in which hung a thin white dress
Of Emily Dickinson's.
I said, "Oh, you mean *Dead Poets' Houses*,"
And the man said, "There's a title,"
Which is the language I've been speaking in lately.
At least it was a mental malapropism that got caught early,
Not like the ones I've been living with for forty years—
Misplaced ideas that are so ingrained in my habits of thinking
That an opening to correctness only flies by
Every once in a while and doesn't land.
It's easy to see how wrong knowledge begins innocently.
My daughter comes home from kindergarten repeating
What she's learned about the world:
Abraham Lincoln was killed during a puppet show,
There are 50 states in a year,
Jesus says that all children are better
Than all adults, so I should just quit yelling.
And that's just the beginning of how we learn
What we don't know. There's also the educational vacation.
Maybe this woman's parents drove her to poet houses

While mine were stuck on Ulysses S. Grant.
Just to make sure, I said, "Are we only talking
Emily Dickinson?" and the woman said,
"No, those dresses are in every poet's house,"
And that it was the tiny pins fastening the dresses
To the wall which frightened her the most.
It didn't make sense. Would Elizabeth Bishop
Pin up dresses? Are there fashion statements
In that house of Carl Sandburg's I keep passing
In Galesburg? The man I didn't know said he had a friend
Who wrote a poem about Hart Crane's house
And historical societies called him up to chat.
It turned out the Crane house lived only in imagination,
And I thought maybe this was true of the dresses too.
I took a train away from the conversation,
Back to a flooded basement and I would have been
Happy to conjure up any other house to live in
But the smell of mildew interfered with reverie.
A bird flew in the window I had opened
To air out the house,
And I thought of Wallace Stevens with all those
Blackbirds whirling by him in his study.

There's a lot of ways the mind could travel with this:
Me, I've decided to be happy for strangers.

CRYSTAL WARREN

Body of Glass

Sometimes I feel trapped in this body of mine.
I look at photographs of myself
and don't recognize the person I see.

Perhaps a symptom of astigmatism;
my eyes have no point of focus,
relying on circles of glass for clarity.

Nothing I see is ever unmediated,
visual perception filtered through a frame
growing thicker through the years.

I see myself reflected in a mirror,
refracted through a camera lens,
with the naked eye—undefined.

The edges of my identity blur:
always an image, evading an answer.
Is this who I really am?

JULENE TRIPP WEAVER

A Family Visit

I must go home periodically to renew my sense of horror.
—Carson McCullers

deep in the darkness of the red-velvet wallpapered room
with its deep dark-red rug that might show no dirt
sunlight dim through maroon curtains
we all congregate, a family
a mother intent on food in your face
an uncle/father plopped in his chair, weighted down
reading glasses on the edge of his nose
a crossword puzzle in hand
a young sister paces by the heavy mahogany sideboard
an older sister visits from out of town
she stands in the darkness noting the room needs to be redone
that this family needs a paint job

the wallpaper, old cracked hangs off its corners
frayed and yellowed
needs to be pulled down stripped off the walls
burned at a stake
the curtains, shabby dense with grease
should be stripped off the windows to let light in
the chandelier, dust it off please
and replace those dead light bulbs
the rug moldy, spotted worn where mites dance
and cats piss
must be pulled up off the floor dragged down the stairs
a trip to the dump must be made

the mother needs a new dress
the uncle a good long walk
the refrigerator needs to be cleaned out
the kitchen windows opened
the mahogany polished
the walls painted something soft
the windows need shades
or breezy white curtains
the mountain fire-yellow faded painting

could be replaced with grandmother's mirror
dusty in the basement, a simple remodel
to share the sunlight and exit the doom

the visiting daughter wants to strip down,
clean up, let light in, degrease everything
she tries to do the dishes
dreams herself a whirling force of change.

BRADEN WELBORN

Paradise Garden

—for Howard Finster (December 2, 1916–October 22, 2001)

i.

First, they say, you were a circuit preacher and clock
maker, rounding country highways and facing time
with waving hands and a voice that just wouldn't let
go. You felt the strain of prophecy: *If the world
started with a beautiful garden, I would like
to see it end with one.* Fifty years back, you bought
this swamp-set plot, tooled geography with vision,
tried to finish in time. Tile, bottles, and melting
visages of dolls cobble paths, stud cement shrines,
trouble the walls. Who'd ever heard of a gospel
built verse by verse, warnings slicing angel wings
with consonants, errant punctuation, promises
and reckonings of God? Your signs stretch their shadows
across skies pocked with flame, fury, cloud. They fly low.

ii.

Photographs of the place never catch more than glare
and gleam, lenses tempted by bricks of mirrored ice,
chains looping lace from ragged ledges. Forever
something's dangling, twinkling, something's moved by wind.
With each glimpse, each careful comment, visitors itch
at what we do not see, what we cannot wrap our eyes
or words around obsessively. Trash cans declare
Jesus Saves. Pennies spell revelation across
the sidewalk's root-humped plain. Mountains of bicycles,
spokes, angles. Serpents circle plastic deer. Shacks
are buried beneath china, marbles, buttons, golf
balls. All our lost things have taken this holy turn
around corners and down ramps, bridging streams, climbing
pines and lining walls with their own apocalyptic dreams.

iii.

For this place is about endings. You built it quick,
you always said, because we'd soon be too late.
Bright missile in the shed trumpets: *There shall be wars*

in last days. Your visions hurried the marriage of flesh
and spine, timber, tin. A sixteen-sided tower
leans from the church. Danger, danger, rusty roof creaks,
steeple sways, and yet it holds, this claptrap temple.
You told of heaven's many realms, but this is what
comes first: our prayers sifting through ossified
junk. Wrecked cars warn, *Before driving check under hood
and fenders for time bombs.* And paradise rises
with the desperate energy of one gone long
without sleep in a booby-trapped world. *One city
block of one hundred thousand things known and unknown.*

iv.
Who will care for the place now—your cutout prophets
with ovular eyes? Have they already shaken
stiffness to wander streamward, rinsing the bird shit
that spackles their limbs? Is old Noah roaming west
Georgia, gathering dogs and hamsters in pairs, words
blooming near his mouth in cartoon balloons as he
sets to work on an ark of lawn chairs and foil? And
Eve, will she make out well in her highway hike, snakes
trailing? No, there must be some child hoarding bits of
broken toys, pie plates, string. Who will one day see your
face swirling in fingerpaint, who will take on time,
this place. Impatient, you visit the child in a
dream, say you have been plundering the shed feathers
of angels, setting aside each broken harpstring.

Ingrid Wendt

Poem at Forty-Five

Summer. July. Hot. And the daredevil spiders,
like an eruption of mushrooms, nightly string the whole of their
faith between the same doomed places:

Volkswagen to Datsun;
picnic table to movable bench; bushes
each side of the front porch step. Look!

These spiders are everywhere. Shiny gold peas,
they'd spin the whole house up if they could.

We'd sleep the ritual hundred years,
we'd have to hack our way out. And yet

each morning I find them
beautiful, go
out of my way to lift, lightly, at least

one nearly invisible polar thread to another,
safer, anchor: each
shimmering, flat, before-Columbus plate of the world

adrift: wheels
within wheels
and the motionless sun at the center,

a solstice
poised in its own
readiness: silent

as some days my own words dissolve
in my hands, middle-aged and amazed
at where they have come from,

where they are going. My daughter,
eighteen, on her own, but connected;

my mother, seventy-eight, on her own,
still, connected; and I

in the knowledge there is no morning
I can not wake up and find the world
forever changed.

LESLEY WHEELER

American Flowers

The girl with crooked braids
snacks on nasturtiums
from a plastic bag: brick-

red, gold, funneling nectar
from her green-lacquered
nails into her rosy throat.

Other arrogant, pretty
children run past her to the hex
jars of lavender honey

or curly piles of Russian kale.
All are safe enough
to trust the long-haired vendors

when they offer fistfuls
of peppery blossom, to chew
with spotless fluoride-

armored teeth, to bruise
and grind those petals
into nutrients. The girl

whose thick soft hair
slips like outrage
from its bindings cries

that piano practice is hard
that someone won't be her friend
that the sun is growing hot

and I want to shout
at her and to feed her
more piano, more flowers

SUSAN WHEELER

In Sky

The high that proved too high, the heroic for earth too hard,
The passion that left the ground to lose itself in sky . . .
—Robert Browning

The girl is waiting in the room to be discovered.
The girl is attempting radiance.
The girl may be a boy, or vice versa.
The girl is anticipating the man's arrival, later.
The girl is anticipating the man's displeasure.
The girl is anticipating the man's disapproval.
The girl takes no guff.
The girl's mendacity has long been remarked upon.
The girl armors up with *chic.*
The girl carries the blooms, the veronicas, the perovskia.
The girl who may be a boy powders the smalt.

The girl fills the room like smoke.
The girl is a deer in the onrush of lamps, she sits on the planks of the pier.
The girl swings her feet above the surface of the water.

The girl presses out, inhales, still fills her seat not.
The seat is an ink room, not-girl, apprehension.
The girl is mottled with self, with indecision.
The girl's amethyst earrings window her eyes.
The girl twirls her cape before the bull.
She refuses her chest.
She refuses "alabaster."
She refuses your volupty at her expense.

The girl is the hole, the cutout.
The box she is punched from throngs with blue spirits.
The ground is blank as a plum, tank-deep.
O water, O silting of dust. Reticulate.
The room's tonnage sags.
The ground is figure to its own ground.
And she, blade of grass at the Battle at Troy.

The girl refuses the stadium seating.
The girl mixes lazule and vivianite.
The girl was or was not a mother, this is irrelevant.
The girl's skin shelters; her skin burns with self.
At the end of the pier, in the house light, she looks up.
Her shade engulfs her.
The girl's blueism offputs the man.

The Girl look't Blew. Blue funked. Cast indigo.
She yelled bloody blue, she talked a blue streak.
The girl blued her bluebacks on linnets and blue duns.
The girl was waiting to be overtaken.
The girl was cruising for a bruiser.
The girl tilted up at the *ciel*: blue-domer.
She struck into space like a bolt from the blue.
Azul ultramarino, when I confessed I repented, the girl said.
She was blue mouldy for the want of that drink.

The girl ardent was: ardent, wracked, and replete.
The girl took the *retablo* from the wall; in her hand its wings shone.
The girl watched, as she listened, the strung lights waver.
The girl's moment for radiance passed.
O she was stippled, O but her room was.
O that the treatment take hold and transform.

The girl swung a gun.
The girl jutted her chin fore.
The girl limped with her sidling and stalled.
She has a fast one, it's in a wheel rut, the girl and her blue ruin, gin and her car.
The girl has veined shoulders.
She passes wind.

The girl's form is landmined: flounces, the flesh.
The girl bats the red lock away from her ear.
The girl takes the synapse and invests it with *scene* (insensible sense).
The girl Rapunzel is (NOT). She disdains.

O discrete make me and blocked.
O scurry me forth on the slate patio, and applaud my every squeak.
O I am helpful like a shill (no groin).
Untransmutable plane with your shadowed door.
The room heats like a vise.

The girl splices the water like a seal or a grouper.
The girl's shell grows a rubbery skin.
The girl looks right back, planted.

The girl holds her thumb piano beneath our view.

She, the girl, regards the chimpanzee.
The chamber loses its ceiling and the stars prick through.

The girl breathes. Her sex bucks out of sight.

The girl, blushing: *O did you see me there? Did you?*

SHARON DOLIN

Essay

I receive the Wom-po discussion list in digest format (once a day). Sometimes, I let many days—even several weeks—go by. But I always catch up by scanning the contents page for discussions that interest me. Sometimes I'll read the poem by a foremother or follow a discussion on an aesthetic issue. Sometimes it's good to know I'm not the only woman writer with gripes against the academy, or publishers, or awards that continue to favor male poets. The List has made me aware of a call for poems, a contest, a magazine, or anthology I didn't know about. And as the director of a chapbook prize, I have been able to spread the word to lots of poets. Most recently the List has been a huge help to me in preparing my course on ekphrasis for adults at the 92nd Street Y in New York City. I invited wompos to send me their poems about visual works of art, since I wanted to include many contemporary examples for my students. I received such an overwhelming array of first-rate poems, sometimes whole book manuscripts that had been published, that I had a hard time choosing which ones to include in my course.

ANN WHITE

The Two Fridas

("The Two Fridas," Frida Kahlo, 1939)

I

I am daily born and like manna
from the sky, rain down from a thundercloud;
I am dulcet blood of the virgin, the accidental spill;
the heart in the throat, the heart out of its cavity;
the chest a mocking hole, the dress mocking birth.
I snip my vein to hold my own;
I spill my blood; I bare the pain.
Jagged and messy behind the white bloom
that surrounds me, the frill that encloses.
Brilliant silence, brown to the bone.

II

Give me clay and I'll chew it.
Give me the serpent and I'll subdue it.
My heart is whole, watch it blossom.
No chest contains it, red breath pure.
These hands, watch how steady,
nothing will deter them.
Wild pelvic upturned, ground heels down flat.
Take *leche* at my breast, forget your deaths.
By eyebrow might, by embalm,
by coptic jar, I will keep you still.

To view the images: http://www.angelo.edu/faculty/rprestia/1301/images/IN522TwFs.jpg.

Radiator

In this light you look half-wolf. Shallow as moonshine, the brightness can't cut through. It only stratifies the shadows, glazes the black blue, so you can't know a face until it's on you, blown flat, collapsed to monochrome. In its blood you're reinvented. In its drift you mean something different. This dream's falling down into the crowd, growing all over the road, confusing what's fabulous with what's just out of control. The danger's in forgetting where you're headed. What you're hunting. What's behind the facades, in the light poles' shadows, below the cobblestones, laying in wait for a little morsel like you. You're never safe going home, but sometimes the signs seem solid as arms, wrapping the story around you, guiding you through the harbor. It's hard to remember that their lights don't flicker for you, not for the lunatics and rodents, the vandals and night crawlers, the lawbreakers, the ingrates. Neon radiates because it has to. You know. For its own sake.

CHRISTINE WHITTEMORE

The Paper-Wasp

I tracked her by the sound her mouthparts made:
rasp, rasp on a dry stick. She straddled it
and worked her jaws, reviving something dead,
collecting shreds of fiber. Once, in Egypt,
strips of plant stem, pressed in crisscross bands,
were made into smooth sheets—a list, a map
of the world beyond, a glove for midwives' hands
so the child, born into papyrus, would not slip.
Rasp, rasp on a dead stalk; she chews old string
to papier-mâché, builds her fluted chambers,
a symmetry of shadows, multiplying.
Her children prosper, folded in the aumbries,
cradled in paper, smocked in the complex fabric,
the house the wasp has made, her enduring book.

CAROLYN WHITTLE

A Break in the Levee

When they hooked her body
caught in the fork of the sunken tree
            they said her life vest was
            full of snakes
                        they said we "slithered"
                        into the water
                                    as they pulled her up
                        don't blame us
                        we didn't kill her
            she drowned
we were just trying to stay warm as long as possible

We got lucky
            found her in the willow
            freshly drowned
                        a warm island in the fast swirl
                        a soft place to hide
            sheesh, we were exhausted
            from swimming so hard
there's not a single bite on her
we swear

She kept us warm,
            we wrapped around her
            in the dark
                        we just *fell* out of her vest and
                        dropped silent into the water
            we didn't slither
            we dove deep
this is where we live
            we were just keeping watch
                        until
                                    you
                                                guys
                                    finally
            arrived

CATHERINE WILEY

The Pink Girls

The Pink Girls shake bootie
as if those skinny hips
were stuck to someone else—
just so boys slide their eyes.

The Pink Girls are the cutest things
this neighborhood has seen,
curls hot-combed and oiled—
back hand if they muss.

The Pink Girls' mom gets mad
when Kool-Aid stains tube-tops,
straps snap on two-inch heels,
sun blacks up their skin.

When the Pink Girls' daddy's mad
he takes the car or else the phone,
hardly ever hits his bitch,
always comes back home.

The Pink Girls strip plum trees
of little hard green fruit,
stuff the balls and spit them out,
pelt the street with flower-heads.

The Pink Girls have to move again:
landlord says they cracked a hose,
peeled the stairs and bent the screens,
scraped his only tree bare.

The Pink Girls ply monkey rings
like angels and dream
of standing still like stars
too big to come undone.

CRYSTAL WILLIAMS

Night Bloom

—for Jade

It makes no sense to say things will get better
because you will not understand until they are better
& they may not get better soon. There is always pain
in the world & you have seen so much of it.
I do not know how to explain other than to say,
I am so sorry your mother has died, Girl,
that her mother has turned her back, that your father
is a rogue & you are having to do this grown-up work alone.
I would like to tell you to be patient
but understand that right now you must only know fear.
Listen, then. & know this: it is okay to be fearful.
& if you cannot believe that things will soften, trust
that I believe for you. You will not remember all of this pain.
But when Darkness insists you attend his party
you will know the trapdoors & gloomy corners of that house.
& you alone will be able to find the garden
where beautiful Cereus is opening her eyes in the pitch black.

SUSAN SETTLEMYRE WILLIAMS

Linnaeus in Eden

One name and one name and one would march
　　　　into infinity, designated, undefined. Uncoupled.

It worries him. (Call it *garden* if by that you mean
　　　　where everything lives, separate, recognizable—

strangling lianas, flesh-eating trumpet plants, unsocial
　　　　desert spikes and spines.) But two names together,

noun and adjective, genus and species, imply relationship,
　　　　the fair sister, the dark sister (and submerged

hierarchy of kinship behind the names—family,
　　　　class, order). Yes, order—for him, not dominion

but classification, a subtler control. In all this greenness,
　　　　using a hand lens to spy similarity, a blade

to discriminate. Reproductive parts in threes or fours
　　　　or fives, arrangement of stamens, ovary superior

or inferior. Organizing *lilies* and *arborvitae* according to
　　　　his metaphor of sex, although they do not mate.

He must account for everything. He is after all not the first
　　　　to dress and keep this place. In sand and marshes, he can see

the long figure-eights of someone else's footprints,
　　　　and he needs to set a double name there too

for this being made from dust, this upright, thumbed,
　　　　and speaking creature, the one wise in magic of names.

CAROLINE WILLIAMSON

Biographies

The trouble with reading a poem
by a woman is you're always looking
behind the words for the life:

Miss Moore, for example, who cast
the same cool eye on a basilisk
and a bowl of nectarines and a grave.

Who shared a house with her mother,
a teacher of English (retired).
Who wore astonishing hats.

And the epigraph to her poems:
'Omissions are not accidents'—
she chose what not to speak of.

And here's Miss Bishop, fresh
out of Vassar, finding her feet
in New York (the best place for a writer)

with her little apartment, and her friends
who would always be friends, and the towers
of the city screening the moon

from the crowded streets: she laughs
at a misprint, imagines a strange
shy monster, casually writes

the first words—and here we sit
after seventy years, decoding
the intricate imaginative tangle:

a death—and a journal—and raindrops
on a steamed-up window—and the silence
of her creature's ghostly city.

Those voices: that conversation
of forty years. Tattooing
and circuses and a fish.

SUSAN R. WILLIAMSON

Nocturne

You up-end the mattress,
over your shoulders,

carry it out under the navy
blue sky, drop it on the lawn.

On the hilltop, all around us,
nebula, Milky Way, Orion's Belt

close enough to unbuckle, the moon
a narrow slit made for pennies.

I lay myself beside you,
cool dark air starlit between us,

my toes painted wet
with cold dew.

Quiet, we wait for night's balm,
against the wide heavens, small,

beached on a remote island
inhabited by unanswered prayers.

ROSEMARY WINSLOW

Palomino

        Gold web of perpetual light, holding us
so gently we don't even know, and with harmony, as

those summers I hung at sunrise from the sisal swing
looped and knotted to the chestnut limb parallel with
the ground and the loose dirt spilling up from my feet's
start-up pacing under my seat and settling, it took me arcing
me and time eased unimpeded by suddenness and terror,
eased out of night's black configurations of memory,
I looked out on fields of timothy bordered by trees.

I loved those millions of stems, each one a cut of light,
and light coasting across to the shape of the wind.
I loved those thousands of hands of trees lifting and
swinging from light sturdy stems, pendulous, weighted by air,
the softer maples' sleeves, and the birches' rattle,
I wanted all they had to give on the top of the world,
I hung suspended in the light gold morning light.

What can I say when I can't see light
until it casts itself to the actual flesh of things?
I try to think, but it comes to me:
I want a quieter song than I've had in my life.
I want, I want
        And then, like agony, a stampede of dust.

SARAH YAKE

Lawn

Burnish the grasses
machine skirmish
with a waspish blade

Banish churlish clover
garish garnish
pointillist blemishes

Furnish uniform hush
the only wish is lush

Essay

I came to Wom-po in 2004 through a chance encounter on the internet, and, unlike most participants, without invitation, from outside academia. Though a lifelong practitioner of the arts of writing and painting, I had made little effort to turn my private work into a public career. Entering Wom-po was like opening a door into a raucous party-house after a years-long amble on a quiet street. While just the thing I needed to leaven my poetry life, Wom-po could also distract and discourage. Every few weeks I would announce to my household, "I've got Wom-po poisoning!," and then retreat: to clear myself and my writing of the clamoring opinions, the overt and covert striving, and what I sometimes thought were harmful, overanalytic approaches to the irreducible magic in poetry.

These undertows excited issues in me I had previously dealt with by remaining isolated in my work. So I kept returning to my in-box to examine these issues more directly and to partake of the devotion, passion, useful information, and vast knowledge also present on Wom-po; together these offer me a nourishing connection to complex and very real aspects of the poetry world.

Wom-po harbors many diversities even though certain demographics predominate. Essays here have addressed gender, race, disability, motherhood, internationality, and other identifications that might twine through or define the life of a poet. This one touches on the marginality and culture-shock one might experience as a nonacademic or noncareer poet on Wom-po.

I've realized the following, however, and it's true for anyone who embodies or holds a nontypical point of view: *I belong to Wom-po because I say I belong.* That is Wom-po's real opportunity, the best thing it offers. Wom-po may feel sometimes like an insider's club, and it might have been limited to that if it were fastened to a physical location. But as an internet phenomenon, its terrain and its scope radically transform. I, or anyone, can participate in this vibrant, vital, credible world arena on the merit of words alone, without having to brandish particular credentials or think or write in a particular way. Knowledge, experience, insight can fly across the great divides—in both directions. All of us individuals, and poetry itself, may benefit from this exchange. This is a personally empowering and perhaps world-changing situation—and a most significant aspect of this anthology.

CHRYSS YOST

Advice for Women

Keep focused on the ceiling and you might
not bite your cheek too hard at the trespass
of cold metal sliding in. And you're right
to feel so pale and exposed (no mas-
ter of your body now!). Clinical light
keeps you composed here, but beyond the glass

window, in the lab next door, a glass
dish cultivates the worst in you. You might
give up the God you heard about in Mass
for antioxidants. There's time to right
your wrongs, and settle scores, before you pass
like breath remade as clouds by winter light

in sharp still mornings. Fluorescent light
rains down on you like blue-white sun in glass
test tubes, like luminescent dynamite.
The gossiping of cells is like a mass
of schoolgirls, watching in the hallway, right
before you stumble. Make small talk to pass

the time. Forget the test, of course you'll pass.
They look for microscopic faults with light
that radiates right through the you on glass.
They'll set aside the parts of you that might
grow into something more. They might amass
more samples, to be sure that you're all right.

Because of course you are. Even if, right
after she turned twenty, my aunt passed
on, mossy black inside her like a mite-
infested paper-white narcissus, glass-
forced to root in a window's filtered light.
Too many women in this family, mass-

acred by cancer rushing them en masse,
as they stood stunned, slashing left and right,
killing and leaving the rest afraid. Passed
on like a recipe, along with light
blue eyes, fears as strong and old as sea glass.
I want to be like them; I fear I might.

For now, breathe lightly as the forceps pass.
A mass is a mass, no more . . . Later, write
Your fragile fate, as quick to break as glass.

ABE LOUISE YOUNG

Make Us

New Orleans, August, 2005

A black bird wakes a bridge.

Morning yells and Earth yanks me to a plot of her black mouth.

Tetrahedron cracked patch, oaks clacking with moss like long wigs, lost wings.

Crank and hoe your earth so dirt can drink.
Scatter your rocks. Diamond-cracked-fissured-foot contradiction-pathway—Door.

Moth mother, hold me in your rumble nest, bald me with your ashy epidermis.

My body bleeds at the base of a tree. Drips mealy blood, my clots and iron ooze, mama-meal in black eggshell
cracks.

Thank you, regal hoop: we give back.
Your flood is full.
You break the banks.

Pull air. Pull out spikes with white roots. Pull hair. Rip the shoots. Eat, harvest, eat our head.

A bed of hair, of stares, of keys.

Yank, thrum, strum taut blind wires.

Add your blood to the swampgrass, muskrat nest, pitcher plants.

The winds begin and the clamor. The water. The water. The water. The water.

Add your oils to the river.

Add our hair to the Great Fires.

Arachnid rock shaped like a brain, ants eating alphabet.
Whose ways are set?
Haiku hep. Rage hangs like wet hair, wet rags, drowned identity.

Grow hurricanes inside a country with a gastric respiratory lock and key,
an endocrine adrenalin. Lock out rescue vehicles, Big Daddy. Let the bodies float and grow bloated in the
streets.

Six babies float by on a box spring.

Everyone paddles but great-grandmother falls.
Mommy Earth, give me your metabolism to stratify time.

Give us our levees, and blur back our crimes in the glowing, broken crescent.

Honey colored curve: an embryo, a bend.

There's liquid quiet radiating crystals at the core. Someone laughs.

Mother Ocean was here,
she gave her grief a moment's name.

We are soon to be a shell, petrified nautilus, curled inward and opening like a trumpet, a gastropod.

Spread out over America like pockets of black crying, white earplugs.

And the drums begin. The tambourines.

A city in a handbag, a century lost in a locket.

Vengeful goddess, do not do nothing
with your boxes of mud, leaves, ovaries, demolished homes and sodden wool.

Be impatient, merciless, tender.
Sit on the side of the river.

Feed the wanderers brass keys.

Reconstitute the tribes and porch-sitters in the delta,

our broken coast, petroleum-sodden, bring the cranes and golden nutria, the black crows, the pelicans and coonasses and people back

to back to back to back

Home. Please make us believe all change is half-possible.

ANDRENA ZAWINSKI

Open Stage

At the Horse & Cart Café, Charleston, SC

You have walked all day the length of streets,
cataloged anything of importance that has been here
before. Tide at the seawall, the cadence of wind,
poems moving in. The church bells chime.
A car starts. Some stranger remarks the brilliance
of sun. Palmettos bow to the weight of air.

You walk until your legs say *sit down. Enter
a café.* The day blows in on door hinge reeds.
You eye the sky so bold a blue, a breathy blinding blue,
you think someone will steal off with it, frame it
in the coarse of sailcloth for a windowless wall.
The register chings. A phone rings. Metal scoops ice.

The room lights up. You read over someone's
shoulder a late edition. Same sex couples marry
in San Francisco. A female astronaut on Mir.
Hyakutake in view, stars spill from the gourd
of dream, do what they please. Poets sort sheaves,
track second thought verse in fine point notes.

A man joins you at your table. You have met
this man before in Pittsburgh, Paris, Charleston.
He buys you coffee, wine, brown sugar pie
in exchange for conversation about his stock
acquisitions, the travels seaside, paintings of sky.
The room's dizzy spirit dances with nerve.

Poets on cue cross the stage. A quivering heart
turns over words, delicate as new shoots on spring
bulbs. A waitress at the cash box sorts checks,
counts the stiffs, searches pockets hoping
she can make it up. Breath beads the window
in a blur. Hummingbirds circle feed.

Sweat glistens the brow. Hand atremble,
an old man's voice cracks like a schoolboy's.
A girl in red, tattooed and pierced, reads fire
between her legs, a passion for learning
as if it's by heart. A man whispers *white trash,*
then relieves himself in a dozen public couplets.

Cadets chuckle the backdrop. You wait for a clearing
in the sound. You think you could inhabit all these
voices all at once, move inside them like babies
about to be born. You are up to read.
The eye quivers, breath starts. The room takes on
a new night chill. The register rings, door swings.

You see the girl has gone, only her scarlet petallike
stain left signing the lip of her cup. A sky, dark,
moans at the glass.

RACHEL ZUCKER

The Moon Has a Reputation for Being Fickle

I read the instructions twice and pee on my hand by mistake.
I wait.
I try again and then, in the 2 minutes 15 seconds it takes to get the First Response
I watch Ponch deliver a baby in a trailer the CHiPs pulled over for speeding.
The woman's screaming.
Ponch pours water from a canteen over his hands and kneels between her legs.
Thirty-five seconds later he emerges from the trailer, pulls on black leather
riding gloves, there's no blood, and
one pink bar
on the plastic view screen.

Who brings us this anthology? Wom-po does, of course,
with poems by womponies, and essays to leaven the verse.
Who edited, made the selection? Whose scruples brought to bear?
It's Wom-po's own creation. We chose what's best for Her
nine years since Annie Finch's cybersphere uncoiled
space for women poets, our letters to the world.
After great pain or frustration, womponies groused online
of odd publishing practices, but then Bright and Levine
said *Want it? Make it happen.* And Moira Richards' plan
set Wom-po teams to action, to make our own print run.
We blogged poems and bios; no judge or referee
needed stand above us. Our skies unmanned are free.
Books brought us together, so we did not protest
when Red Hen heard the ruckus, and called us to her List.

—D'Arcy Randall

Afterword

Letters to the World is the culmination of an unusual effort. This anthology was planned, compiled, and edited through the collaborative interaction of a group of self-selected women and brought into physical form almost entirely through the nonphysical medium of the internet.

The collaborators, volunteers possessing widely varied levels of publishing experience, worked from five countries on three continents. We exchanged files and philosophies, questions, and suggestions through e-mail on a private internet discussion forum separate from the Wom-po LISTSERV. We assembled ourselves in small groups to deal with specific tasks. Sometimes we "backchanneled" each other, communicating through e-mail outside of the public Wom-po LISTSERV or the editorial forum. However, an unspoken rule of openness largely ensured there were no major decisions made without whole-group participation.

This collaborative ethic made working on this book surprising, frustrating, and fruitful in turn. The editorial vision of this anthology *is* its inclusive process; by design, every participant had equal authority in the book's content, and no individual had editorial veto power. We groped and stumbled toward an efficient process that remained true to our collective vision—and this was made even more difficult by the fluid nature of any listserv, the changing cast of participants. In fact, the continual diversification and change in the make-up of the Wom-po LISTSERV led us to reopen the call for submissions at a point when the book, as comprised by those who had responded to the first call, was nearly complete.

Over the course of our collaboration, questions of procedure and leadership naturally arose. Was it polite, some of us wondered, to offer or comment on ideas for aspects of the book another person was working on? How were we to handle and resolve conflict and disagreement? Sometimes we ignored differences, allowing them to cool or melt away. At other points, especially as we neared completion, we addressed conflicts directly and worked together persistently until a solution emerged.

The word "emergence" characterizes both this project and our process. As the idea for this anthology emerged from the Wom-po community and volunteers stepped forward to make it happen, likewise the necessary skills and time to work on the project became miraculously available in our self-selected group. The book's gestation over more than a year allowed familiarity and trust to develop among us. The mostly level field of our collaboration encouraged playfulness, creative thinking, and risk-taking. In every case, and through numerous routes, a "way through" opened up.

The internet has opened new avenues for far-flung collaborations. The feminist movement has given us new models for acting and interacting powerfully and effectively. *Letters to the World,* the book and the process that led to it, is our enthusiastic response to these twin invitations.

Moira Richards (George, South Africa—in the Southern Cape region) coordinated the entire project by e-mail, mail, and fax. She facilitated initial discussion among the members of the listserv and, later, the labors of the editorial group; created the original blog from which the manuscript was formed; organized opinions and resources; took the lead in creating streamlined work plans and editorial processes at several stages; and acted as liaison between Red Hen and the collective participants in the book. She recalls, "I almost lost my nerve in the very early days of the project when I opened an e-mail from a Distinguished Professor of Creative Writing who offered her skills to do, 'whatever! . . . I can hold the gate open.' I've since come to appreciate that Eloise Klein Healy's offer epitomises the extraordinary richness of expertise and generosity that is the Wom-po LISTSERV."

Rosemary Starace (Pittsfield, Massachusetts, U.S.) managed and prepared the manuscript, assembling its contents and creating order and consistency among its many parts. She also kept track of, implemented, and evaluated changes as the manuscript evolved during multiple stages of proofreading and discussion.

Rosemary Starace and **Lesley Wheeler** (Lexington, Virginia, U.S.) proposed, collected, edited, and arranged the short essays, intending to provide a polyvocal expansion of the Preface and Introduction. As in the poems themselves, however, each author had final say over the content of her own piece.

Annie Finch (Portland, Maine, U.S.), founder of the Wom-po LISTSERV, wrote the Preface. Her enthusiastic participation also drew many contributors to the project from the outset and again at the end of 2006, when we reopened submissions to poets who had recently joined the list.

D'Arcy Randall (Austin, Texas, U.S.), researched and wrote the Introduction.

Margo Berdeshevsky (Paris, France) designed several possible covers, describing each piece as "a collage and a montage, both, made of my own photographs, added in many layers, torn, cropped, colored, erased, transparent—much akin to painting—all in my computer . . . Much of my work, both in language and in the visual, builds in metaphors that collect tiny and ragged understandings and visions," as does this anthology.

Several people contributed to the proofreading and the process of coordinating the proofing of poems and biographies among many dispersed contributors, including Ellen Goldstein (Beverly, Massachusetts, U.S.), who headed the "in-house" proofreading effort and researched our questions on style and usage, Rachel Dacus (San Francisco, California, U.S.), Ann Hostetler (Goshen, Indiana, U.S.), Louisa Howerow (London, Ontario, Canada), Athena Kildegaard (Morris, Minnesota, U.S.—"prairie pothole country"), D. O. Moore (Washington, D.C., U.S.), and Cynthia Trammell (Los Angeles, California, U.S.). Assigned to proofread one section of the manuscript, Ann Fisher-Wirth (Oxford, Mississippi, U.S.) proofread the whole thing "and admired the spirit of community that informed every step of this anthology." Cynthia Trammell collected each contributor's contract and the acknowledgements for previously published poems. Ann Fisher-Wirth, Moira Richards, Rosemary Starace, and Lesley Wheeler contributed editorial suggestions to the Preface and Introduction and D'Arcy Randall to the Preface and Afterword; Annie Finch made editorial contributions to the Introduction and, with Alicia Ostriker and Yerra Sugarman, added to discussions on the cover and title.

Lillian Baker Kennedy (Auburn, Maine, U.S.) collected and compiled the biographical notes, assisted by Ren Powell (Stavanger, Norway) and Louisa Howerow.

Louisa Howerow organized several rounds of additional collecting and proofreading in the second phase with the same willingness and generosity evidenced by all of "team editorial." Ann Hostetler applied her imagination in ways that increased tolerance among us for widely divergent viewpoints and helped us to move forward at a critical juncture. Ann Hostetler, Lillian Kennedy, and Kay Day (Jacksonville, Florida, U.S.) began planning publicity before the manuscript was even complete.

Eloise Klein Healy (Los Angeles, California, U.S.) contacted Mark E. Cull and Kate Gale at Red Hen Press in the first place about the possibility of publishing the anthology, which then existed in blog form.

These people and many other wompos contributed to the project in less formal ways, usually by e-mail. They offered publishing expertise; weighed in on how to arrange the anthology and how to title it; helped to design processes for collecting and editing various materials; and discussed how the Preface, Introduction, short essays, and this Afterword might best complement the poems themselves. The contributors sustained our morale with their frequent messages of support and gratitude.

In "This is my letter to the World," Emily Dickinson wrote of messages committed "to Hands I cannot see—". The poems in this anthology, like Dickinson's, are also being offered as a gift to unseen hands. But this anthology is a gift *from* many unseen hands as well: the hands of all those who may never meet one another, yet worked together across continents and time zones to create the book you hold. We remain amazed by the process, though not surprised by its outcome, and thankful for the many acts of faith and generosity that brought this unique anthology into being.

—Moira Richards, Rosemary Starace, and Lesley Wheeler
April 2007

Biographical Notes

Diana Adams is an Alberta-based writer with work published in several journals. Her work has appeared previously in the *Del Sol Review*, *Perihelion*, *Pindeldyboz*, *Pagitica*, *Jones Av.*, and *Bayou*. Her first book of poetry, *Like Antlers*, is slowly making its way through the mail system.

Mary Alexandra Agner's poetry appears in *North American Review*, *Passages North*, *Puerto del Sol*, and *The Literary Review*. Currently, she's at work on a novel-in-verse, *Queen of the Steppe*. All her life she's observed the universe and written about it. She can be found online at http://www.pantoum.org.

Kelli Russell Agodon was born and raised in Seattle and educated at the University of Washington and Pacific Lutheran University. She is the author of two books of poems, *Small Knots* and *Geography*, winner of the 2003 Floating Bridge Press Chapbook Award. Currently, she is editing the *Poetry Broadside Series: The Making of Peace*. Her website is www.agodon.com.

Malaika King Albrecht's poems have recently been published or are forthcoming in *Kakalak: An Anthology of Carolina Poets*, *Shampoo*, *4am*, *Hiss Quarterly Review*, *The Bedside Guide to No Tell Motel—Second Floor*, *Fire in the Womb: Mothers and Creativity*, and other online and print magazines. She has taught creative writing to sexual abuse survivors, to addicts and alcoholics in therapy groups, and also volunteers in schools. She currently lives in North Carolina.

Meena Alexander was born in India. Her work includes books of criticism, novels, poems, and essays (*Shock of Arrival: Reflections on Postcolonial Experience*, 1997). She is the editor of the anthology *Indian Love Poems* (Knopf/Everyman's Library, 2005). Her volumes of poetry include *Illiterate Heart*, winner of the 2002 PEN Open Book Award, and *Raw Silk*, 2004. Her memoir *Fault Lines* (Publishers Weekly Choice, Best Books of 1993) was reissued in 2003 with an added chapter "Lyric in a Time of Violence." She is Distinguished Professor of English at the Graduate Center and Hunter College, City University of New York.

Kelly Lenox Allan's poems and translations have been published in *RHINO*, *Ellipsis*, *MARGIN*, *RATTLE*, *Big Bridge*, *Gobshite Quarterly*, *Switched-On Gutenberg*, *Hubbub* (forthcoming in 2007), and other online and print magazines. Her translations of Slovenian poets have been published in *Six Slovenian Poets* (United Kingdom: Arc Publications) and *Voice in the Body* (Slovenia: Litterae Slovenicae, 2005). The chapbook *Chasms* (PM Books), translations of the Slovene poet Barbara Korun, was published in 2003. She is a contributing editor for *Hunger Mountain* and is currently editing an anthology of contemporary Slovenian poetry.

Celia Lisset Alvarez holds an MFA in creative writing from the University of Miami. Her poetry has appeared in *The Powhatan Review*, *TarWolf Review*, *Iodine Poetry Journal*, and in two collections, *The Stones* (Finishing Line Press, 2006) and *Shapeshifting* (Spire Press, 2006), winner of the 2005 Spire Press Poetry Award. She teaches composition and literature at St. Thomas University in Miami, where she lives with her husband and their extended family.

Ivy Alvarez received a MacDowell Colony Fellowship (United States) and a Hawthornden Castle Fellowship (United Kingdom) in 2005. She is the author of three chapbooks; the latest one is titled *what's wrong*. Previously published in *c-side*, her poem "length" also appears in *Mortal* (Red Morning Press, 2006).

Jean Anaporte-Easton's work has appeared recently in *One Trick Pony*, *13th Moon*, *Mid-American Review*, and *Contemporary Literary Criticism*. A recipient of fellowships from Yaddo and the West Virginia Commission on the Arts, she is the editor of *Breathing from the Belly: Etheridge Knight on Poetry and Freedom* (University of Michigan Press, forthcoming in 2007). She has taught poetry in universities, schools, prisons, and mental health facilities. Presently she is a professor of English at West Virginia State University.

Judith Arcana's writing has recently been or is forthcoming in *Poetica*, *Junctures*, *Michigan Avenue Review*, *Diner*, *Women's Lives*, *Not What I Expected*, *White Ink*, and *FreshWater*. Among her prose books is *Grace Paley's Life Stories, A Literary Biography*. Her newest book, *What if your mother* (Chicory Blue Press), is poetry focused on rarely offered motherhood themes: abortion, adoption, and the biotechnology of contemporary conception/pregnancy in the United States. Judith was a teacher for over forty years; as a performer/speaker, she works for reproductive justice with campus and community groups (see her profiles at www.womenarts.org and www.speakersclearinghouse.org).

Marilyn Arnold lives in Launceston, Tasmania. She has had poems published in many Australian literary journals including *Island Magazine*, *Famous Reporter*, and *Poetry Australia*. She has published two chapbooks, *The Loom of Time* and *Soft Windows*. She is a regular reader at the Tasmanian Poetry Festival and runs a monthly poetry night (Poetry Pedlars) in Launceston. She has an honors degree in literature and history. She loves being on the Wom-po list.

Renée Ashley is the author of three volumes of poetry: *Salt*, Brittingham Prize in Poetry (University of Wisconsin Press), *The Various Reasons of Light*, and *The Revisionist's Dream* (Avocet Press), as well as a novel, *Someplace Like This* (The Permanent Press). She has received fellowships from the New Jersey State Council on the Arts and the NEA, and is on the faculty of Fairleigh Dickinson University's low-residency MFA Program in Creative Writing.

Felice Aull is a physiologist and medical humanities scholar at New York University School of Medicine. She uses poetry and fiction with medical students to consider the illness experience and is founding editor of a web resource, The Literature, Arts, and Medicine Database. In 2001 she received an MA in humanities and social thought, and started writing poetry. A poem is forthcoming in *Poet Lore* and others were published in *Ekphrasis*, *Facets*, and elsewhere.

Lana Hechtman Ayers grew up in New York and spent a decade in New Hampshire before moving to Washington State two years ago. She's worked at a myriad of professions, from insurance actuary to therapist, and is currently a nonfiction book editor and publisher of the Concrete Wolf Chapbook Series. Her own poetry has appeared in many national publications, including *Slant*, *The Bitter Oleander*, and *Seattle Woman*. She holds an MFA from New England College. Her first chapbook, *Love Is a Weed*, is available from Finishing Line Press.

Anny Ballardini is a translator and interpreter, teaches at high school, is the editor of the "Poets' Corner," an online poetry site (http://www.fieralingue.it/modules.php?name=poetshome), and writes a blog: "Narcissus' Works." Her book: *Opening and Closing Numbers* (Moira Editions, 2005) can be found online or bought on lulu.com. Among her translations: *In_Ri by Henry Gould*; *On the Trail of Words* by Larry Jaffe; *Smokestacks Allegro* by Rita Cominolli; *Metaphysical Reference* by Kenneth Hirst, from English into Italian; and from Italian into English: *The Renaissance of the Self* and the *Notebook of Positano* by Arturo Onofri.

Hadara Bar-Nadav's recent publications appear or are forthcoming in *Beloit Poetry Journal*, *Chelsea*, *Indiana Review*, *The Journal*, *Prairie Schooner*, *TriQuarterly*, *Verse*, and other journals. Her book of poems, *A Glass of Milk to Kiss Goodnight*, was chosen by Kim

Addonizio for the MARGIE First Book Prize and will be published in spring 2007. She currently lives in Minnesota and teaches in the English department at St. John's University.

Judith Barrington is the author of three volumes of poetry, most recently *Horses and the Human Soul* (Story Line Press, 2004). *Lifesaving: A Memoir* was the winner of the Lambda Book Award and finalist for the PEN/Martha Albrand Award. Her best-selling text: *Writing the Memoir: From Truth to Art* is used in numerous writing programs. She has won many awards for poetry and received the ACLU Freedom of Expression Award and the Stuart Holbrook Award from Literary Arts for outstanding contributions to Oregon's literary life. She is published widely in journals and teaches workshops across the United States and in Britain.

Jeanne Marie Beaumont is the author of *Curious Conduct* (BOA Editions, 2004) and *Placebo Effects* (Norton, 1997), and coeditor, with Claudia Carlson, of *The Poets' Grimm: 20th Century Poems from Grimm Fairy Tales*. She lives in Manhattan, where she teaches at the Unterberg Poetry Center of the 92nd Street Y.

Kimberly L. Becker lives in the Washington, D.C. area, although as a Southerner she prefers the Blue Ridge to the Beltway. She holds degrees from the University of North Carolina—Chapel Hill (BA in English with highest honors in creative writing; MA in German) and Virginia Theological Seminary (MDiv). She has held a state fellowship in fiction (New Jersey). Her work appears in print and online journals, including *Borderlands*, *Georgetown Review, ken*again, Snowy Egret*, *South Carolina Review, storySouth*, *Westview*, and *Words-Myth*.

Lynn Behrendt is the author of three chapbooks: *The Moon as Chance, Characters*, and *Tinder*. Her work has appeared in *26, Matter 7, How2*, and at the *Cosmic Baseball Association*. She lives and writes in New York's Hudson Valley.

Kate Bernadette Benedict lives in New York City and publishes *Umbrella*, an online poetry journal. Her book of poems, *Here from Away*, was Editor's Choice in *The Philadelphia Inquirer* in February 2006. Among her journal credits are *Able Muse, The Blue Moon Review, The Cortland Review, Kalliope, Sing Heavenly Muse!*, and *Slant*. Visit her online at www.katebenedict.com.

Margo Berdeshevsky lives in Paris, won The Robert H. Winner Award from Poetry Society of America, Chelsea Poetry Award, Sue Saniel Elkind Award, and placed in Pablo Neruda and Ann Stanford Awards, Border's Books/Honolulu Magazine Grand Prize for Fiction, and has received three Pushcart nominations. She has been published in *Poetry International*, *Chelsea, Nimrod, Kalliope, The Southern Review, Runes, New Letters, Many Mountains Moving, Rattapallax, Southern California Anthology, Van Gogh's Ear, ACM*, and *WSQ*. Her images, exhibited at The Pacific Center of Photography, La Galerie Etienne De Causans in Paris, and "The Ghosts of Versailles," at http://www.galeriebenchaieb.com/flash_fr.html. Her poetry manuscript, *But a Passage in Wilderness*, will be published by The Sheep Meadow Press in 2007.

Mary Rose Betten's "My Voice" was published in *Hanging Out with Loose Words* (Foothills Publishing, New York, January 2005). She spoke as a Hollywood character actress/playwright, forever in the mind of others. At seventy she retired and free verse, she tells us, whooshed out at half blast and blew her inner life all over the page. She says, "To my ear, voice in my own poems belongs to a thief, a window cleaner, recluse in a bell tower, cleaning lady caught in the rain. I can't be held responsible."

Tara Betts, a Chicago-to-New-York transplant, is a writer/educator/performer. She's studied with Lucille Clifton, Anne Waldman, and Alicia Ostriker, among others. She has appeared in *Vagina Monologues* and *The Empress Has Red Clothes* (a performance piece on menstruation). She cofounded the women's performance space, Women OutLoud, and a young women's workshop, GirlSpeak.

Publishing credits: *Obsidian III*, *Columbia Poetry Review*, *FEMSPEC*, *Women's Studies Quarterly*, *Essence*, *That Takes Ovaries!*—and the upcoming *Home Girls Make Some Noise: Hip Hop Feminism*. Steppenwolf Theater's *Words on Fire*, HBO's "Def Poetry Jam," and Jessica Care Moore's "SPOKEN" also featured her work. She is a New England College MFA candidate. Learn more at www.tarabetts.net.

Paula Bohince's poems have appeared in *Agni*, *Crazyhorse*, *Field*, *Poetry Northwest*, *Shenandoah*, and *Poetry Daily*. She is the author of *Incident at the Edge of Bayonet Woods* (Sarabande Books, 2008). She has received the Grolier Prize, residencies from the MacDowell Colony, and artist's grants from the Puffin Foundation and the Vogelstein Foundation. In 2008, she will be the Amy Clampitt Resident Fellow in Lenox, Massachusetts. She lives in Pennsylvania.

Lisa Bourbeau shares a mountainside with three aging greyhounds and an ancient hellhound, and to feed them, runs a contract cleaning firm that operates along the eastern seaboard. An associate editor of *Talisman House*, she was a 2003 recipient of the State of New Hampshire Individual Arts Fellowship. Her work has appeared in a wide range of journals, including *Yankee*, *Ploughshares*, *First Intensity*, *Nedge*, and the *Turkish Edebiyat Ve Elestiri*. Her first book, *Cuttings from the Garden of Little Fears*, was published by First Intensity in 2003.

Karen Braucher is the author of *Aqua Curves*, winner of the 2005 Stevens Manuscript Competition (selected by Peter Meinke, NFSPS Press), and *Sending Messages Over Inconceivable Distances*, finalist for the Oregon Book Award (selected by Maxine Kumin, The Bacchae Press), as well as two chapbooks, *Mermaid Café* and *Heaven's Net*. Her poems have appeared widely, including in *Diner*, *Pool*, *Puerto del Sol*, *Nervy Girl*, *the new renaissance*, *Nimrod*, *Oregon Review*, *Paterson Literary Review*, *RATTLE*, *The Spoon River Poetry Review*, *The Worcester Review*, and other places, including Portland's buses and trains through the national Poetry in Motion program.

Susan Bright is a poet, author of 19 books of poetry, and publisher of Plain View Press, a feminist publishing house, which since 1975 has published the work of more than 300 poets, fiction writers, and writers of issue-based nonfiction.

Patricia Brody's work has appeared in Canadian and U.S. journals including *Poet Lore*, *Barrow Street*, *Room of One's Own*, *Western Humanities Review*, and *The Paris Review* and also featured on *Poetry Daily* and in a new anthology, *Chance of a Ghost*. She is editing an anthology, *SURVIVAL of the SOUL: Artists Living with Illness*. Awards include two Academy of American Poets awards and two Pushcart nominations. Brody, a family therapist in private practice (LCSW, Columbia University), teaches American literature at Boricua College in Harlem. Her NYC-raised children are 20, 15, and 11.

Elaine Brown originates from Alaska, and now lives in Montreal, Quebec, where she is engaged in a PhD in philosophy at McGill University. Her poems and prose have appeared or are forthcoming in *Fulcrum*: *An Annual of Poetry and Aesthetics*, *Poetry Midwest*, *Squaw Valley Review*, and *Voices from Prague: An Anthology*.

Debra Bruce's third book, *What Wind Will Do*, was published by Miami University Press of Ohio. She's had work in *The Atlantic*, *The Formalist*, *Poetry*, *Ploughshares*, *The Virginia Quarterly Review*, *Prairie Schooner*, and other journals. She has been the recipient of grants and awards from the National Endowment for the Arts, National Endowment for the Humanities, The Illinois Arts Council, The Poetry Society of America, and Poetry magazine.

Beverly Burch's recent poetry appears in *New England Review*, *Barrow Street*, *Poetry Northwest*, *The Antioch Review*, *Ontario Review*, *Southern Humanities Review*, *Mississippi Review*, and *North American Review*. Her book, *Sweet to Burn*, won the Gival Poetry Prize and the Lambda Literary Award. She is a psychotherapist in Berkeley, California.

Rebecca Byrkit's poems have appeared in *Best American Poetry 1997*, *Best of Exquisite Corpse 2000*, *Fever Dreams: Poets of the American Southwest*, *Night Out: Poems about Hotels, Motels, Restaurants and Bars*, as well as dozens of excellent literary journals (*Ploughshares*, *Black Warrior Review*, *Phoebe*, *Crazyhorse*). Her first book, *zealand*, was a Western States Book Award finalist. Becky has lived on the islands of Patmos and on Maui, and currently directs the Northern Arizona Book Festival.

Wendy Taylor Carlisle lives in Texas. She has published one full-length book of poetry, *Reading Berryman to the Dog* (Jacaranda Press, 2000) and one poetry chapbook, *After Happily Ever After* (#15 in the 2River Chapbook series, 2004). Her poetry is available most recently in *Windhover*, *2RiverView*, *Cider Press Review*, and *Cafe Review*.

Nancy Naomi Carlson is the author of *Kings Highway* (WWPH), *Complications of the Heart* (Texas Review Press), and *Imperfect Seal of Lips* (Poems & Plays). She is an associate editor for Tupelo Press and an instructor at the Bethesda Writer's Center. Nominated five times for a Pushcart Prize, her work has appeared in such journals as *Poetry*, *Shenandoah*, *Prairie Schooner*, *Chelsea*, and *The Southern Review*. Her translations of René Char have appeared in *Denver Quarterly* and *Colorado Review*.

Sherry Chandler is the author of two poetry chapbooks, *Dance the Black-Eyed Girl* (Finishing Line) and *My Will and Testament Is on the Desk* (FootHills Publishing). Her work has been nominated for the Kentucky Literary Award in poetry and has won the Betty Gabehart Award from the Women Writer's Conference. She has received professional development funding from the Kentucky Arts Council. Her work has appeared in many print and online magazines, including *Spillway*, *The Louisville Review*, *Wind*, *nth position*, and *Tears in the Fence*.

Laura Cherry is the author of a chapbook, *What We Planted*, which was awarded the 2002 Philbrick Poetry Award by the Providence Athenaeum. Her work has been published or is forthcoming in online and print journals including *Asphodel*, *Literary Mama*, *Argestes*, *Forklift: Ohio*, *Agenda*, and the *Vocabula Review*. It has also appeared in the anthologies *Present Tense: Writing and Art by Young Women* (Calyx Press) and *Vocabula Bound* (Marion Street Press). Laura received an MFA from Warren Wilson College. She lives near Boston with her partner and their three-year-old daughter.

Kathleen Clancy is in the Stonecoast MFA Program at the University of Southern Maine, and is currently writing poems and studying the development of free verse from the formal tradition in Canadian poetry. Her poems have appeared in some journals including *The Purple* and *The Shuylkill Valley Journal of the Arts*. She lives on the New Hampshire seacoast.

Katharine Coles has published two novels and three collections of poems: *The Golden Years of the Fourth Dimension*, *A History of the Garden*, and *The One Right Touch*. She served on the design team for Salt Lake City's Passages Park; her collaboration with artist Maureen O'Hara Ure has resulted in two installations and an artist's book, *Swoon*. She is on the faculty of the creative writing program and directs the Utah Symposium in Science and Literature at the University of Utah. She lives in Salt Lake City with her husband and a small menagerie.

Virginia Conn's work has appeared in *Cimarron Review*, *Primavera*, *Mobius*, *2RiverView*, and *A.I.M.*, among other publications. She is the author of two chapbooks: *Trouble is My Business* and *Barbie in a Box*. She lives in Tucson, Arizona.

Nicole Cooley grew up in New Orleans, Louisiana. Her first book of poetry, *Resurrection*, won the 1995 Walt Whitman Award and was published by LSU Press in 1996. Her second book of poetry, *The Afflicted Girls*, about the Salem witch trials of 1692, came out with LSU Press in April 2004. Her book in progress is called *Stabat Mater*. She is an associate professor of English at Queens College—CUNY and lives in New Jersey with her husband and two young daughters.

Chella Courington pursued a doctorate in literature at the University of South Carolina and studied with James Dickey. In 2002 she moved to California with an economist and two cats before returning to poetry. Now teaching at Santa Barbara City College, she has poetry published in several journals and anthologies. Her first chapbook, published by Foothills Publishing of New York in November 2004, is entitled *Southern Girl Gone Wrong*.

Mary Cresswell was born and raised in Los Angeles, and educated at University of California, Riverside, and Stanford. She has lived in New Zealand since 1970 and is a freelance science editor. She has published poems in New Zealand, the United States, Canada, Australia, and online. She is coauthor of *Millionaire's Shortbread* (University of Otago, 2003). Her new book, *Trace Fossils*, is at the forthcoming-assuming-funding stage and should appear in 2007.

Alison Croggon is a writer who lives in Melbourne, Australia. She has published several collections of poetry, the most recent being *The Common Flesh* (Arc Publications, United Kingdom). She also writes fantasy novels for young adults, which are published in Australia, the United Kingdom, and the United States, edits the e-zine *Masthead* (masthead.net.au), and writes theater criticism on theatrenotes.blogspot.com.

Barbara Crooker's new book, *Radiance*, recently won the Word Press First Book Award. Her poems appear in many journals and anthologies, including *Good Poems for Hard Times* (Garrison Keillor, editor, Viking Penguin). She has won a number of awards, including the 2004 Yeats Society of New York Prize (Grace Schulman, judge), the 2004 Pennsylvania Center for the Book Poster Competition, the 2003 Thomas Merton Poetry of the Sacred Prize (Stanley Kunitz, judge); three Pennsylvania Council on the Arts Fellowships in Literature; 23 nominations for the Pushcart Prize; and 11 residencies at the Virginia Center for the Creative Arts.

Rachel Dacus's new poetry collection is *Femme au chapeau* (David Robert Books). It follows her first collection, *Earth Lessons*, and two poetry CDs: *A God You Can Dance* and *Singing in the Pandaleshwar Caves*. Her poetry has appeared in *Atlanta Review's 10th Year Anthology*, *Bellingham Review*, *Prairie Schooner*, *Swink*, and *Ravishing DisUnities: Real Ghazals in English*. More of her writing can be found at www.dacushome.com.

Catherine Daly has been a member of Wom-po since its inception; she was even Webster for a time. She began reviewing with the encouragement of listers, and she's published two books with presses supportive of Wom-po: Salt and Tupelo. Her poem in this anthology was originally posted to the list as part of a discussion about poems on lingerie.

DeLana Dameron is a native of Columbia, South Carolina, who studies history at the University of North Carolina—Chapel Hill. She is on a life quest to marry the historical and the literary. Her current project is a full-length manuscript *of jasmine & clover: poems for palestine*. She is a Cave Canem fellow and a member of the Carolina African American Writer's Collective.

Kay Day is the author of three books. Her collection *A Poetry Break* (Ocean Publishing, 2004) was the only Florida poetry title nominated by SEBA as a book of the year selection for 2005. Her memoir *Killing Earl* (OP, 2005) received second prize in competition sponsored by Florida State Association, National League of American Pen Women. A full-time freelancer, Day has published over 500 articles in newspapers like *The Florida Times Union* and *Christian Science Monitor*, and magazines like *The Writer*. She has won awards for poetry, fiction, and nonfiction, and she lives in Jacksonville, Florida, with her husband and daughters.

Martha Deed retired early from her psychology practice to write full-time instead of "between times." She lives on the Erie Canal near its mouth in North Tonawanda, NY. Recent publications include *The Iowa Review Web* (with wompo Millie Niss), *Shampoo*, *Gypsy*, *Moria*, *Big Bridge*, and *Unlikelystories*. Her mini-chap is #9 in Furniture Press's PO25centsEM series. Whether writing poetry, multimedia installations, or traditional print pieces, she often uses ordinary events to interpret a broader social, political, and literary world. Her website: www.sporkworld.org/Deed.

Shira Dentz's poems have appeared in various journals including *Denver Quarterly*, *Colorado Review*, *Field*, *American Letters & Commentary*, *Chelsea*, *Seneca Review*, *Salt Hill Journal*, *Electronic Poetry Review*, *Painted Bride Quarterly*, *The Journal*, *How2*, *Web del Sol*, and *Barrow Street*. She has been the recipient of the Poetry Society of America's Lyric Poem Award, Electronic Poetry Review's Discovery Award, and Painted Bride Quarterly's poetry prize. Her poetry has aired on National Public Radio and been featured on *Poetry Daily*. She has received fellowships from the Vermont Studio Center, the Ragdale Foundation, Squaw Valley Writers' Community, and the MacDowell Arts Colony.

Jessica G. de Koninck's poems appear in *The Jewish Women's Literary Annual*, *Bridges*, the *Paterson Literary Review*, *US 1 Worksheets*, the *Edison Literary Review*, and other journals and anthologies. Her work has been nominated for a Pushcart Prize. A former councilwoman and resident of Montclair, New Jersey, she is a graduate of Brandeis University and Boston University School of Law. When not engaged in poetry, Jessica is the Director of Legislative Services for the New Jersey Department of Education.

Annie Deppe is the author of *Sitting in the Sky* (Summer Palace Press, Ireland, 2003). Her work has been anthologized in the *Forward Book of Poetry 2004* (England). She received a title-by-title individual grant from the Irish Arts Council and was selected by Poetry Ireland for their Introductions reading series. Her work has appeared in *Poetry Ireland*, *Sou'wester*, *The Stinging Fly*, *THE SHOp*, and elsewhere.

Michelle Detorie lives in Goleta, California, and edits *WOMB*, an online magazine for poetry by women (www.wombpoetry.com). Her poems have appeared or are forthcoming in *FOURSQUARE*, *Blackbird*, *Chelsea*, and *The Bedside Guide to No Tell Motel—Second Floor*. Michelle is a 2007 National Endowment for the Arts literary fellow.

Joanie DiMartino, winner of the 2003 Betty Gabehart Award for poetry, is a founding member of the women's poetry group, Mosaic. Her work has appeared in *Thema*, *Calyx*, *Wicked Alice Poetry Journal*, *Modern Haiku*, and in *Sideshow*, a collaborative exhibit displaying poetry and art at several venues in Lexington, Kentucky.

Ana Doina, a Romanian-born American writer, left Romania during the Ceausescu regime due to political pressure and social restrictions. She holds an MA in history and philosophy. Her poems and essays have been published in many literary journals and anthologies, such as *War*, *Literature*, and the *Arts*, *Pinyon Poetry*, *Vision International*, *North American Review, Argestes*, *RATTLE*, *California Quarterly*, *White Pelican*, *Paterson Review*, *Eclectica*, *Crab Orchard Review*, *Inside Grief*, *American Diaspora: Poetry of Exile*, *RedWhite and Blue*, *One hundred poets against the war*, and *Approaching literature in the 21st Century*. Two of her poems have been nominated for the Pushcart Prize.

Sharon Dolin is the author of *Realm of the Possible* (Four Way Books, 2004), *Serious Pink* (Marsh Hawk Press, 2003), and *Heart Work* (The Sheep Meadow Press, 1995), as well as four poetry chapbooks. Ms. Dolin directs The Center for Book Arts Annual

Letterpress Poetry Chapbook Competition, and is a curator of the Center Broadsides Reading Series. She is Poet-in-Residence at Eugene Lang College, The New School for Liberal Arts, and also teaches at the 92nd Street Y and Poets House in New York City.

Carol Dorf's poems have appeared in *Runes*, *Five Fingers Review*, *Poetica*, *Feminist Studies*, *Edgz*, *NewVerseNews*, *Caprice*, *The NeoVictorian*, *Heresies*, and elsewhere. Her chapbook, *A Breath Would Destroy that Symmetry*, was published by eg press. She's taught in a variety of venues: as a California Poet in the Schools, at Lawrence Hall of Science, and at a large, urban high school.

Katherine Drabek was awarded an MFA in poetry from Vermont College in January 2006. She loves cats, dogs, downtime, friends, and poetry—a list that's in alphabetical order, not in order of importance. She received a PhD in European language from the University of Oregon in 1983. Stanford Studies in Literature published her book *Vision and Revision: A Study of Inspiration in Thomas Mann's Fiction* in 1987. She was way busy for a long time, but got over that recently.

Camille T. Dungy, author of *What to Eat, What to Drink, What to Leave for Poison* (Red Hen Press, 2006), has received fellowships from organizations including the National Endowment for the Arts, The Virginia Commission for the Arts, and The American Antiquarian Society. Associate Editor of *Gathering Ground: A Reader Celebrating Cave Canem's First Decade* (University of Michigan Press, 2006), she is an associate professor in the Creative Writing Department at San Francisco State University.

Rishma Dunlop is the author of three books of poetry: *The Body of My Garden*, *Reading Like a Girl*, and *Metropolis*. She is coeditor of *Red Silk: An Anthology of South Asian Canadian Women Poets*. Winner of the 2003 Emily Dickinson Award, her work includes essays, memoir, radio drama, and fiction. She currently edits *Studio*, an electronic poetry journal. She is a professor of English and creative writing at York University, Toronto.

Lisken Van Pelt Dus is a poet, teacher, and martial artist living in Pittsfield, Massachusetts. Her work can be found in *Conduit*, *Main Street Rag*, *The South Carolina Review*, *The Sow's Ear Poetry Review*, and other journals. She has earned awards from *The Comstock Review* and *Atlanta Review*.

Jilly Dybka is a computer network engineer and webmaster, and a student in the MFA program in Creative Writing at Queens University of Charlotte. When she isn't pushing bytes or writing poems, Jilly can be found in front of the dials of her ham radio, sending Morse code with an old WWII telegraph key. She lives near Nashville, Tennessee, with her husband, Darryl, a Grammy-winning record producer and jazz musician. Her poetry news blog is at www.poetryhut.com.

Lynnell Edwards is the author of two books of poetry, *The Farmer's Daughter* (Red Hen Press, 2003) and *The Highwayman's Wife* (Red Hen Press, 2007). She is a regular reviewer for *Pleiades*, *Rain Taxi*, and *The Georgia Review*, and the recipient of an Al Smith Fellowship from the Kentucky Arts Council, 2007. She lives in Louisville, Kentucky. (http://www.lynnelledwards.com)

Moira Egan's first book of poems, *Cleave* (WWPH, 2004) was nominated for the National Book Award and was a finalist for the ForeWord Book of the Year Award. Recent poems have appeared in *Gargoyle*, *Notre Dame Review*, *Passages North*, *Poems & Plays*, *Poetry*, *Prairie Schooner*, *Smartish Pace*, *32 Poems*, and *West Branch*, among many others. Her work is also featured in the anthologies *Kindled Terraces: American Poets in Greece* and *Lofty Dogmas: Poets on Poetics*. Two of her Bar Napkin Sonnets won first prize in the Baltimore City Paper Poetry Contest, 2005.

Susan Elbe is the author of *Eden in the Rearview Mirror* (Word Press, 2007) and *Light Made from Nothing* (Parallel Press, 2003). Her poems have appeared or are forthcoming in many journals including *Ascent*, *Blackbird*, *Calyx*, *Crab Orchard Review*, *MARGIE*, *North American Review*, *Passages North*, and *Smartish Pace*. She is the winner of the Calyx Lois Cranston Memorial Poetry Prize and a Rowland Foundation fellowship to the Vermont Studio Center. She lives in Madison, Wisconsin.

Julie R. Enszer is a writer and lesbian activist living in Maryland. She has previously been published in *Iris: A Journal About Women*, *Room of One's Own*, *Long Shot*, the *Web Del Sol Review,* and the *Harrington Lesbian Literary Quarterly*, among many other periodicals. She is at work on a poetry collection, *Limnings*, a novel, and a feminist history of the nuclear age. You can learn more about her work at www.JulieREnszer.com.

Nancy Esposito's first book of poems was *Changing Hands* (Quarterly Review of Literature Contemporary Poetry Series). *Mêm' Rain*, a winner of the National Looking Glass Poetry Chapbook Competition, was published in 2002 by Pudding House Publications, which also published *Greatest Hits 1978–2001* in 2003. She received the Discovery/*The Nation* Award, Massachusetts Arts Lottery Grant, the Colladay Award, PSA Gordon Barber Memorial Award, a Fulbright Grant to Egypt, and grants to Vietnam and Cambodia. Her poems and translations have appeared in such journals as *APR*, *The Nation*, *Southwest Review*, *Indiana Review*, *Denver Quarterly*, and *Stand*. Her poems have been translated into Spanish and Vietnamese.

Kate Evans, a California native, lives in San Jose by way of Santa Cruz, Seattle, and Yokohama, Japan. Her poetry collection, *Like All We Love* (Q Press) was nominated for a Los Angeles Times Book Prize and a Lambda Literary Award. She is also the author of a book about LGBTQ teachers, *Negotiating the Self* (Routledge), and a forthcoming novel (*For the May Queen*). She teaches at San Jose State University. Her website is www.kate-evans.com.

Dina Ripsman Eylon, who has her PhD in post-biblical Hebrew language and literature from the University of Toronto, has been teaching biblical and modern Hebrew at Carleton University and the University of Toronto. She is the editor of *Women in Judaism: A Multidisciplinary Journal*. Her book *Reincarnation in Jewish Mysticism and Gnostism* was published by Edwin Mellen Press in 2003. Eylon is the founder of the Vaughn Poets' Circle. She also serves as the Thornhill branch manager of the Ontario Poetry Society. Her poems were published in *Convergence: Poets for Peace*, *Kinesis*, *Verse Afire*, and in the anthology *Stress(full) Sister(hood)*.

Marcia Falk's poems have appeared in *American Poetry Review*, *Prairie Schooner*, *Runes*, and many other places. She is the author of *The Book of Blessings*, a re-creation of Jewish prayer in poetic forms (Beacon Press, 1999), and several books of translations, including *The Song of Songs: Love Lyrics from the Bible* (Brandeis University Press/University Press of New England, 2004), *The Spectacular Difference*, poems by the modern Hebrew mystic Zelda (Hebrew Union College Press, 2004), and *With Teeth in the Earth*, poems by the Yiddish modernist Malka Heifetz Tussman (Wayne State University Press, 1992). She is also a painter; her art can be viewed at www.marciafalk.com.

Annie Finch's books of poetry are *Calendars* (Tupelo Press, 2003), *The Encyclopedia of Scotland* (Salt, 2004), and *Eve* (Story Line Press, 1997). Other works include a translation of the poems of Louise Labé, (University of Chicago Press, 2006) and an opera libretto based on the life of Marina Tsvetaeva (American Opera Projects, 2003). Her most recent of several anthologies and books on poetics is *The Body of Poetry: Essays on Women, Form, and the Poetic Self* (University of Michigan Press, 2005). She directs the Stonecoast Brief-Residency MFA in Creative Writing at the University of Southern Maine.

Margaret Rockwell Finch of Maine, born in New Jersey in 1921, has been a poet for eighty years. Her work has appeared in *The Saturday Review*, *Voices*, *The Christian Science Monitor*, and elsewhere, including the anthologies *Japan: Theme and Variations*, *Poems of*

War Resistance, The Poets' Grimm (2003), and also *Coming Home Twice* (2005) from the Maine Poets' Society, for which she was editor-in-chief. In 1973 she won an Annual Members' Award from the Poetry Society of America, and in 1996 she published *Davy's Lake, 101 Selected Poems from 1936 to 1995*. Her recent chapbook is *The Barefoot Goose: Poems of Love* (Just Write Books, 2006).

Ann Fisher-Wirth is the author of two books of poems—*Blue Window* and *Five Terraces*—and two chapbooks—*The Trinket Poems* and *Walking Wu Wei's Scroll*. Her awards include a 2003 Malahat Review Long Poem Prize, and, in 2004, the Rita Dove Poetry Award, the Poetry Award from the Mississippi Institute of Arts and Letters, and a Poetry Fellowship from the Mississippi Arts Commission. Her poems have appeared widely in journals, online, and in anthologies. She teaches at the University of Mississippi. She is the president of the 1000-member international Association for the Study of Literature and Environment.

Barbara Flaherty has published poems and essays in anthologies, journals, and e-zines. Her first book of poems is *Holy Madness* (Chanting Press, 2006). The poem "Dark Raven" was the recipient of the Drogheda Amergin Poetry Prize in 2005. Barbara has toured through a chautauqua speakers bureau funded by the National Endowment for the Humanities, and facilitates ecospirituality retreats and post–secondary educational tours of Alaska. By trade she is polydiagnosis clinician and behavioral health professional trainer.

Kathleen Flenniken lives in Seattle, Washington. Her first collection, *Famous*, winner of the 2005 Prairie Schooner Prize in Poetry, was released in fall 2006 by the University of Nebraska Press. Her poems have appeared in *The Iowa Review*, *Poetry*, and *Poetry Daily*, and she is the recipient of fellowships from the NEA and Artist Trust.

Cherryl Floyd-Miller is the 2006 inaugural winner of the Poetry Daily–Virginia Arts of the Book Companion Poems Contest. Also a produced playwright and a quilter, she is the author of three volumes of poems: *Utterance: A Museology of Kin* (2003), *Chops* (Nexus Press, 2004), and *Exquisite Heats* (Salt Publishing, 2007). She is currently working on The Race Quilt, a collaborative poetry and fiber art project among 30 U.S. writers.

Ruth E. Foley lives in Massachusetts, where she teaches English for a local adult literacy nonprofit. Her poems have appeared in over 50 print and web journals including *RATTLE*, *Confrontation*, *Poetry Midwest*, and *Hanging Loose*.

Audrey Friedman is an eighth grade English teacher in Rhode Island and received an MFA in poetry from Vermont College in January 2005. Her work has been published in a number of small press literary journals, including but not limited to *The California Quarterly*, *Urban Spaghetti*, *The Newport Review*, *The Griffin*, the *Black Buzzard Review*, and *The Comstock Review*. Audrey's chapbook, *Gallery of the Surreal*, has been published by Premier Poets of Portsmouth, Rhode Island. Audrey's work has also been anthologized in *Regrets Only: Contemporary Poets on the Theme of Regret*, published by Little Pear Press.

Suzanne Frischkorn's most recent collection, *Spring Tide*, was selected by Mary Oliver for the 2004 Aldrich Poetry Award. She is the author of *Red Paper Flower* (Little Poem Press, 2004), *Exhale* (2000), and *The Tactile Sense* (1996). *A Shore Without Silence*, a poetry CD, was released by Alsop Review Press in 2004. Her poems have appeared most recently, or are forthcoming, in *Indiana Review*, *MARGIE*, *88*, *Poet Lore*, *Mot Juste*, and in many other journals as well as eight anthologies. Suzanne is also associate editor of *Samsāra Quarterly*. She lives in Connecticut with her husband and their three children.

Helen Frost is the author of *Skin of a Fish, Bones of a Bird* (Ampersand, 1993, now on CAPA at http://capa.conncoll.edu/frost.sfbb.html), and three novels-in-poems, all from Farrar, Straus, and Giroux (Frances Foster Books): *Keesha's House*, a Printz honor book, 2003; *Spinning through the Universe*, 2004; and *The Braid*, 2006. Her website can be found at www. helenfrost.net. "First Deep Breath" is a mason sonnet; it is also a genethliacum (poem of blessing for a new baby) for Althea Crane Finch Brand, sent to the Wom-po list when Althea was born to Annie Finch on December 21, 1998.

Gloria Frym's most recent book of poems, *Solution Simulacra*, was published by United Artists in 2006. A previous collection, *Homeless at Home*, won an American Book Award in 2002. She is also the author of two books of short stories, *Distance No Object* (City Lights Books) and *How I Learned* (Coffee House Press), and several other volumes of poetry. She teaches at California College of Arts in the Bay Area.

Diane Gage was born in a very small town on the Montana highline and studied English literature at Duke and Arizona State University. Her poems have appeared in such publications as *Plainsongs*, *Puerto del Sol*, *Chattahoochee Review*, *Rattapallax*, *Seattle Review*, *Phoebe*, and *Wind*. She is also a visual artist who works as an expressive arts counselor, using art processes to help people make desired or necessary changes in their lives. She is currently working on a project called Walking in Birdland, a series of daily haiku about her So-Cal suburban neighborhood.

Jeannine Hall Gailey is a Seattle-area writer whose first book of poetry, *Becoming the Villainess*, was recently published by Steel Toe Books. Poems from the book were featured on NPR's *The Writer's Almanac* and *Verse Daily*. Her work has appeared in journals such as *The Iowa Review*, *The Evansville Review*, and *The Columbia Poetry Review*. Her chapbook, *Female Comic Book Superheroes*, is available from Pudding House Press and from her website www.webbish6.com/poetry.htm.

Alicia Zavala Galván is primarily a poet with six published bilingual collections of poetry. She has translated the Spanish work of other poets and published them through her own small press (at www.galvart.com). Her research is on the seventeenth-century feminist nun of colonial Mexico, Sor Juana Inés de la Cruz. Her literary and scholarly works in English and Spanish have been presented before popular and academic audiences in the United States, Mexico, and South America.

Jennifer J. Gandel grew up in the San Francisco Bay Area. She is currently working on her MFA at the University of Alabama in Tuscaloosa, where she teaches creative writing and serves as poetry editor for *Black Warrior Review*.

Lisha Adela García is a bilingual, bicultural poet who has México, the United States, and that land in between (Spanglish) in her work. She has an MFA from Vermont College and currently resides in Arizona. She is influenced by the American Southwest, the ghosts that haunt her labyrinth, and border culture. Lisha is also a simultaneous interpreter and translator, and most recently translated into English the Mexican poet Luis Armenta Malpica's book, *The Will of Light*. Her day job is with local government working in neighborhoods. Lisha also has a Master's Degree in International Business from Thunderbird.

Alice George lives in Evanston, Illinois, where she coedits *RHINO* magazine (www.rhinopoetry.org). She also teaches poetry to kids as an artist-in-residence in area schools. Recent and forthcoming publications (including collaborations with Cecilia Pinto) include work in *Bellingham Review*, *Court Green*, *Sentence*, *New Orleans Review*, and *Quarter after Eight*. Alice was awarded an Illinois Arts Council Fellowship for Poetry in 2005. The anthology poem is from her chapbook manuscript, optimistically entitled *The Beautiful Atheist*.

Bernadette Geyer is author of the poetry chapbook *What Remains* (Argonne House Press) and was twice selected as a Jenny McKean Moore Poetry Scholar at George Washington University. Her poems have appeared in *Hotel Amerika*, *South Dakota Review*, *The Midwest*

Quarterly, *The Marlboro Review*, *32 Poems*, and elsewhere. Geyer's full-length manuscript, *Dead Men*, was a finalist for the OSU Press/*The Journal* Poetry Prize and for the Richard Snyder Memorial Publication Prize.

Ellen Goldstein was raised in Charlottesville, Virginia, and currently lives in Beverly, Massachusetts. Her poems have appeared in *pettycoat relaxer*, *Southern Poetry Review*, *The Formalist*, *Streetlight*, and *The New Hampshire Review*. She was a finalist for the 2007 Ruth Stone Prize in Poetry from *Hunger Mountain*.

David Graham is professor of English at Ripon College in Wisconsin. His poetry, essays, and reviews have appeared widely. His most recent poetry collections are *Stutter Monk* (Flume Press) and *Greatest Hits* (Pudding House). With Kate Sontag, he coedited the essay anthology *After Confession: Poetry as Autobiography* (Graywolf Press). His website (www.ripon.edu/faculty/GrahamD) includes an online poetry library with many links and resources related to poets and poetry.

Neile Graham, Canadian by birth and inclination, currently lives in Seattle, Washington. The Bumbershoot Arts Festival described her work as "breathtaking and stern, abducting her audience into a realm of disturbing yet beautiful detail and experience." In *Arc* magazine, Barry Dempster wrote (about her third collection, *Blood Memory*): "I love how intensely she leads us into greater and greater complexities, history and mythology and the most secretive parts of the heart all colliding in a grand burst of energy...the page lighting up like a meteor shower." Her poem here is from a collection in progress, an idiosyncratic travelogue of Scotland.

Arielle Greenberg is the author of *My Kafka Century* (Action Books, 2005) and *Given* (Verse/Wave Books, 2002) and teaches at Columbia College Chicago. A former contributing editor for *How2*, she is a co-editor of the journal *Court Green* and the poetry editor for *Black Clock*, and founder of the poet-moms listserv. She lives in Evanston, Illinois with her family.

Kate Greenstreet was born in Chicago and has lived mostly on the east and west coasts of the United States, currently back on the Atlantic side, in New Jersey. Her chapbook, *Learning the Language*, was published by Etherdome Press in 2005, and her first full-length book, *case sensitive*, is due from Ahsahta Press in September 2006. For more information, visit her website: kategreenstreet.com.

Susan Grimm is a native of Cleveland, Ohio. Her poems have appeared in *West Branch*, *Poetry Northwest*, *Rattapallax*, *The Journal*, and other publications. Her book of poems, *Lake Erie Blue*, was published by BkMk Press in 2004. She edited *Ordering the Storm: How to Put Together a Book of Poems*. Currently, she teaches at Cleveland State University and is the series editor of the Cleveland State University Poetry Center.

Eve Grubin's first book of poems is *Morning Prayer* (The Sheep Meadow Press, 2005). Her poems have appeared in *The American Poetry Review*, *Barrow Street*, *Conjunctions*, *The New Republic*, *The Virginia Quarterly Review*, and elsewhere. She teaches at The New School University, and she is a fellow at the Drisha Institute for Jewish Education.

Susan Gubernat's first book of poems, *Flesh,* won the Marianne Moore Prize and was published by Helicon Nine Editions. She is an opera librettist whose work was recently showcased by the New York City Opera. Her awards include fellowships from the New York and New Jersey State Arts Councils and a Woodrow Wilson Grant in Women's Studies, as well as residencies at Yaddo and MacDowell. She is on the permanent faculty of the English department at California State University, East Bay.

Cindy Williams Gutiérrez is a poet who collaborates with artists in theater, music, and visual art. Her work has been published in *Crab Orchard Review*, *ZYZZYVA*, *The Grove Review*, *Open Spaces*, among others. In 2005, her poems were exhibited in *People, Places and Perceptions: A Look at Contemporary Northwest Latino Art* at the Maryhill Museum of Art in Goldendale, Washington. She is currently pursuing her MFA in the Stonecoast program at the University of Southern Maine.

Tami Haaland is the author of *Breath in Every Room*, which won the 2001 Nicholas Roerich Prize from Story Line Press. Her work has appeared in various journals and anthologies, including *Rattapallax*, *5 AM*, *High Desert Journal*, and *Ring of Fire: Writers of the Yellowstone Region*. She teaches creative writing at Montana State University-Billings.

Marilyn Hacker's most recent book is *Desesperanto* (W.W. Norton, 2003). She received the Lenore Marshall Award of the Academy of American Poets in 1995 for *Winter Numbers*; her *Selected Poems* received the Poets' Prize in 1996. Her translations from the French include *Birds and Bison* (Sheep Meadow Press, 2005) poems by Claire Malroux, and *She Says* (Graywolf Press, 2003) poems by Vénus Khoury-Ghata. Hacker received an Award in Literature from the American Academy of Arts and Letters in 2004. She teaches at the City College and at the CUNY Graduate Center.

Anne Haines lives in Bloomington, Indiana, where she is employed by the Indiana University Libraries. Her work has appeared or is forthcoming in journals and anthologies including *Calyx*, *Rattle*, *Poetry Midwest*, *Cortland Review*, and *Poetry from Sojourner: A Feminist Anthology*. Her poem "Windows" was nominated for a Pushcart Prize in 2005. She shares a tiny house with two rather large and suspiciously self-satisfied cats.

Kendra Hamilton's work has appeared in *Callaloo*, *The Southern Review*, and *Shenandoah*, among others, as well as in *Bum Rush the Page: A Def Poetry Jam*, *The Best of Callaloo*, and *The Ringing Ear: Black Poets Lean South*. She has won fellowships from the Cave Canem Foundation as well as the Rockefeller Foundation's prestigious Bellagio residency program. Her debut collection, *The Goddess of Gumbo*, was published in 2006.

Maryanne Hannan has published poetry in *Carquinez Poetry Review*, *Clare*, *Hampden-Sydney Poetry Review*, *Sport Literate*, *Windhover*, and *Xavier Review*. She lives in upstate New York.

Lois Marie Harrod won a 2003 fellowship, her third, from the New Jersey Council on the Arts for her poetry. Her seventh book of poetry, *Put Your Sorry Side Out*, has just been published by Concrete Wolf. Her sixth book of poetry, *Spelling the World Backward* (2000), was published by Palanquin Press, University of South Carolina Aiken, which also published her chapbook, *This Is a Story You Already Know* (1999), and her book *Part of the Deeper Sea* (1997). Her poems have appeared in journals from *American Poetry Review* to *Zone 3*, and online in *Verse Daily*.

Mary Senior Harwood is a Vermont writer whose prose work has appeared in a variety of publications, including *Vermont Voices I* and *Vermont Voices II*. Primarily a fiction writer, Mary is currently completing a novel. She is a degree candidate in the University of Southern Maine Stonecoast Low-Residency MFA program. This poem came out of her work on a critical thesis examining writers who publish prose and poetry.

Farideh Hassanzadeh-Mostafavi is an Iranian poet and translator. She published her first book of poetry at age 22. Her poems appear in various anthologies. Here are her works: *The Last Night with Sylvia Plath: Essays on Poetry*, *Eternal Voices: Interviews* *with Great Poets*, and other bilingual anthologies of American, African, and Latin American poetry. She has translated the poems of T. S. Eliot, Marina Tsvetaeva, Jaroslav Seifert, Pablo Neruda, and Adonis.

Dolores Hayden's most recent poetry collection is *American Yard*. Her work has appeared in *The Kenyon Review*, *The Yale Review*, *Southwest Review*, *Michigan Quarterly Review*, *Slate*, *Margin*, and many other journals and anthologies. She has won the Boyle Farber Award for the best poem in form from the New England Poetry Club and been runner-up for their Motton Award for best book. She's received The Writer Magazine/Emily Dickinson Award from the Poetry Society of America. A former Guggenheim and NEA fellow, the author of nonfiction about American landscapes, she is a professor of architecture and American studies at Yale.

Ava Leavell Haymon is a poet, playwright, and teacher. Her poems have appeared in journals, including *Poetry*, *The Southern Review*, *Prairie Schooner*; in five chapbooks; and in two collections, *The Strict Economy of Fire* and *Kitchen Heat* (2006), both from LSU Press. She teaches poetry writing in Louisiana and directs a writers' and artists' retreat center in New Mexico.

Eloise Klein Healy, Distinguished Professor of Creative Writing Emerita and founding chair of the MFA in Creative Writing Program at Antioch University Los Angeles, is the author of five books of poetry; the most recent is *Passing* (Red Hen Press). Healy's work has been anthologized in *The World in Us: Lesbian and Gay Poetry of the Next Wave*, *The Geography of Home: California's Poetry of Place*, *Another City: Writing from Los Angeles*, and *California Poetry: From the Gold Rush to the Present*. She is the cofounder of ECO-ARTS (www.eco-arts.net), and originator of the Red Hen Press imprint Arktoi Books.

Allison Adelle Hedge Coke is a professor of writing at the Institute of American Indian Arts. Her lineage includes: Huron, Cherokee, Creek, Metis, French Canadian, Portuguese, English, Irish, Scot, French, and Swiss blood. Her award-winning publications include the volumes *Dog Road Woman* and *Off-Season City Pipe* (poetry, Coffee House Press); *Rock, Ghost, Willow, Deer* (memoir, University of Nebraska Press); and *Blood Run* (verse-play, Salt Publishing). She is a labor/environmental poet and has had fellowships from the Black Earth Institute Think Tank and the MacDowell Colony.

Liz Henry has published poems, translations, and essays in *Lodestar Quarterly*, *Poetry Flash*, *other*, *Two Lines*, *Cipactli*, *caesura*, *Literary Mama*, *Convergence*, and *Strange Horizons*. In the 90s she edited the riot grrl zines *Vanilla Milkshake* and *Slut Utopia*. Through Tollbooth Press, she publishes a small magazine, *Composite: Multiple Translations* (http://www. compositetranslation.com). Her current projects include translating poems by Nydia Lamarque, Juana de Ibarbourou, and Nestor Perlongher. She blogs about poetics, translation, and politics at http://liz-henry.blogspot.com and http://literarytranslators.blogspot.com.

R. Joyce Heon grew up a field urchin in New England, reciting nursery rhymes and song lyrics. Today she gleefully claims the perks of great-grandmotherhood. She believes all credentials should be—like your driver's license—left in your pocket until someone with a badge requires them. There is some argument amongst those with poetry badges whether her poems are truly ekphrasis or whether the artwork is just a springboard for invention—an argument she dodges, reaching for another photograph, leaving the poems to speak for themselves. Her ethnic heritage is Finnish, which, she says, explains a whole lot (see any of the above).

Anne Higgins teaches English at Mount Saint Mary's University in Emmitsburg, Maryland. She has had about seventy poems published in *Yankee*, *Commonweal*, *Spirituality and Health*, *The Melic Review*, *The Drexel Online Journal*, and a variety of small magazines. Her book of poetry, *At the Year's Elbow*, was published by the Mellen Poetry Press in 2000.

Erin Shannon Hollowell lives in Cordova, Alaska, a small fishing town on Prince William Sound off the road system. She has published in small literary magazines and was one of the poets featured in 2005 on the Alaska state website during National Poetry Month. In 2004, she was commissioned to write poems to be made into a play for the University of Alaska Humanities Forum. She shares her life with her husband, two dogs, and the beautiful Copper River Delta.

Ann Hostetler grew up in Pennsylvania but has spent much of her adult life in the American Midwest, learning to love plains and big skies. Her first collection of poetry, *Empty Room with Light*, was a finalist for the Arlin G. Meyer Prize in 2005. She is also the editor of *A Cappella: Mennonite Voices in Poetry*, the first comprehensive anthology of poetry by writers from Mennonite contexts, published by University of Iowa Press. She teaches literature and creative writing at Goshen College in Goshen, Indiana. She can be found on the web at http://www.goshen.edu/~anneh.

Louisa Howerow has a home in Ontario, Canada, and writes wherever she finds herself to be.

Bette Lynch Husted lives and writes in rural Oregon. Pudding House published her chapbook *After Fire* in 2002. *Above the Clearwater: Living on Stolen Land* (Oregon State University Press, 2004) was a finalist for both the 2004 Oregon Book Award and the 2005 WILLA award in creative nonfiction.

Karla Huston has published poetry, reviews, and interviews in several journals including *Cimarron Review*, *Ecletica Magazine*, *5 AM*, *Margie*, *North American Review*, *One Trick Pony*, *Pearl*, *RATTLE*, *Smartish Pace* (online), and others. She is the author of five chapbooks of poetry, most recently: *Flight Patterns* (winner of the 2003 Main Street Rag chapbook contest), *Virgins on the Rocks* (Parallel Press, an imprint of UW Libraries, 2004), and *Catch and Release* (Marsh River Editions, Marshfield, Wisconsin, 2005).

Luisa Igloria, www.luisaigloria.com (previously published as Maria Luisa Aguilar-Carino) is originally from Baguio City, Philippines, where she lived before coming to the United States on a Fulbright in 1992. She has degrees from the University of the Philippines, Ateneo de Manila University, and the University of Illinois in Chicago. She edited *Not Home, But Here: Writing from the Filipino Diaspora* (Anvil, 2003), and authored eight books including *Encanto* (Anvil, 1994), *In the Garden of the Three Islands* (Moyer Bell/Asphodel, 1995), and most recently *TRILL & MORDENT* (WordTech Editions, 2005). She teaches in the MFA program at Old Dominion University.

Judy Jensen's poems have appeared in journals and anthologies such as *The International Prose Poem*, *Poetry Miscellany*, and *What Will Suffice: Contemporary American Poets on the Art of Poetry*. She's been nominated for a Pushcart Prize and has placed in the Austin International Poetry Festival.

Liesl Jobson is a bassoonist in the Johannesburg Philharmonic Orchestra. She received an honorable mention in the 2006 Commonwealth Short Story Competition and won the 2005 POWA Women's Writing Poetry Competition. Her flash fiction manuscript, "100 Papers," won the Ernst van Heerden Creative Writing Award from the University of the Witwatersrand, and her poetry book *Underground Work* will be published by the Timbila Poetry Project, Limpopo, in 2007.

Judith E. Johnson's recent books are *Cities of Mathematics and Desire* and *The Ice Lizard* (Sheep Meadow Press, 2005 and 1992). Her first book, *Uranium Poems*, won the 1968 Yale Series of Younger Poets Prize. Professor of English and Women's Studies at University at Albany, State University of New York, former president of the Board of Associated Writing Programs and of the Poetry Society of America, she edits the feminist literary periodical, *13th Moon*. Before 1985, she published as Judith Johnson Sherwin.

Adrianne Kalfopoulou is the author of *Wild Greens*, poetry; *Figs*, a chapbook-contest winner that was translated into Polish; *The Untidy House*, a critical study on female discourses and the American Dream; and *Broken Greek*, *a language to belong*, a memoir. She lives and teaches in Athens, Greece, and is part of the Scottish Universities' International Summer Program (SUISS) at the University of Edinburgh.

Julie Kane is the author of *Rhythm & Booze* (University of Illinois Press, 2003), which was Maxine Kumin's selection for the National Poetry Series and a finalist for the 2005 Poets' Prize. She is also the coeditor of *Umpteen Ways of Looking at a Possum: Critical and Creative Responses to Everette Maddox* (Xavier Review Press, 2006). Her work can be found in such journals as *The Southern Review*, *The Antioch Review*, *Prairie Schooner*, *Feminist Studies*, *London Magazine*, *Verse Daily*, and *The Formalist*. She is an associate professor of English at Northwestern State University in Natchitoches, Louisiana.

Julia Spicher Kasdorf has published two collections of poetry with the University of Pittsburgh Press, *Eve's Striptease* and *Sleeping Preacher*, which won the Agnes Lynch Starrett Prize and the Great Lakes Award for New Writing. She has also published a collection of essays, *The Body and the Book: Writing from a Mennonite Life*, a biography, *Fixing Tradition: Joseph W. Yoder, Amish American*, and with Michael Tyrell, she edited *Broken Land: Poems of Brooklyn*. She is associate professor of English and women's studies at Pennsylvania State University.

Pratibha Kelapure was born in Mumbai, India, and currently lives in California.

Bridget Kelley-Lossada is a Los Angeles poet who received her Master of Fine Arts in poetry from Antioch University Los Angeles. Bridget's poetry has appeared in various journals and anthologies such as *Inkwell*, *51%*, *Moondance*, *Invisible Plane*, *A Pagan's Muse*, and will appear in a forthcoming anthology from Tebot Bach.

Robin Kemp (BA Georgia State, MFA University of New Orleans) is a poet, teacher, and journalist. She was born in New Orleans on Mardi Gras Day. A Hambidge Poetry Fellow, her work appears in *Texas Poetry Journal*, *Ascent*, *Ellipsis*, *Texas Review*, *Common Lives Lesbian Lives*, *Verse Daily*, *Valparaiso Poetry Review*, *Able Muse*, and *Mesechabe*. She has published articles on Kate Chopin, William Stafford (Oxford Encyclopedia of American Literature, 2000), Turner Cassity, and New Formalism (Greenwood Encyclopedia of American Poetry, 2006). Robin runs hurricanepoetscheckin.blogspot.com, which coordinates aid for Hurricane Katrina's surviving poets, and is coediting a post-Katrina anthology of New Orleans poets.

Diane Kendig, a poet, writer, and translator, is the author of three chapbooks, most recently *Greatest Hits, 1978–2000* (Pudding House). Her poetry and nonfiction have appeared in such journals as *Colere*, *Ekphrasis*, *Minnesota Review*, *Mid-American Review*, *U.S. 1*, and *Slant*, as well as the anthologies *Modern Poems of Ohio* and *Those Winter Sundays: Female Academics and their Working-Class Parents*. A recipient of two Ohio Arts Council Fellowships in Poetry, a Fulbright lectureship in translation, and a Yaddo Fellowship, she currently lives in Lynn, Massachusetts. http://dianekendig.com

Lillian Baker Kennedy, author of *Tomorrow After Night* (Bay River Press, 2003) and *Notions* (Pudding House, 2004), coedited *A Sense of Place, Collected Maine Poems* (Bay River Press, 2002) and *Leavings* (Bay River Press, 2005). Kennedy's poetry has been exhibited with the sculpture of Kerstin Engman (Earthly Beatitudes, USM L/A College, 2003), included in *Off the Record*, an anthology of poetry by lawyers (Legal Studies Forum, James R. Elkins, Editor), and journals including *Cider Press Review*, *Words & Images*, and *The Cafe Review*. Kennedy practices law and lives in an old cape bordered by wild roses in Auburn, Maine.

Laura Kennelly is a freelance arts writer from Texas who now lives in Berea, Ohio, where she also works as an editor. She has taught creative writing and English at the University of North Texas and at Texas Woman's University. A former president of the Texas Association of Creative Writing Teachers, she has published one chapbook, *The Passage of Mrs. Jung* (Norton Coker Press, 1990) and edited *A Certain Attitude: Poems by Seven Texas Women* (Pecan Grove Press, 1995).

Judith Kerman has published eight books or chapbooks of poetry, most recently *Galvanic Response* (March Street Press, 2005) and the bilingual collection, *Plane Surfaces/Plano de Incidencia* (Santo Domingo: CCLEH, 2002). Her book of translations, *A Woman in Her Garden: Selected Poems of Dulce María Loynaz* (Cuba; Cervantes Prize laureate, 1992), was published by White Pine Press in 2002. Kerman was a Fulbright Senior Scholar to the Dominican Republic in 2002, translating the poetry and fiction of contemporary Dominican women. She publishes Mayapple Press and was founding editor of *Earth's Daughters*.

Claire Keyes is Professor Emerita at Salem State College in Massachusetts, where she served as English Department Chair and Coordinator of the Graduate English Programs. She is the author of *The Aesthetics of Power: The Poetry of Adrienne Rich*. Her reviews and poems have appeared (or are forthcoming) in such journals as *Calyx*, *ReviewRevue*, *The Women's Review of Books*, *Spoon River Poetry Review*, *Zone 3*, and *Blueline*. Her chapbook, *Rising and Falling*, won the Foothills Poetry Competition. She lives in Marblehead, Massachusetts, with her husband, Jay Moore.

Athena Kildegaard lives in Morris, Minnesota, where she is the director of a nonprofit cultural organization and a roster artist with the COMPAS/Writers and Artists in the Schools program. Her book *Rare Momentum* was published in fall 2006 by Red Dragonfly Press.

Sally Rosen Kindred's chapbook *Garnet Lanterns* won the 2005 Anabiosis Press Chapbook Competition (available at http://garnetlanterns.quietmoon.com). Her poems have appeared in *Spoon River Poetry Review*, *The Florida Review*, *Poetry Northwest*, *Earth's Daughters*, and *Runes*. She teaches poetry writing online for the Johns Hopkins Center for Talented Youth.

Amy King is the author of the poetry collection, *Antidotes for an Alibi* (Blazvox Books), a Lambda Book Award finalist, and the chapbook, *The People Instruments* (Pavement Saw Press Chapbook Award, 2002). Ms. King currently teaches creative writing and English at Nassau Community College and teaches a workshop of her own design, Making the Urban Poetic, at Poets House in Manhattan. She is also the NYC interview correspondent for MiPO Radio. Please visit www.amyking.org for more.

Janet R. Kirchheimer's work has appeared in journals such as *Potomac Review*, *Kalliope*, *Natural Bridge*, *Lilith*, *Alimentum*, *PoetryNZ*, *Kerem*, *Confrontation*, *Main Street Rag*, and *Nashim*. She was a semi-finalist in the Discovery/The Nation contest, and a finalist in the Portlandia and Concrete Wolf chapbook contests. Janet is the recipient of a Drisha Arts Award for 2006–07. She is completing a poetry manuscript about the Holocaust. She is Director of Community Development and Assistant to the President at CLAL—The National Jewish Center for Learning and Leadership, and she teaches adults and teens about Judaism using poetry and creative writing.

Kaaren Kitchell's 2003 book of poems, *The Minotaur Dance,* was published by Spout Graphic Press. In 2005, she received an MFA in creative writing from Antioch University Los Angeles. Mythology is her passion; Calliope, her muse. With husband, Richard Beban, she teaches Living Mythically: How to Embody Myth in Your Daily Life. The Getty Museum commissioned a fine art manuscript of two of their poems. She and Beban live in Playa del Rey, California, and Paris.

Katrina Kostro writes on recovering from childhood illness and the process of healing. Her poems have been published in *Columbus* magazine and will appear in *SURVIVAL of the SOUL: Artists Living with Illness*. She has an older and younger brother, a Siamese cat, and lives in New York City.

Ann Neuser Lederer was born in Ohio and has also lived and worked in Pennsylvania, Michigan, and Kentucky. Her poems and creative nonfiction have been published in such journals as *Cross Connect*, *Brevity*, *Diagram*, *Moria*, *No Tell Motel*, *Wind*, and *Kalliope*, in various anthologies, and in chapbooks, *Approaching Freeze* (Foothills) and *The Undifferentiated* (Pudding House). She is employed as a visiting nurse.

Donna J. Gelagotis Lee's forthcoming book, *On the Altar of Greece*, won the 2005 Gival Press Poetry Award. Donna's poetry has appeared in numerous literary and scholarly journals, including *CALYX: A Journal of Art and Literature by Women*, *Descant*, *Feminist Studies*, *The Massachusetts Review*, *The Midwest Quarterly*, and *The Seattle Review*. Donna earned a BA, cum laude, in English and creative writing from Sweet Briar College. She lived in Athens, Greece, for many years. She was a researcher for *CLASSIC: The Magazine About Horses & Sport* in New York City. Currently a resident of New Jersey, Donna has been a contributing editor of a number of textbooks and an editor of many scientific journal articles.

Sharon Leiter is the author of *Critical Companion to Emily Dickinson: A Literary Reference to Her Life and Work*; a volume of poetry, *The Lady and the Bailiff of Time*; and *Akhmatova's Petersburg*, a literary study of the Russian poet Anna Akhmatova. Her poetry has appeared in such journals as *Atlanta Review*, *Cimarron Review*, *Georgia Review*, and *Virginia Quarterly Review*. She is poetry editor of *Streetlight*.

Amy Lemmon's poetry and criticism have appeared in *New Letters*, *Verse*, *Prairie Schooner*, *Crab Orchard Review*, *Cincinnati Review*, and elsewhere. Her manuscript *Fine Motor* was a finalist in the 2006 Center for Book Arts chapbook competition. A contributing editor of *Barrow Street*, Amy holds a PhD in English/creative writing from the University of Cincinnati and is Assistant Chair of English at the Fashion Institute of Technology in New York City.

Carol Levin's poetry appears or is forthcoming in *The Massachusetts Review*, *Rock Salt Plum Review*, *Tundra*, *Seattle Woman Magazine*, *Third Coast*, *The Seattle Review*, *The Comstock Review*, and *The Cortland Review*. Her poems have been performed as a choral work. *Sea Lions Sing Scat* was semifinalist in Finishing Line Press' 2006 Open Chapbook Competition and is being published. A chapbook, *Red Rooms and Others*, is due from Pecan Grove Press. Carol teaches Alexander Technique in Seattle.

Anne-Marie Levine lives in New York City. A poet and scholar who began writing while touring as a concert pianist, she's the author of three books of poetry: *Euphorbia, Bus Ride to a Blue Movie*, and *Oral History*. Her work also appears in the anthologies *Poetry after 9/11* and *Literature as Meaning*. She's published essays on Gertrude Stein's politics, and on art and trauma, and has received grants from the NYFA, Puffin, and Vogelstein Foundations. She performs solo theater pieces based on her poems, and is currently working on a Commonplace Book and a visual arts project called *Box Poems*.

Karen L. Lewis is a transplanted Canadian writer, editor, and photographer. She is a teaching artist for Just Buffalo Literary Center and a contributing editor for *Traffic East* magazine (www.trafficeast.com). Her work has been published by such journals as *Poetry Daily*, *The Buffalo News*, *Slipstream*, *Moondance*, *Stirring*, and *Sacred Stones*. She has an essay in The Writing Group Book published by Chicago Review Press. Her poem "Even If" was nominated for a 2005 Pushcart Prize.

Barbara E. Lightner grew up in backcountry Tennessee before moving to the Arkansas Ozarks. Her poetry has appeared in *The Table Rock Review* and *Poesia*. A personal narrative of her life as a dairy farmer was published in Margaret Cruikshank's *Lesbian Path*. Her performance poetry reflects her work as a civil rights activist and an environmentalist. A chapbook, *In the Going forward of that Run*, is due out in September 2007.

Frannie Lindsay's second volume, *Lamb* (Perugia Press), was the 2006 runner-up for the Laughlin Award. Her first, *Where She Always Was* (Utah State University Press, 2004), won the May Swenson Award. She has held fellowships from the National Endowment for the Arts and the Massachusetts Cultural Council. Her poems have appeared or are forthcoming in *The Atlantic Monthly*, *Hunger Mountain*, *The Yale Review*, *Field*, *Prairie Schooner*, *Salamander*, *Runes*, *Poetry Daily*, *Black Warrior Review*, *Poetry East*, and *Bat City Review*.

Julia Lisella's forthcoming collection, *Terrain*, will be published by WordTech editions in summer 2007. She is also the author of *Love Song Hiroshima*, a chapbook (Finishing Line Press, 2004). Like most working poets, she writes in other genres too, reviews and scholarly essays mostly, and teaches American literature and writing at Regis College in Weston, Massachusetts. She has been a member of the Wom-po LISTSERV since meeting Wom-po member Catherine Daly several years ago at a panel about the poet H. D.

Diane Lockward is the author of *Eve's Red Dress* and *What Feeds Us* (Wind Publications, 2003, 2006). Her poems have been anthologized in *Poetry Daily: 366 Poems from the World's Most Popular Poetry Website* and in Garrison Keillor's *Good Poems for Hard Times*. Her poems have also appeared in such journals as *The Beloit Poetry Journal*, *Spoon River Poetry Review*, *Poet Lore*, and *Prairie Schooner*. She has received several Pushcart Prize nominations and a poetry fellowship from the New Jersey State Council on the Arts. A former high school English teacher, Diane now works as a poet-in-the-schools. (www.dianelockward.com)

Rachel Loden is the author of *Hotel Imperium*, which won the Contemporary Poetry Series Competition and was named one of the ten best poetry books of the year by *The San Francisco Chronicle*. Loden has also published four chapbooks, including *The Last Campaign*, which won the Hudson Valley Writers' Center Chapbook Prize, and *The Richard Nixon Snow Globe*. Her work appears in numerous anthologies including *Western Wind: An Introduction to Poetry* and *Best American Poetry 2005*. Other awards include a Pushcart Prize and a fellowship in poetry from the California Arts Council.

Judy Longley has three books of poetry published: *My Journey Toward You*, *Parallel Lives*, and *Rowing Past Eden*. Her poems have appeared in *Paris Review*, *Poetry*, *Western Humanities Review*, and *The Southern Review*. She was poetry editor five years for *Iris: A Journal for Women*, published by the University of Virginia. Currently she's poetry editor for *Tough Times Companion*, published by the Virginia Foundation for the Humanities.

Bobbi Lurie's poems have appeared or are forthcoming in *The American Poetry Review*, *New American Writing*, *Gulf Coast*, *Puerto del Sol*, *Nimrod*, and elsewhere. She is the author of two volumes of poetry: *Letter from the Lawn* (CustomWords, 2006) and *The Book I Never Read* (CustomWords, 2003).

Glenna Luschei is the founder of Solo Press, now in its 40th year. She was appointed Poet Laureate of San Luis Obispo City and County for the year 2000. She is also an avocado rancher in the Carpinteria Valley and has served as a medical interpreter for the Hispanic population. For many years she conducted poetry workshops at Atascadero State Hospital and California Men's Colony. She has recently filed her dissertation in Hispanic languages and literatures under the title, "Fatal Attractions in Luso-Brazilian Literature" at the University of California, Santa Barbara.

Catherine MacDonald lives in Richmond, Virginia, where she is a candidate for an MFA in creative writing at Virginia Commonwealth University.

Shawn Maeder holds an MA in linguistics from the University of Pennsylvania and currently teaches English at The Baldwin School in Bryn Mawr, Pennsylvania. Her interests include the history of the English language, queer poetics, and cooking with her daughters. The poem "The Needle" is from a series exploring feminine consciousness in middle age.

Marie-Elizabeth Mali lives in New York City and Housatonic, Massachusetts. Prior to focusing more exclusively on poetry, she was a licensed acupuncturist and life coach. Her work has appeared or is forthcoming in the journals *2River View* and *Hobble Creek Review*. She is a student in the MFA in Poetry program at Sarah Lawrence College.

Charlotte Mandel is a poet, editor, and independent scholar. Six books of poetry include her recent collection, *Sight Lines* (Midmarch Arts Press) and two poem-novellas, *The Life of Mary* (foreword by Sandra M. Gilbert, Saturday Press) and *The Marriages of Jacob* (Micah Publications). She edited *Saturday's Women*, the Eileen W. Barnes Award anthology of women poets over 40. A series of articles on the role of cinema in the life and work of poet H. D. have appeared in journals such as *Women's Studies* and *Literature/Film Quarterly*. She teaches poetry writing at Barnard College Center for Research on Women.

Argie Manolis is the service-learning coordinator at the University of Minnesota, Morris, where she also teaches creative writing and composition courses. She has an MFA from Arizona State University. Her poems have been published in such journals as *Bellingham Review*, *Mochila Review*, and *So To Speak: A Feminist Journal of Language and Art*. Much of her writing focuses on her Greek-American heritage, her lesbian and feminist identities, and life in a small, rural community.

Louise Mathias was born and raised in England and Los Angeles. She is the author of *Lark Apprentice*, chosen by Brenda Hillman for the New Issues Poetry Prize and published by New Issues Press in 2004. Recent poems appear in *Triquarterly*, *Denver Quarterly*, and *The Laurel Review*. Critical work is forthcoming in *Slope*. She makes her home by the sea in Long Beach, California, and works at a public television station.

Janet McCann is an old Texas poet, has taught at Texas A&M for 36 years, poems published hither and yon. She spends her spare time reading murder mysteries and attempting to help feral cats—who are not always grateful.

Wanda McCollar has taught English to high school students for half a century in the United States, Japan, and Germany. She now lives in Germany and manages a worldwide online writing project she designed for the DoDEA OnLine Academy (DOLA) for students enrolled in the U.S. Department of Defense overseas schools. When she was seventy, she began writing the poetry that had been living within her those many years. Her first poems have been published in *Del Sol Review*, *Perihelion*, *Chile Verde*, and the collected works, *Rites of Spring*, and *Radio, Radio!*

Gwyn McVay is the author of two chapbooks of poems; her first full-length collection, *Ordinary Beans*, is forthcoming from Pecan Grove Press in 2007. Her work has appeared in numerous publications and anthologies including *Prairie Schooner*, *Boulevard*, *Ploughshares*, and *New American Writing*. She teaches at the Pennsylvania College of Art & Design and Millersville University of Pennsylvania, where she recently appeared in *The Vagina Monologues*.

Susan Meyers is the author of *Keep and Give Away* (University of South Carolina Press, 2006), selected by Terrance Hayes for the 2005 South Carolina Poetry Book Prize. Her chapbook *Lessons in Leaving* was selected by Brendan Galvin for the 1998 Persephone Press Book Award. A long-time writing instructor, she holds an MFA from Queens University of Charlotte. She lives with her husband in the rural community of Givhans, near Summerville, South Carolina.

Ann E. Michael is a poet, essayist, and librettist who lives in eastern Pennsylvania, where she teaches part-time at several colleges. She has received a Pennsylvania Council on the Arts fellowship in poetry. Her poems and essays have appeared in numerous literary and commercial publications. Her chapbook *More than Shelter* is available from Spire Press (2004). (www.annemichael.com)

Peggy Miller's poetry has recently appeared in *Karamu*, *Astropoetica*, and *Paper Street*. Her chapbooks include *Martha Contemplates the Universe* (Frith Press). Her full-length collection *What the Blood Knows* is forthcoming in 2007 from Custom Words. She serves as an editor for the *Comstock Review*. She lives in Florida with her husband Phil Wolfson.

Shayla Mollohan grew up in north Alabama, home to rockets, cotton, and numerous caves; it is also where Andrew Jackson's ghost haunts Huntsville's railroad depot. Her professional life has been just as motley: from working with children to government contracting. She received a BA from the University of Alabama and has published poetry in numerous publications: *Poem*, *Amelia*, *Touchstone Literary Review*, and, recently, *Amaze*. Her first book is near completion and she is included in *Whatever Remembers Us: Anthology of Alabama Poetry* (Negative Capability Press).

Judith H. Montgomery's poems appear in *The Southern Review*, *Gulf Coast*, *Northwest Review*, and *The Bellingham Review*, among other journals and several anthologies. She's been awarded fellowships in poetry from the Literary Arts and the Oregon Arts Commission, residencies from Soapstone and Caldera, and prizes from the National Writers Union, *Americas Review*, and *Red Rock Review*. Her chapbook, *Passion*, received the 2000 Oregon Book Award. Her next collection, *Red Jess*, appeared in February 2006. She is the first poet-in-residence at Central Oregon Community College.

Ellen Moody has translated the poetry of Vittora Colonna and Veronica Gambara, two Renaissance Italian women poets. She has published essays and reviews on the writings of English women writers from the Renaissance through the mid–nineteenth century and on film adaptations. Her published book is on Anthony Trollope (*Trollope on the Net*). Her website includes e-text editions of novels by eighteenth-century French women writers. She teaches at George Mason University. (http://www.jimandellen.org/ellen/emhome.htm)

D. O. Moore is a poet and translator living in Hyattsville, Maryland, and has had poetry appear in a variety of publications, such as *The Literary Review*, *Fugue*, *Confrontation*, *Barrow Street*, and *Elixir*. Moore's translations of contemporary Latin American poets and fiction writers have appeared in *Mid-American Review*, *The Literary Review*, and *TriQuarterly*.

LouAnn Shepard Muhm is a poet and teacher from Park Rapids, Minnesota. Her poems have appeared in *Dust & Fire*, *The Talking Stick*, *North Coast Review*, *Alba*, *Red River Review*, *Eclectica*, *Poems Niederngasse*, and *CALYX*, and she is a recipient of the 2006 Minnesota State Arts Board Artist Initiative Grant in Poetry. Her chapbook, *Dear Immovable*, was published in 2006 by Pudding House Press.

Aimee Nezhukumatathil owns a geriatric miniature dachshund named Villanelle who is afraid of frogs and pots. She (Aimee, not Villanelle) is the author of *Miracle Fruit*, winner of the Tupelo Press Prize and ForeWord Magazine's Poetry Book of the Year award. Her poems have appeared in *Tin House*, *Shenandoah*, *Beloit Poetry Journal*, and *Prairie Schooner*. She is assistant professor of English at SUNY—Fredonia and can be found online at www.aimeenez.net.

Joyce Nower is the author of three books of poetry: *Year of the Fires* (1983), *Column of Silence* (2001), and *The Qin Warriors and Other Poems* (2003), the last two published by Avranches Press. Her poems have appeared in *Slant*, *GR Review*, *The Evansville Review*, *Common Ground*, *Grasslands Review*, *Taproot, Terminus*, *The Raven Chronicles*, *The American Poetry Journal*, *Andwerve*, and *Visions International*. Currently she writes a poetry column called "Intersections" for *The Alsop Review* (www.alsopreview.com).

Mendi Lewis Obadike is the author of *Armor and Flesh* and *The Sour Thunder*. Her poetry and text-based new media art have been exhibited internationally. She often works collaboratively with her husband, Keith Obadike. Their work has been commissioned by the Whitney Museum of American Art, Yale University, and the New York African Film Festival/Electronic Arts Intermix. They recently developed *Four Electric Ghosts* (songs and stories based on Amos Tutuola's novel *My Life in the Bush of Ghosts* and the video game Pac Man) in Toni Morrison's Atelier at Princeton University, where Mendi is a 2006–09 Cotsen postdoctoral fellow.

Anne Britting Oleson lives and writes from the mountains of central Maine. Her work has appeared in *Exit 13*, *Poetry Motel*, *Confluence*, *The Tulane Review*, and *Valparaiso Poetry Review*. Her first book of poetry, *The Beauty of It*, is scheduled for publication in 2007.

Alicia Ostriker has published eleven volumes of poetry, most recently *The Volcano Sequence* (2002) and *No Heaven* (2005). Twice a finalist for a National Book Award, she has also received the William Carlos Williams Award, the Paterson Poetry Prize, the San Francisco State Poetry Center Award, and two Pushcart prizes, among others. As a critic she is the author of *Stealing the Language: The Emergence of Women's Poetry in America* (1986) and *Dancing at the Devil's Party: Essays on Poetry, Politics and the Erotic* (2000) as well as numerous essays. Ostriker teaches in the low-residency poetry MFA program of New England College. Homepage: http://www.rci.rutgers.edu/~ostriker/home.htm.

Christina Pacosz has been writing and publishing prose and poetry for almost half a century and has several books of poetry, the most recent, *Greatest Hits, 1975–2001* (Pudding House, 2002). Her work has appeared recently in *Jane's Stories III*, *Women Writing Across Boundaries*, and one of her poems has been accepted for publication online by *Pemmican*. She lives with her husband of almost twenty years and teaches urban youth in Kansas City, Missouri.

Shin Yu Pai is the author of *The Love Hotel Poems* (Press Lorentz), *Works on Paper* (Convivio Bookworks), *Unnecessary Roughness* (xPress(ed)), *Equivalence* (La Alameda), and *Ten Thousand Miles of Mountains* and *Rivers* (Third Ear Books). Visit her website at http://shinyupai.com.

Cheryl Pallant lives in Richmond, Virginia, where she teaches poetry, dance, and a blend of the two at the University of Richmond. Her books and chapbooks include *Uncommon Grammar Cloth*, *Spontaneities*, *Into Stillness*, *The Phrase*, and *Contact Improvisation*. Her poetry, prose, and dance criticism are published widely in places like *Women's Studies Quarterly*, *Fence*, *Tarpaulin Sky*, and *Sleeping Fish*. Her website is www.cherylpallant.com.

Susan Firghil Park has worked as a psychotherapist and editor. Her chapbook, *Estuary Light*, was published in 2005 by Finishing Line Press. She is currently a student in the low-residency MFA program of the Rainier Writers Workshop at Pacific Lutheran University.

Cynthia Parker-Ohene is a graduate of the MFA program at the Saint Mary's College of California where she was the Chester Aaron Scholar in Creative Writing Excellence. She has received fellowships from Naropa University and Indiana University/Bloomington. Her poems have appeared in *The Ringing Ear: Black Poets Lean South* (Nikkey Finney, editor), *nocturnes (re)view*, and *x literary journal* (London), among others.

Elise Paschen is the author of *Infidelities*, winner of the Nicholas Roerich Poetry Prize, and *Houses: Coasts*. Her poems have been published in *The New Republic*, *Poetry*, *Shenandoah*, among others, and in numerous anthologies, including *Reinventing the Enemy's Language: Contemporary Native Women's Writings of North America*, and *A Formal Feeling Comes*. She is coeditor of *Poetry in Motion*, *Poetry in Motion from Coast to Coast*, and *Poetry Speaks*, and editor of *Poetry Speaks to Children*. Former Executive Director of the Poetry Society of America, she teaches in the Writing Program at The School of the Art Institute of Chicago.

Lynn Patmalnee is a born and bred Jersey Girl who worked in cinemas, record stores, and on the Asbury Park boardwalk before breaking into the music business. As Lynn Crystal, she hosts the long-running Carnival of Song radio program on WFDU FM 89.1, Teaneck, New Jersey, and http://www.carnivalofsong.com.

Molly Peacock is the author of five volumes of poetry, including *Cornucopia: New and Selected Poems*, published by W.W. Norton and Company. Her poems have appeared in *The New Yorker*, *The Nation*, *The New Republic*, *The Paris Review*, as well as *The Best of the Best American Poetry* and the *Oxford Book of American Poetry*. Currently she is touring with her one-woman show in poems *The Shimmering Verge*, now part of an Off Broadway Festival of One-Woman Shows at Urban Stages. She is a member of the graduate faculty of the Spalding University Brief Residency MFA. Her website is www.mollypeacock.org.

Carol Peters writes from her home in Charleston, South Carolina. She received her MFA in creative writing from Queens University of Charlotte. Carol's blog is http://carolpeters.blogspot.com.

Katha Pollitt is the author of *Antarctic Traveller* (Knopf), which won the National Book Critics Circle Award for poetry, and three collections of prose: *Reasonable Creatures*, *Subject to Debate*, and *Virginity or Death!* (Random House, 2006). Her poems have appeared in many magazines, including *The New Yorker*, *The New Republic*, *Poetry*, and *Paris Review*, and she is the recipient of many grants and prizes including a Whiting Award and a Guggenheim Fellowship. She is a columnist for *The Nation*, and lives in New York City, where she is at work on a collection of personal essays.

Cati Porter is a poet, artist, freelance writer, and reviewer, and editor of the online all-poetry journal, *Poemeleon*. Her poems and reviews have recently appeared or are forthcoming from *Literary Mama*, *kaleidowhirl*, *Poetry Southeast*, *Galatea Resurrects*, and others.

Ren Powell is a native Californian living on the west coast of Norway. She has published ten books of translations, and is the author of a series of children's books (Min San Publishing, 2006) and two volumes of poetry in bilingual editions from Wigestrand Press: *Fairytales and Soil*, 1999, and *Mixed States*, 2005. She is a graduate of Texas A&M and Lancaster University, and is currently the editor of the International Cities of Refuge Network website and webzine (www.icorn.org). Her personal website is www.renpowell.com.

Kristin Prevallet is a poet, critic, educator and editor of the online journal *materialworld.com*. Recent books include *Scratch Sides: Poetry, Documentation and Image-text Projects* (Skanky Possum, 2004) and *Shadow Evidence Intelligence* (Factory School, 2006). She lives in Brooklyn and teaches at St. John's University in Queens, NY.

Sina Queyras is the author of three collections of poetry including *Lemon Hound*. She recently edited *Open Field: 30 Contemporary Canadian Poets*. Queyras lives in Brooklyn and teaches at Rutgers.

Ellen Rachlin's chapbook, *Waiting for Here*, was published by Finishing Line Press, 2004. Her poems have appeared in various journals including *American Poetry Review*, *Confrontation*, *The Comstock Review*, and *Court Green*. She serves as Treasurer of the Poetry Society of America.

Beverly Rainbolt, author of a collection of poetry, *The Altar of this Moment*, and coeditor of *Women Poets Workshop Into Print*, holds an MFA from the University of New Orleans Creative Writing Workshop. She has had works published in various journals and anthologies. A lifelong resident of Louisiana, she now spends most of her time and love trying to live in and otherwise help in small and prosaic ways to rebuild the city of her heart—New Orleans—and the surrounding Gulf Coast area.

D'Arcy Randall is a writer, editor, and teacher in Austin, Texas, where she cofounded *Borderlands: Texas Poetry Review*. Before moving to Texas, she worked for nine years as fiction editor for the University of Queensland Press in Brisbane, Australia. Her awards include Michener Fellowships and the Roy Crane Award from the University of Texas at Austin, *The Malahat Review* Long Poem Prize, and an AWP *Intro* prize.

Elizabeth Rees' poetry has appeared in *North American Review*, *Partisan Review*, *Kenyon Review*, *The New England Review*, *River Styx*, *Mid-American Review*, *Agni*, and *Puerto Del Sol*, among many other journals. Her first chapbook, *Balancing China*, won Sow's Ear Review's 1998 contest. A second chapbook, *Hard Characters*, was published in 2002 by March Street Press. She recently won first place in the *Swink* Poetry Contest, and second place in the Ann Stanford Contest. Her first collection of poems, *Returning From Egypt*, has been a finalist more times than she can count.

Martha Rhodes is the author of three poetry collections: *At the Gate* (Provincetown Arts, 1995), *Perfect Disappearance* (winner of the 2000 Green Rose Prize from New Issues), and *Mother Quiet* (Zoo Press, 2004). She teaches at Sarah Lawrence College and in the MFA Program for Writers at Warren Wilson College. She is a founding editor and the director of Four Way Books.

Susan Rich lives in Seattle, but has previously lived and worked in Bosnia, Niger, South Africa, West Bank, and Gaza; she's worked as an electoral supervisor, human rights trainer, Peace Corps Volunteer, and scholar. Poems appear in *Alaska Quarterly Review*, *Bellingham Review*, *Christian Science Monitor*, *Massachusetts Review*, *North American Review*, *Poetry International*, and *Witness*. She teaches at Highline Community College, Antioch University's MFA Low Residency Program, and is a founding board member of the Somali Rights Network. Her books include *The Cartographer's Tongue*, winner of the PEN USA Poetry Award, and *Cures Include Travel*, both from White Pine Press. Visit her online at http://www.susanrich.org.

Moira Richards. Google "Moira Richards" to find links to her essays on women abuse, her reviews of woman-authored books, and to other writing and editing work she does for various print and e-publications. She can often be found lounging about the staff rooms of womenwriters.net, absolutewrite.com, and moondance.org—usually sipping tea, sometimes Jack Daniels. Off-line, she teaches accounting and other numberly subjects to students at the Nelson Mandela Metropolitan University in South Africa. And writes a poem or two.

Margaret Ricketts has studied creative writing at American University and the University of Kentucky. Her poetry has appeared in *Long Shot*, *The Redneck Review*, *Open City*, and *Wind*, among others. Margaret has been the recipient of grants from both the Kentucky Arts Council and the Kentucky Foundation for Women. She is a regular contributor to the Sunday book page of the *Lexington Herald-Leader*.

Eve Rifkah is editor of *Diner*, a literary journal, and cofounder of Poetry Oasis, Inc., a nonprofit poetry association dedicated to education, promoting local poets, and publishing *Diner*. Poems have or will appear in *Bellevue Literary Review*, *The MacGuffin*, *5 AM*, *ParthenonWest*, newversenews.com, *PoetryMagazine.com*, *Chaffin Journal*, *Porcupine Press*, *The Worcester Review*, *California Quarterly*, *ReDactions*, *Jabberwock Review*, *Southern New Hampshire Literary Journal*, and have been translated into Braille. Her chapbook, *At the Leprosarium*, won the 2003 Revelever chapbook contest. A professor of English at Worcester State College, she received her MFA in writing from Vermont College and lives with her husband, poet Michael Milligan.

Kim Roberts is the editor of *Beltway Poetry Quarterly* and author of a book of poems, *The Wishbone Galaxy*. She has published widely in literary journals throughout the United States, as well as in Canada, Ireland, France, and Brazil. She is the recipient of grants from the National Endowment for the Humanities, the D.C. Commission on the Arts, and the Humanities Council of Washington, and has been awarded writers' residencies at ten artist colonies.

Aleida Rodríguez was born in Güines, Cuba. Her first book, *Garden of Exile*, won the Kathryn A. Morton Prize in Poetry and the PEN USA 2000 Literary Award. *Garden of Exile* garnered critical acclaim and was listed as a "Best Book of 2000" by the *San Francisco Chronicle*. Recipient of many awards, including an NEA fellowship, Aleida's work has been published in the United States for 30 years, and more recently in Great Britain, Czechoslovakia, and Holland. Her prose collection, *Desire Lines*, derives its name from the landscape-design term for the worn footpaths made when people veer off the established paths.

Lois Roma-Deeley's full-length poetry collection *Rules of Hunger* (Star Cloud Press, 2004) earned her a National Book Award nomination. She is an Emily Dickinson Award in Poetry Competition winner (Universities West Press), third place, as well as the 2005 Allen Ginsberg Awards in Poetry Competition winner (Passaic Review), third place, and Editor's Choice. Her poetry has earned the Arizona Governor's Arts Awards nomination and a Pushcart nomination. She has been published nationwide, including in six anthologies and numerous literary journals. Further, Roma-Deeley has published various poetry reviews in several literary journals. *NorthSight*, her second poetry collection, was published by Singularity Press in January 2006. (http://www.singularitypress.biz/)

Rachel Rose is a dual Canadian/American citizen whose work has been published in journals in both countries, including *Poetry*, *Verse*, *The Malahat Review*, and *The Best American Poetry 2001*. Her first book, *Giving My Body to Science* (McGill/Queen's University Press), was a finalist for The Gerald Lampert Award, The Pat Lowther Award, and the Grand Prix du Livre de Montreal, and won the Quebec Writers' Federation A. M. Klein Award. Her second book, *Notes on Arrival and Departure*, was published by McClelland & Stewart in 2005.

Cynthia Roth was born in Mississippi and grew up in Tennessee. Her poems have appeared in *Dogwood*, *Poetry Midwest*, *The Pittsburgh Quarterly*, *Moxie*, and elsewhere. In 2003 she won an Illinois Arts Council Fellowship in Poetry. In 2002 she was a Tennessee Williams Scholar in Poetry at the Sewanee Writers' Conference and a semifinalist in the Yale Series of Younger Poets competition. She lives in Murphysboro, Illinois, where she and her husband own a sculpture studio. Roth holds MFA degrees in fine art and creative writing from SIU Carbondale. She coedits the online poetry journal *Mot Juste*. (www.motjustepoetry.com)

Helen Ruggieri lives in Olean, New York, and has a book of poems, *Glimmer Girls*, available from mayapplepress.com and a book of haibun, *The Character for Woman*, from foothillspublishing.com.

C. J. Sage edits *The National Poetry Review* and teaches at De Anza and Hartnell Colleges. Her poems have appeared or are forthcoming in *Ploughshares*, *Shenandoah*, *The Antioch Review*, *The Threepenny Review*, *Prairie Schooner*, and *Black Warrior Review*, among others. A book-length terza rima, *Odyssea*, is forthcoming from Turning Point Books in spring 2007. Previous books are *Field Notes in Contemporary Literature*, *And We the Creatures*, and *Let's Not Sleep*. CJ lives in Rio del Mar, California.

cin salach performs and publishes her work widely. An Illinois Arts Council award recipient, Ragdale Fellow, and program director of Words@Play: an after school poetry collaboration with the Chicago Park District and Children's Humanities Fest, cin and her band *ten tongues* recently released their first full-length CD, *a wide arc*, now available on CD Baby. Her work can also be found in *Columbia Poetry Review*, *ACM*, and *Court Green* as well as the anthologies *The Spoken Word Revolution*, *Power Lines*, and *Poetry Slam*. *Looking for a Soft Place to Land*, her first book, was released in 1996.

Metta Sáma (previously Lydia Melvin) did not get an MLA interview. She resides in upstate New York, where she sighs and wonders about her future. She has work published or forthcoming in *Torch and Pebble Lake*, *Sojourn*, *Zone 3*, *Kestrel*, *Paterson Literary Review*, *Crab Orchard Review*, *Verse online*, among others, and is author of *South of Here* (New Issues Press, 2005). Sigh. No AWP either.

Rati Saxena is an eminent Hindi poet, translator, and Sanskrit scholar. She has authored three collections of poems in Hindi and one each in English and Malayalam (in translation). In addition, she has written several research articles on Vedic literature and Indology and published critical studies. Her poems are translated in different languages. She is the editor of the poetry journal, *Kritya* (www.kritya.in).

Ada Jill Schneider, winner of the Galway Kinnell Poetry Prize, is the author of *Fine Lines and Other Wrinkles* (1993), *The Museum of My Mother* (1996), *Poems for Grandma and Me* (2001), and *Saudades: The Jewish-Portuguese Connection* (2005). *Aviary* is forthcoming from Premier Poet Chapbook Series. Her reviews and poetry have been published in a number of journals including *Midstream*, *The Sow's Ear Poetry Review*, *Lizzie Borden Quarterly*, *Diner*, *Nedge*, and *The Newport Review*. Ada received her MFA in writing from Vermont College and currently directs "The Pleasure of Poetry," a program she initiated at the Somerset Public Library in Massachusetts.

Penelope Scambly Schott has published four chapbooks and four books of poetry. Her books include *The Perfect Mother* (1994); *Penelope: The Story of the Half-Scalped Woman* (1999), a narrative about an early New Jersey settler; *The Pest Maiden: A Story of Lobotomy* (2004); a documentary narrative; and most recently, *Baiting the Void* (2005), winner of the Orphic Prize from Dream Horse Press. She has been a resident at the Fine Arts Work Center in Provincetown, Massachusetts; the Vermont Studio Center in Johnson, Vermont; and the Helene Wurlitzer Foundation in Taos, New Mexico. In her next life, she wishes to return as her own dog.

Margaret Peters Schwed is a writer living in NYC. Recently, her poems have appeared in *Raritan*, *Rattapallax*, *Ekphrasis*, *River Oak Review*, *Nimrod*, and Phil Miller and Gloria Vando's *Chance of a Ghost* anthology, and are forthcoming in several other anthologies. She has reviewed books for the *Sunday Times Book Review*, *The Wall Street Journal*, *The Chicago Review*, and *Pleiades*.

Elaine Sexton's poems, essays, and book reviews have appeared in numerous journals including *American Poetry Review*, *Poetry*, *Prairie Schooner*, *New Letters*, *ARTnews*, *Art New England*, and the *Women's Review of Books*. *Sleuth*, a collection of poems, came out with New Issues (Western Michigan University) in 2003. She teaches at the Writing Institute at Sarah Lawrence College and works in magazine publishing.

Deema K. Shehabi is a Palestinian-American poet who grew up in the Arab world. She arrived in the United States in 1988, where she completed an MS in journalism. Her poems have appeared or are forthcoming in *Atlanta Review*, *Bat City Review*, *Crab Orchard Review*, *Drunken Boat*, *DMQ Review*, *The Kenyon Review*, *The Poetry of Arab Women*, *White Ink*, and *Arab-American and Diaspora Literature*. She resides in Northern California with her husband and two sons.

Evie Shockley's two poetry collections, *a half-red sea* (2006) and *The Gorgon Goddess* (2001), were published by Carolina Wren Press. Her work, which includes criticism and fiction, appears in such publications as *Beloit Poetry Journal*, *African American Review*, *Dark Matter: A Century of Speculative Fiction from the African Diaspora*, *HOW2*, *Rainbow Darkness*, and *nocturnes (re)view*. She is a Cave Canem fellow and received a residency from Hedgebrook in 2003. Shockley teaches at Rutgers University, New Brunswick.

Peggy Shumaker's most recent book of poems is *Blaze*, a collaboration with the painter Kesler Woodward (Red Hen Press). *Just Breathe Normally*, a book of her lyric nonfiction, will be published by University of Nebraska Press in fall 2007. Professor Emerita at University of Alaska Fairbanks, Shumaker teaches in the low-residency Rainier Writing Workshop. Her web site is www.peggyshumaker.com.

Shoshauna Shy is a member of the Prairie Fire Poetry Quartet, and in May 2004, she founded a program called Poetry Jumps Off the Shelf with the mission of placing poetry in public places where it is not expected. Her poems have been published in numerous journals and magazines, which include *Poetry Northwest*, *Cimarron Review*, *The Comstock Review*, and *Rosebud*. One of her poems was selected for the Poetry 180 Library of Congress program, "A Poem a Day in American High Schools," launched by Billy Collins.

Martha Silano was born in New Jersey and educated at Grinnell College and the University of Washington. She is the author of two volumes of poetry, *Blue Positive* (Steel Toe Books) and *What the Truth Tastes Like* (Nightshade Press). She has received fellowships from the Seattle Arts Commission and The University of Arizona Poetry Center. Currently, she teaches at Bellevue and Edmonds Community Colleges. Her website is www.marthasilano.com.

Ellen McGrath Smith teaches writing and literature at the University of Pittsburgh, where she earned an MFA in poetry in 1993. Her poems have appeared in *CQ*, *5 AM*, *Café*, *Oxford Magazine*, *Pig Iron*, *The Prose Poem*, *Pearl*, *Zone 3*, *Southern Poetry Review*, *The Pittsburgh Quarterly*, *Sistersong*, *Descant* (Canada), and others. Her work has received the *Zone 3* Rainmaker Award and the Ascher Montandon Award (HyperAge). She has critical work in *The Denver Quarterly*, *The Pennsylvania Review*, and other journals. Regular contributor, *Sentence*; recent honorable mention, Lynda Hull Award, *Crazyhorse*. She's been a wompo for five years.

Elizabeth Smucker grew up in Milwaukee, Wisconsin. She recently completed a BA in creative writing at Indiana University in Bloomington. In addition to writing poetry, she works as an artisan baker and spends time painting and walking in the woods.

Heidi Lynn Staples was a recipient of the New Issues Poetry Prize for *Guess Can Gallop*, her debut collection of poems. Her second book, *Dog Girl*, has been selected by Carolyn Forché for publication by Ahsahta Press. Her work has appeared or is forthcoming in numerous literary journals and anthologies, including *Best American Poetry 2004*, *Chicago Review*, *Denver Quarterly*, *Ploughshares*, and *Salt Hill*. She lives in Rosslare, Ireland.

Rosemary Starace is a native of New York City who now lives in western Massachusetts. A visual artist as well as a writer, she's put examples of her work in both arenas online at www.rosemarystarace.com. She has a poem forthcoming in *Orion*.

Francine Sterle is the author of *The White Bridge* (Poetry Harbor, 1999), *Every Bird is One Bird* (Tupelo Press, 2001), and *Nude in Winter* (Tupelo Press, 2006), a collection of ekphrastic poems. Awards include a Loft-McKnight Foundation Award, a Jerome Foundation Travel and Study Grant, four Pushcart Prize nominations, a Fellowship Grant and a Career Opportunity Grant from the Minnesota State Arts Board, as well as residencies at the Anderson Center for Interdisciplinary Studies, the Blacklock Nature Sanctuary, and the Leighton Studios at the Banff Centre for the Arts.

Diana Stokes, former editor for Wom-po Newsletter, lives and writes in Crowsnest Pass, Alberta. Her poetry has appeared in literary journals, anthologies, and trade publications. Diana, a member of the League of Canadian Poets, continues to work on her manuscript.

Yerra Sugarman received the 2005 PEN/Joyce Osterweil Award for Poetry for her first collection, *Forms of Gone*, published by The Sheep Meadow Press in 2002. She also has received a Discovery/*The Nation* Prize, a Chicago Literary Award from *Another Chicago Magazine*, a George Bogin Award from the Poetry Society of America, and an Academy of American Poets Prize. Some of her poems have been translated into French and have appeared in the French journals *Siècle 21* and *Europe*. She teaches creative writing and English at The City College of New York.

Kathleen Sullivan has been a practicing psychotherapist for many years. She comes to writing late in life, but not too late to pursue an MFA in poetry at Stonecoast in Maine, where Annie Finch taught her about the feeling of formal poetry by dancing iambs and trochees in the attic of the Stone House. Kathleen is interested in the similarity between the language of psychotherapy and poetry and is experimenting with the therapeutic use, with clients, of poems triggered by compelling or confusing aspects of their work together.

Amanda Surkont lives and writes in the Northeast Kingdom of Vermont. She is poetry editor of *Rhode Island Roads Magazine*. Through her poetry she hopes to preserve lost voices.

Barbara A. Taylor writes: "Each day demands that I write and that my fingers touch and feel the earth." Barbara has published prose and poetry in print in Australia, the United Kingdom, and the United States, on community, local, and national ABC radio, and in various literary e-zines. She is a regular reader and slammer at Live Poets evenings. Barbara writes from the sub-tropical Rainbow Region of New South Wales, Australia, where inspiration, peace, and freedom to create comes from the serenity and beauty of this special area. Samples of her diverse poetry with audio are at http://batsword.tripod.com.

Marilyn Taylor's poems have appeared in *Poetry*, *The American Scholar*, *The Formalist*, and many other journals. Her work won first place in recent competitions sponsored by *Dogwood*, *Passager*, *The Ledge*, and *GSU Review*, and she has received three Pushcart Prize nominations. Her second full-length collection, titled *Subject to Change* (David Robert Books, 2004), was nominated for the Poets

Prize in 2005. Marilyn is a Contributing Editor for *The Writer* magazine, where her articles on poetic craft appear regularly. She has taught for many years at the University of Wisconsin—Milwaukee, and served as Poet Laureate of Milwaukee in 2004/05.

Diane Thiel is the author of six books of poetry, nonfiction, and creative writing pedagogy: *Echolocations* (Nicholas Roerich Prize, 2000), *Writing Your Rhythm* (2001), *The White Horse: A Colombian Journey* (2004), *Resistance Fantasies* (2004), *Crossroads: Creative Writing Exercises in Four Genres* (2005), and *Open Roads: Exercises in Writing Poetry* (2005). Her work appears in *Poetry*, *Best American Poetry 1999*, and is reprinted in over 25 major anthologies. She received her BA and MFA from Brown University, and has traveled and lived in various countries in Europe and South America. A recent Fulbright Scholar, she is associate professor at the University of New Mexico. (www.dianethiel.net)

Ann Townsend is the author of two collections of poetry, *The Coronary Garden* (Sarabande Books, 2005) and *Dime Store Erotics* (Silverfish Review Press, 1998), and is the editor of a collection of essays, *Radiant Lyre: On Lyric Poetry* (with David Baker), forthcoming from Graywolf Press in 2007. Her poetry has appeared in *Poetry*, *The Paris Review*, *The Nation*, *The Georgia Review*, and many other magazines. She is the recipient of a National Endowment for the Arts Fellowship, an individual artist's grant from the Ohio Arts Council, and the Discovery/*The Nation* prize. A professor of English at Denison University, she lives in Granville, Ohio.

Cynthia Trammell, a native Californian, is pursuing an MFA in Creative Writing at Antioch University of Los Angeles. She is currently an intern with Red Hen Press.

Elizabeth Treadwell is the author of seven books, including two poetry collections to be published in 2007: *Wardolly* (Chax Press) and *Birds & Fancies* (Shearsman Books). She was born in Oakland, California, in 1967 and lives there now with her family. Since 2000, she's served as the director of Small Press Traffic Literary Arts Center in San Francisco. More information is available at elizabethtreadwell.com.

Patricia Valdata writes poetry, fiction, and nonfiction. She lives in Elkton, Maryland.

Diane Vance is a poet who lives in Hyattsville, Maryland. Her work has appeared in *The North American Review*, *The Southwestern Review*, and the anthologies *My Lover is a Woman* (Ballantine Books) and *Women Poets, Workshop Into Print* (In(her)itance Press).

Wendy Vardaman, Madison, Wisconsin, holds a PhD in English from University of Pennsylvania. After teaching at Penn, Helsinki University, and University of Washington, she quit to stay home with her three children and write. She has received three Pushcart nominations, and has recent and forthcoming poems, interviews, and reviews in *Main Street Rag*, *Nerve Cowboy*, *Wisconsin People and Ideas*, and *Free Verse*, among others. Her first chapbook, *Obstructed View*, is forthcoming.

Kathrine Varnes was born near Köln, Germany, on the day after John F. Kennedy was shot. From the age of four, she grew up in Los Angeles, learning to keep her cool around famous people. Some of her odd jobs have included filing engine gaskets, painting the names on boats, and singing in bars. One of the first five wompos, Varnes is the author of a book of poems, *The Paragon* (Word Tech, 2005), coeditor with Annie Finch of *An Exaltation of Forms* (University of Michigan Press, 2002), and a coordinator of collaborative sonnet crowns.

Pramila Venkateswaran, author of *Thirtha*, published by Yuganta Press, has poems in *Paterson Literary Review*, *Ariel*, *Atlanta Review*, *Prairie Schooner*, *Kavya Bharati*, and *CALYX*, and the anthologies *A Chorus for Peace* and *En*(Compass). She has performed her poems nationally, most recently in the Geraldine R. Dodge Poetry Festival. She is currently engaged in doing multimedia performances that include dance, poetry, and music. She teaches English and women's studies at Nassau Community College, New York.

Lynn Wagner's poems have appeared in *Shenandoah*, *Chautauqua Literary Review*, *Two Rivers Review*, *Painted Bride Quarterly*, and other journals, and in the anthology *Breath of Parted Lips*, volume 2 (CavenKerry Press, 2004). Lynn received an MFA from the University of Pittsburgh, where she won the Academy of American Poets prize in 2002. She has been a fellow at the Virginia Center for the Creative Arts. A lurker on Wom-po since 2000, Lynn curates the Pittsburgh Poetry Calendar on www.poetz.com.

Gale Renee Walden is the author of *Same Blue Chevy*, published by Tia Chucha Press. She resides in Urbana, Illinois.

Crystal Warren was born and raised in Port Elizabeth and now lives in Grahamstown, having spent her entire life in the Eastern Cape Province of South Africa. With degrees in librarianship and literature she works as a researcher at the National English Literary Museum and teaches a creative writing course at Rhodes University. Her poems and stories have been published in many South African literary journals over the years and her first collection of poems, *Bodies of Glass*, appeared in 2004.

Julene Tripp Weaver (formerly June Arlene Eggler) has her BA in creative writing from City University of New York. She graduated with Honorable Mention of the Mary M. Fay Award in poetry at Hunter College. She has a masters in applied behavioral science from the Leadership Institute of Seattle, and works as an HIV/AIDS case manager. She won third prize for poetry from the Unfinished Works Contest sponsored by AIDS Services Foundation Orange County, December 2005. This year Nerve Cowboy awarded her third prize for her chapbook *Case Walking: An AIDS Case Manager Wails her Blues*.

Braden Welborn is a PhD student in literature and American culture studies at Washington University in St. Louis. She is a graduate of the MFA Program in Creative Writing at the University of Alabama, where she served as poetry editor for *Black Warrior Review*. She has taught at the University of Alabama, The Capitol School, and the Alabama School of Fine Arts, and her writing appears or is forthcoming in *Crab Orchard Review*, *Prairie Schooner*, *Lifeboat: A Journal of Memoir*, *Diagram*, and *Georgetown Review*.

Ingrid Wendt's books of poems include *Surgeonfish* (winner of the 2004 Editions Prize), *The Angle of Sharpest Ascending* (winner of the 2003 Yellowglen Award), *Blow the Candle Out*, *Singing the Mozart Requiem* (Oregon Book Award), and *Moving the House*. She coedited the anthologies *In Her Own Image: Women Working in the Arts* and *From Here We Speak: An Anthology of Oregon Poetry*. A mother and grandmother, Ingrid lives in Eugene, Oregon, with her husband, writer Ralph Salisbury. She also sings second alto with The Motet Singers, a women's a cappella ensemble. She is on the web at www.ingridwendt.com. Listen and order CDs at http://www.singers.com/choral/motetsingers.html.

Lesley Wheeler's poems appear in *Agni*, *Prairie Schooner*, *Crab Orchard Review*, and other journals. Her book, *The Poetics of Enclosure: American Women Poets from Dickinson to Dove*, appeared in 2002. She is currently at work on two manuscripts: a poetry collection called *Heathen* and a scholarly study of poetic voice. She teaches at Washington and Lee University in Lexington, Virginia.

Susan Wheeler is the author of four books of poetry, most recently *Ledger* from the University of Iowa Press, and a novel, *Record Palace*, from Graywolf Press. The recipient of a Guggenheim Fellowship and the Witter Bynner Prize for Poetry from the American Academy of Arts and Letters, she teaches at Princeton University and the New School in New York City.

Ann White is a native Floridian and multiple-genre writer. She started writing poetry in 2003, after working in magazine and newspaper markets, and publishing a newspaper on women business owners. Her poems have appeared in various journals, including *Blue Fifth Review*, *Triplopia*, *HLFQ*, *Modern Haiku*, and *Bay Windows*. Ann is a Pushcart Prize nominee and a candidate for an MFA in the Creative Writing Program at Antioch University Los Angeles. During the week, Ann coordinates an ESL program at a community college in north Florida.

Brandy Whitlock is a poet and librarian finishing her first collection in Maryland, her native state. Other poems from the collection have appeared or are forthcoming in *New Orleans Review*, *The Cream City Review*, *Baltimore Review*, *Clackamas Literary Review*, *Salt Hill*, *LUNGFULL!*, and *CALYX*.

Christine Whittemore was born and grew up in England, lived in Italy for five years, then moved to New York with her American husband. Since 1988 they and their three children have lived in northeast Pennsylvania; youngest child is now in college. New horizons for all? Her poetry and essays have appeared in various publications including *Hunger Mountain*, *The American Scholar*, *Plains Poetry Review*, *Parabola*, and *Islands*. Awards include a 1998 Fellowship in Literature from the Pennsylvania Council on the Arts. Recurring themes are the meaning of place and the rewards of looking closely.

Carolyn Whittle earned an MA in English from the University of Chicago and MBA from Columbia University. A former college teacher, environmentalist, legislator, and officer of a global bank, she writes poetry to prevent her left brain from taking over. When not traveling, she lives on the Hudson River, the river that flows both north and south, depending on the movement of the tides. Her poetry has been published in *Margie Review*, *Byline Magazine*, *Tiger's Eye*, *Yale Poetry Circle*, and *Rattapallax*. She was a finalist in the Margie Award for Poetry in 2005.

Catherine Wiley was born in Rochester, New York, and teaches at the University of Colorado at Denver. Her poems appear or are forthcoming in *Salamander*, *Kalliope*, *Calyx*, *Phoebe*, *Copper Nickel*, and other venues; and her 2003 chapbook *Failing Better* was a finalist for the Colorado Book Award.

Crystal Williams is a native of Detroit, Michigan, and is the author of two collections of poetry. She currently lives in Chicago, Illinois.

Susan Settlemyre Williams's poetry has recently appeared in *Mississippi Review*, *River City*, *Shenandoah*, *Sycamore Review*, *The Cream City Review*, and *Poetry Southeast*, among other journals, and in *Best New Poets 2006*. Her chapbook *Possession* (Finishing Line Press) was published in April 2007. She was the cowinner of the 2006 Diner Poetry Contest. She is book review editor and associate literary editor of the online journal *Blackbird* and lives in Richmond, Virginia.

Caroline Williamson started out in London, and has also lived in Oxford, Cambridge, Newcastle, Beijing, and now Melbourne, Australia. Has been writing poetry since she learnt to write. Works as a freelance editor. One son, nine years old. Now doing a Masters in creative writing, struggling with critical theory, but having a ball. Recently published in *Heat* and *Eureka Street* (both Australian journals), *Poets Against the War* (U.S. website), and *True North*, with Alana Kelsall and Meg McNena (Waterline Press, Melbourne, 2006).

Susan R. Williamson's poems have appeared in *Lumina*, *Streetlight*, *LINK*, *StorySouth*, *Three Candles*, *The Virginia Quarterly Review*, and other journals. She is the managing editor of *Streetlight*, *A Journal of Art and Literature*, and founder of Rives Street Poets. She was previously associate publisher at Tupelo Press, on the board of the Charlottesville Writing Center, and on the publisher's day committee of the Virginia Festival of the Book. An MFA candidate at Virginia Commonwealth University, she lives and works in Charlottesville, Virginia.

Rosemary Winslow's poems have appeared in several anthologies, including *Voices from Frost Place*, and in publications such as *32 Poems*, *Innisfree*, *Pinstripe Fedora*, *Poet Lore*, *The Southern Review*, and *Valparaiso Poetry Review*. Her work has received three Larry Neal Awards for Poetry, including first place in 2006, and fellowship grants from the District of Columbia Arts Commission and the Vermont Studio Center. An associate professor at The Catholic University of America, she has published widely on prosody, style, American poetry, rhetoric, and teaching writing. A swimming and hiking enthusiast, she lives in downtown Washington, D.C., with her husband, John, a visual artist.

Sarah Yake has been a bookseller and a sales rep for a major publisher. She's now on the other side of the publishing fence, working as a literary agent's assistant. She lives with her husband and six-year-old daughter in Paoli, Pennsylvania, holds a MA in English literature from West Chester University, and loves nothing better than a really good used book sale at the local library.

Chryss Yost is a poet, editor, and graphic designer. She is the author of two chapbooks and coeditor of two anthologies, *Poetry Daily: A Year of Poems* and *California Poetry*. Her poems have been widely anthologized and published in the *Hudson Review*, *Quarterly West*, *Crab Orchard Review*, among other journals. She is a former editor of *Solo: A Journal of Poetry*, book editor for the *Santa Barbara Independent*, and currently edits the *Journal of Haitian Studies* at the University of California, Santa Barbara. She has one daughter, Cassidy.

Abe Louise Young is a poet, teacher, and activist who delights in generating connections between poetry and other disciplines. A Louisiana native, she currently lives in Austin and directs "Alive in Truth: The New Orleans Disaster Oral History Project." Her poems have received a Grolier Poetry Prize, an Academy of American Poets Anne Bradstreet Prize, and others, and have recently been published in *New Letters*, *Bloom*, and *Hawai'i Review*. She is a contributor to the *Austin Chronicle*, a graduate of the James Michener Center for Writers, and an Affiliate at the Benjamin Hooks Institute for Social Change.

Andrena Zawinski, born and raised in Pittsburgh, Pennsylvania, and educated at the University of Pittsburgh, now lives and teaches writing in Oakland, California. Her poetry appears widely online and in print. She is features editor at *PoetryMagazine.com*. (www.poetrymagazine.com/zawinski)

Rachel Zucker is the author three books of poetry, most recently, *The Bad Wife Handbook* published by Wesleyan University Press. She is currently the Poet-in-Residence at Fordham University and also works as a certified labor doula. More information about her can be found at www.rachelzucker.net.

Acknowledgements

Adams, Diana: "Trees." Originally appeared in *Perihelion,* Vol. 5, Issue 1, 2005. Copyright © by Diana Adams. Reprinted with permission of the author.

Agner, Mary Alexandra: "Longest Night." Originally appeared in *Hidden Oak*, Fall/Winter 2003. Reprinted with permission of the author.

Agodon, Kelli Russell: "In the 70's, I Confused Macramé and Macabre." Originally appeared in *RHINO* Vol. 5, Issue 1, 2005. Reprinted with permission of the author.

Albrecht, Malaika King: "We Can't Step into the Same River Twice." Originally appeared on the North Carolina Arts Council website, NCARTS.org in November 2005. Copyright © 2005 by Malaika King Albrecht. Reprinted with permission of the author.

Alexander, Meena: "Triptych in a Time of War."Originally appeared in *Raw Silk* (Triquarterly Books/ Northwestern University Press, 2004). Reprinted with permission of Northwestern University Press.

Alvarez, Celia Lisset: "What It Takes to Be Lois Lane." Originally appeared in *The Stones* (Finishing Line Press, 2006). Copyright © 2006 by Celia Lisset Alvarez. Reprinted with permission of the author.

Alvarez, Ivy: "length." Originally appeared in *C-side* <*www.c-side.com.au*>. Reprinted with permission of the author. Copyright © 2005 by Ivy Alvarez.

Anaporte-Easton, Jean: "poem for the new year." Originally appeared in *Corroboree*, Vol. 1, No. 1, 1991. Reprinted with permission of the author.

Arcana, Judith: "Facts of Life." Originally appeared in *Prairie Schooner*, Spring 2004 (University of Nebraska Press). Reprinted with permission of the University of Nebraska Press.

Ashley, Renée: "The Weaving: Her Voice." Previously appeared in *The American Voice,* Fall 1995 and *The Revisionist's Dream*, 2001. Copyright © 2001. Reprinted with permission of the author.

Aull, Felice: "Alice Neel Paints a Portrait." Originally appeared in *Ekphrasis*, Vol. 3, No. 5, Spring/Summer 2005. Reprinted with permission of the author.

Ayers, Lana Hechtman: "Near Winter Solstice." Originally appeared in *White Pelican Review* Vol. 6, No. 1, Spring 2005. Reprinted with permission of the author.

Ballardini, Anny: "Apples." Originally appeared in *Opening and Closing Numbers* (Moira Poetry, 2005). Reprinted with permission of the author.

Bar-Nadav, Hadara: "Night with Wings." Originally appeared in *The Journal*, Vol. 29, No. 2, 2005. Reprinted with permission of the author.

Barrington, Judith: "Souls under Water." Originally appeared in *He Drew Down Blue from the Sky to Make a River* (The Arvon International Poetry Competetion Anthology, 2004). Copyright © 2006. Reprinted with permission of the author.

Becker, Kimberly L.: "The Fallen Apples." Originally appeared in *Southern Hum*, Vol. 2, Issue 2, December 2006. Copyright © 2006 by Kimberly L. Becker. Reprinted with permission of the author.

Benedict, Kate Bernadette: "Sheela-na-gig." Originally appeared in *Wild Plum*, Vol. 1, No. 1, Spring 2004. Reprinted with permission of the author.

Berdeshevsky, Margo: "But a Passage in Wilderness." Originally appeared in *Chelsea*, Issue 76, 2004. Copyright © 2004 by Margo Berdeshevsky. Reprinted with permission of the author.

Betten, Mary Rose: "My Voice." Originaly appeared in *Hanging Out with Loose Words* (Foothills Press, 2005). Reprinted with permission of Foothills Press.

Bohince, Paula: "Acrostic: Queen Anne's Lace." Originally appeared in *FIELD*, No. 73, 2005. Copyright© 2005 by Paula Bohince. Reprinted with permission of the author.

Bourbeau, Lisa: "Collage." Originally appeared in *First Intensity*, No. 20, Fall 2005. Reprinted with permission of the author.

Braucher, Karen: "Medusa in the Checkout Line." Originally appeared in *Aqua Curves* (NFSPS Press, 2005).Reprinted with permission of the author.

Bright, Susan: "Enheduanna Wrote on Stone." Previously appeared in *Women's Way*, 1991, *House of the Mother* (Plain View Press, 1994), *Next to the Last Word* (Plain View Press, 1998), and *The Layers of Our Seeing* (Plain View Press, 2002). Reprinted with permission of the author.

Brody, Patricia: "Dangerous to Know, Even After Death." Previously appeared in *Paris Review*, No. 171, Fall 2004, and *Poetry Daily*, December 2004. Reprinted with permission of the author.

Bruce, Debra: "The Unmothering." Originally appeared in *Poetry*, Vol. 178, August 2001. Reprinted with permission of the author.

Burch, Beverly: "Referred Pain." Originally appeared in *Terminus*. Reprinted with permission of the author.

Byrkit, Rebecca: "Number Four Is Heroin." Previously appeared in *Exquisite Corpse*, February 2000, and *The Salt River Review,* Fall 2004. Reprinted with permission of the author.

Carlisle, Wendy Taylor: "In the 9th Ward." Originally appeared in *storySouth*, Winter 2006. Reprinted with permission of the author.

Carlson, Nancy Naomi: "What Floats through Me." Originally appeared in *Poetry,* Vol. 178, No. 5. Reprinted with permission of the author.

Chandler, Sherry: "Skin Out a Woman." First appeared in *Dance the Black-Eyed Girl* (Finishing Line Press, 2003). Reprinted with permission of the author.

Cherry, Laura: "The Nurse and the Principal." Previously appeared in *Vocabula Review*, Vol. 4, No. 10, October 2002, and *What We Planted*, 2002. Reprinted with permission of the author.

Coles, Katharine: "Outside Newton's House." Originally published by *Western Humanities Review*, Vol. 54, No. 1, Spring 2000. Reprinted with permission of the author.

Cooley, Nicole: "Grief As Is." Originally appeared in *Washington Square*, 2002. Reprinted with permission of Washington Square.

Courington, Chella: "Summer at Thirteen." Previously appeared in *Ibbetson Street Press*, Issue 15, June 2004, the anthology *CloudView Poets* (Arctos Press, 2005), and the book *Southern Girl GoneWrong* (Foothills Publishing, 2004). Reprinted with permission of the author.

Cresswell, Mary: "Free on Board." Originally appeared in *Landfall*, Vol. 207, 2004. Reprinted with permission of the author.

Crooker, Barbara: "All that Is Glorious around Us." Originally appeared in *Radiance* (Word Press, 2005). Reprinted with permission of the author.

Dacus, Rachel: "Femme au chapeau." Originally appeared in *Femme au chapeau* (David Robert Books, 2005). Reprinted with permission of the author.

Day, Kay: "Volunteer Reading Lesson with Mira." Previously appeared in *Fairfield Review*, Fall/Winter 2000, and *A Poetry Break* (Ocean Publishing, 2004). Reprinted with permission of the author.

De Koninck, Jessica G: "Chagall's Windows." Originally appeared in *Earth's Daughters*, No. 66, 2005. Reprinted with permission of the author.

Deed, Martha: "Illegal Entry." Originally appeared in *Artvoice*, Vol. 3, No. 14, April 2004. Reprinted with permission of the author.

Dentz, Shira: "Poem for my mother who wishes she were a lilypad in a Monet painting." Originally appeared in *Chelsea,* 2003. Reprinted with permission of the author.

Deppe, Annie: "The Throat Singers." Previously appeared in *Sitting in the Sky* (Summer Palace Press, 2003). Reprinted with permission of the author.

Detorie, Michelle: "Elegy for a Sleepwalker." Originally appeared in *Dusie,* Issue 5, Winter 2006. Reprinted with permission of the author.

DiMartino, Joanie: "Ultrasound." Originally appeared in *Wicked Alice Poetry Journal*, Winter 2004. Reprinted with permission of the author.

Dolin, Sharon: "Envy Ghazaled." Originally appeared in *Whisky Island Magazine*, No. 49, Summer 2005. Reprinted with permission of the author.

Dorf, Carol: "Liminal." Originally appeared in *Runes*, Vol. 6, Issue 1. Reprinted with permission of the author.

Dungy, Camille T.: "Almost Like They Wanted It." Originally appeared in *MiPOesias*. Reprinted with permission of the author.

Dunlop, Rishma: "Naramata Road." Originally appeared in *Red Silk* (Mansfield Press, 2004). Reprinted with permission of Mansfield Press and the author.

Dus, Lisken Van Pelt: "Broken Things." Originally appeared in *The Comstock Review*. Copyright © 2006 by Lisken Van Pelt Dus. Reprinted with permission of the author.

Edwards, Lynnell: "The Farmer's Daughter; or Persephone's Return." Originally appeared in *The Farmer's Daughter* (Red Hen Press, 2003). Reprinted with permission of the author.

Egan, Moira: "Questions Midway." Previously appeared in *Verse Daily*, November 8, 2004, and *Cleave* (Washington Writers' Publishing House, 2004). Reprinted with permission of the author.

Elbe, Susan: "Drought, 1937." Originally appeared in *Calyx, A Journal of Art and Literature by Women* Vol. 22, No. 3, Summer 2005. Reprinted with permission of the author.

Enszer, Julie R.: "Reparations." Originally appeared in *Long Shot*, Vol. 27, 2004. Reprinted with permission of the author.

Esposito, Nancy: "Snake Charmer." Previously appeared in *Southwest Review*, Vol. 74, No. 4, Autumn 1989, and *Greatest Hits 1978–2001* (Pudding House Publications, 2003). Reprinted with permission of the author.

Evans, Kate: "Middle Age." Reprinted from *Like All We Love* (Q Press, 2006). Used by permission of the author. Copyright © 2006 by Kate Evans.

Eylon, Dina Ripsman: "Tragic Figures." Originally appeared in *Kinesis*, April 2000. Reprinted with permission of the author.

Falk, Marcia: "After Astounding Evil, the Promise of More to Come." Previously appeared in *The Women's Review of Books*, Vol. 20, No. 5, February 2003, and *September 11, 2001: American Writers Respond*, 2002. Reprinted with permission of the author.

Finch, Annie: "Letter for Emily Dickinson." Originally appeared in *Calendars* (Tupelo Press, 2006). Reprinted with permission of the author.

Finch, Margaret Rockwell: "The Seventeenth Day of May." Originally appeared in *Davy's Lake* (Caribou Press, 1996). Reprinted with permission of the author.

Fisher-Wirth, Ann: "Blue Window." Originally appeared in *Blue Window* (Archer Books, 2003). Copyright © by Ann Fisher-Wirth. Reprinted with permission of the author.

Flaherty, Barbara: "Dark Raven." Originally appeared in *Holy Madness* (Chanting Press, 2006). Reprinted with permission of the author.

Flenniken, Kathleen: "It's Not You, It's Me." Originally appeared in *Famous* (University of Nebraska Press). Copyright © 2006 by the Board of Regents of the University of Nebraska. Reprinted with permisson of the University of Nebraska Press.

Floyd-Miller, Cherryl: "Otherness." Originally appeared in *storySouth*, Fall 2005. Copyright © by Cherryl Floyd-Miller. Reprinted with permission of the author.

Foley, Ruth E.: "Triolet for Eric." Originally appeared in *Rattle,* Vol. 8, No. 2. Reprinted with permission of the author.

Friedman, Audrey: "The Morgan Health Center." Originally appeared in *The Comstock Review*, Vol. 18, Fall/Winter 2004. Reprinted with permission of the author.

Frischkorn, Suzanne: "Mermaid." Originally appeared in *Margie*, Vol. 4, 2005. Reprinted with permission of the author.

Frost, Helen: "First Deep Breath." Originally appeared in *Kalliope,* Vol. 25, No. 2, 2003. Reprinted with permission of the author.

Frym, Gloria: "Medicate Specific." Previously appeared in *New American Writing*, No. 23, May/June 2005, and the book *Solution Simulacra* (United Artists Books, 2006). Reprinted with permission of the author.

Gage, Diane: "Reading Anne Sexton." Originally appeared in *Chattahoochee Review*, Vol. 24, No. 2/3, Winter/Spring 2004. Reprinted with permission of the author.

Gailey, Jeannine Hall: "Female Comic Book Superheroes." Originally appeared in *Becoming the Villainess* (Steel Toe Books, 2006). Reprinted with permission of the author.

Gandel, Jennifer J.: "A Toilet." Originally appeared in *Reed,* Vol. 56, 2003. Reprinted with permission of the author.

George, Alice: "The wingless atheist remarks the number of birds." Originally appeared in *Diagram*, Vol. 5, No. 3, 2005. Reprinted with permission of the author.

Geyer, Bernadette: "The Naming of Bones." Originally appeared in *The Pedestal Magazine,* Issue 14, February 2003. Reprinted with permission of the author.

Goldstein, Ellen: "Meadowbrook Sapphics." Originally appeared in *The New Hampshire Review*, Issue 1, Vol. 1, Summer 2005. Reprinted with permission of the author.

Graham, David: "Long Overdue Note to My College Professor Who Broke Down and Cried One Morning in 1974 While Teaching Yeats." Originally appeared in *Stutter Monk* (Flume Press, 2000). Reprinted with permission of the author.

Graham, Neile: "On Skye." Previously appeared in *And No One Knows the Blood We Share: Poems from the Feminist Caucus*, 2005, *Vintage 95,* 1996, *The Alsop Review*, and *PoetsWest*. Reprinted with permission of the author.

Greenstreet, Kate: "Lives of the Saints." Originally appeared in *The Massachusetts Review*, Vol. 44, No. 3, Fall 2003. Reprinted with permission of the author.

Grubin, Eve: "Modesty." Originally appeared in *Morning Prayer* (Sheep Meadow Press, 2005). Reprinted with permission of the author.

Gubernat, Susan: "Hades." Originally appeared in *Pleiades*, Vol. 25, No. 1, 2005. Reprinted with permission of the author.

Haaland, Tami: "Reasons to Fly." Originally appeared in *Rattapallax*, Issue 12. Reprinted with permission of the author.

Hacker, Marilyn: "Ghazal: In Summer." Originally appeared in *Bat City Review*, Vol. 1, No. 1, Fall 2005. Reprinted with permission of the author.

Haines, Anne: "Let X Equal . . . ." Originally appeared in *Northwest Review*, Vol. 30, No. 3, 1992. Reprinted with permission of the author.

Hannan, Maryanne: "To You Who Speak of Audre Lorde." Originally published in *ELM*, Vol. 13. No.2, Spring 2005. Copyright © 2003 by Maryanne Hannen. Reprinted with permission of the author.

Harrod, Lois Marie: "His Mouth." Originally appeared in *The Literary Review*, Vol. 48, No.1. Reprinted with permission of the author.

Hayden, Dolores: "On the Hundred-Percent Corner." Originally appeared in *The Yale Review*, Vol. 90, January 2002. Copyright © by Dolores Hayden. Reprinted with permission of the author.

Haymon, Ava Leavell: "Pose, Flammable." Originally appeared in *Bellingham Review*, Vol. 29, No. 1, Issue 57, Spring 2006. Reprinted with permission of the author.

Hedge Coke, Allison Adelle: "Ghosts." Originally appeared in *Blood Run* (Salt Publishing Ltd., 2007). Reprinted with permission of Salt Publishing Ltd.

Henry, Liz: "Kissing Nadine in the Rain." Originally appeared in *Cuts From the Barbershop* (Tollbooth Press, 2004). Reprinted with permission of the author.

Heon, R. Joyce: "High Flying." Originally appeared in *Poets in the Galleries* by the Worchester County Poetry Association in collaboration with the Worchester Art Museum. Reprinted with permission of the author.

Hostetler, Ann: "Resisting Geometry." Previously appeared in *The American Scholar*, 1995, and *Empty Room with Light* (Pandora Press U.S., 2002) Reprinted with permission of Pandora Press.

Howerow, Louisa. "Forewarned." Originally appeared in *The Pedestal Magazine*, Issue 27, 2005. Copyright © 2005 by Louise Howerow. Reprinted with permission of the author.

Husted, Bette Lynch: "Tending Adobe." Originally appeared in *Triplopia*, Vol. 4, Issue 2, April 2005. Reprinted with permission of the author.

Huston, Karla: "Monuments." Originally appeared in *Eclectica Magazine*, Oct./Nov. 2004. Reprinted with permission of the author.

Jensen, Judy: "Past Perfect." Previously appeared in *Silver Visions II, Visions-International*, No. 72, 25th Anniversary Edition (Black Buzzard Press). Copyright © 2005 by Judy Jensen. Reprinted with permission of the author.

Jobson, Liesl: "Vocal Warm-Up at the Co-Op." Originally appeared in *Mississippi Review* online, Vol. 10, No. 4, 2004. Reprinted with permission of the author.

Kalfopoulou, Adrianne: "The Meal." Originally appeared in *Columbia Poetry Review*, No. 18, Spring 2005. Reprinted with permission of the author.

Kasdorf, Julia Spicher: "Poetry in America." Originally appeared in *Pleiades,* Vol. 20, No. 2, Spring 2000. Reprinted with permission of the author.

Kelley-Lossada, Bridget: "In Morocco." Originally appeared in *Inkwell*, Issue 9, Winter 1999. Reprinted with permission of the author.

Kemp, Robin: "New Breast." Originally appeared in *Texas Review*, Vol. 23, Fall/Winter 2002. Reprinted with permission of the author.

Kendig, Diane: "Marie Blanchard, 1914." Originally appeared in *Slant: A Journal of Poetry*, Vol. 12, 1998. Reprinted with permission of the author.

Kennedy, Lillian Baker: "Notions." Originally appeared in *Notions* (Pudding House Publications, 2004). Reprinted with permission of the author.

Kennelly, Laura: "Helen with Insomnia, at the Clavier." Previously appeared in *San José Studies*, 1992, and *A Certain Attitude* (Pecan Grove Press, 1995). Reprinted with permission of the author.

Kerman, Judith: "One-Book Poet." Previously appeared in *House Organ*, January 2005, and *Galvanic Response* (March Street Press, 2005). Reprinted with permission of March Street Press.

Keyes, Claire: "Bridge to Savannah." Originally appeared in *Onset Review*, Summer 1998, and *Rising and Falling* (Riverstone Press, 1999). Reprinted with permission of the author.

Kildegaard, Athena: "Aria." Originally appeared in *Willow Springs*, Vol. 45, 2000. Reprinted with permission of the author.

Kindred, Sally Rosen: "To Eve." Previously appeared in *Poetry Northwest* , Vol. 35, No. 2, Summer 1994, and *Garnet Lanterns* (Anabiosis Press, 2006). Reprinted with permission of the author.

King, Amy: "Cynthia McKinney Cast the Lone Dissenting Vote." Originally appeared in *Order & Decorum*. Reprinted with permission of the author.

Kirchheimer, Janet R.: "Dogs." Originally appeared in *Potomac Review,* Issue 39, Spring/Summer 2005. Copyright © 2005 by Janet R. Kirchheimer. Reprinted with permission of the author.

Lederer, Ann Neuser: "The Undifferentiated." Previously appeared in *Pudding,* Vol. 32, 1996, and *The Undifferentiated* (Pudding House, 2003). Reprinted with permission of Pudding House.

Lemmon, Amy: "Karyotype." Originally appeared in *Barrow Street*, Fall 2005. Reprinted with permission of the author.

Levin, Carol: "The Perfumer." Originally appeared in *Third Coast*, Spring 2003. Copyright © 2003. Reprinted with permission of the author.

Levine, Anne-Marie: "Four November 9ths." Originally appeared in *Bus Ride to a Blue Movie* (Pearl Editions, 2003). Reprinted with permission of the author.

Lewis, Karen L.: "Even if." Originally appeared in *Slipstream*, Issue 25, 2005. Reprinted with permission of the author.

Lindsay, Frannie: "Walking an Old Woman into the Sea." Previously appeared in *Valparaiso Poetry Review*, Vol. 8, No. 1, Fall/Winter 2006-2007, and *Lamb* (Perugia Press, 2006). Copyright © 2006 by Frannie Lindsay. Reprinted with permission of Perugia Press.

Lisella, Julia: "Rosebush." Originally appeared in *Many Mountains Moving*. Copyright © 2004 by Julia Lisella. Reprinted with permission of the author.

Lockward, Diane: "Losing the Blues." Originally appeared in *Eve's Red Dress* (Wind Publications, 2003). Reprinted with permission of the author.

Loden, Rachel: "Miss October." Originally appeared in *The Richard Nixon Snow Globe* (Wild Honey Press, 2005). Copyright © 2005 by Rachel Loden. Reprinted with permission of the author.

Longley, Judy: "We Knock upon Silence for an Answering Music." Originally appeared in *Tough Times Companion*, Vol. 2, 2005. Reprinted with permission of the Virginia Foundation for the Humanities.

Lurie, Bobbi: "Ane the Shoes Will Take Us There In Spite Of The Circumference." Originally appeared in *Wild Plum* Vol. 1, Issue 1, 2004, and *Letter from the Lawm* (Custom Words, 2006). Reprinted with permission of the author.

Luschei, Glenna: "Kestrel." Originally appeared in *Parnassus: Poetry in Review*. Reprinted with permission of the author.

MacDonald, Catherine: "Grace." Originally appeared in *Washington Square*, Issue 17, Winter 2006. Reprinted with permission of the author.

Mali, Marie-Elizabeth: "Walking in Winter." Originally appeared in *The 2River View*, Vol. 11, No. 2, Winter 2006. Reprinted with permission of 2River.

Mandel, Charlotte: "Still Life." Originally appeared in *The National Poetry Review*, Vol. 3, No. 4, Spring/Summer 2005. Reprinted with permission of the author.

Mathias, Louise: "Desert Flux." Previously appeared in *Denver Quarterly*, Vol. 39, Issue 3, Fall 2004, and *Lark Apprentice* (New Issues Press, 2004). Reprinted with permission of the author.

McCann, Janet: "Answering Machine." Previously appeared in *Pascal Goes to the Races* (Custom Words, 2004). Reprinted with permission of the author.

McCollar, Wanda: "Oh, Radio." Originally appeared in *Radio! Radio!* (Pecan Grove Press, 2000). Copyright © 2000 by Pecan Grove Press. Reprinted with the permission of Pecan Grove Press.

McVay, Gwyn: "In the Dirt." Originally appeared in *Willow Springs*, Winter/Spring 1996. Reprinted with permission of the author.

Meyers, Susan: "Awaiting My Brother's Pathology Report, My Husband and I Take to the River." Previously appeard in *Crazyhorse*, Fall 2005, and *Keep and Give Away* (University of South Carolina Press, 2006). Reprinted with permission of University of South Carolina Press.

Michael, Ann E.: "Stabled." Originally appeared in *Sojourn*, Fall 2005. Reprinted with permission of the author.

Miller, Peggy: "*Aedes albopictus*: Getting Things in Context." Originally appeared in *Paper Street*, Vol. 3., No. 3, Spring 2006. (Paper Street Press, 2006). Reprinted with permission of the author.

Montgomery, Judith H.: "Sonata for Tide and Light." Previously appeared in *The Comstock Review*, Vol. 18, No. 2, Fall/Winter 2004 (The Comstock Writers Group), and the book *Red Jess* (Cherry Grove Collections, 2006). Reprinted with permission of the author.

Moore, D. O.: "Splitting Oaks." Originally appeared in *Interdisciplinary Humanities*, Special Issue 2003. Reprinted with permission of the author.

Muhm, LouAnn Shepard: "Waitress." Originally appeared in *Calyx, A Journal of Art and Literature by Women,* Vol. 20, No. 2. Copyright © 2002 by LouAnn Shepard Muhm. Reprinted with permission of the author.

Nezhukumatathil, Aimee: "Last Aerogramme to You, with Lizard." Originally appeared in *At The Drive-In Volcano* (Tupelo Press, 2007). Reprinted with permission of the author.

Obadike, Mendi Lewis: "Strut." Originally appeared in *Bloom*, Vol. 1, No. 2. Reprinted with permission of the author.

Oleson, Anne Britting: "Looking Back Up the Hospital Drive." Originally appeared in *Valparaiso Poetry Review,* Vol. 7, No. 2, Spring/Summer 2005. Copyright © 2006 by Anne Britting Bowman. Reprinted with the permission of the author.

Ostriker, Alicia: "Everywoman Her Own Theology." Originally appeared in *Imaginary Lover* (University of Pittsburgh Press, 1986). All rights are controlled by the University of Pittsburgh Press. Reprinted with permission of the University of Pittsburgh Press.

Pai, Shin Yu: "it does a body good." Originally appeared in *How 2*, Vol. 2, No. 4, Summer 2006. Reprinted with permission of the author.

Pallant, Cheryl: "A Declaration of Independence." Originally appeared in *Fence*, Vol. 9, No. 1, Winter/Spring 2006. Copyright © 2006 by Cheryl Pallant. Reprinted with permission of the author.

Park, Susan Firghil: "Prayer." Originally appeared in *Estuary Light* (Finishing Line Press, 2005). Reprinted with permission of Finishing Line Press.

Parker-Ohene, Cynthia: "Weather Report." Originally appeared in *nocturnes 4 (re)view of the literary arts,* Issue 4, 2005. Copyright © 2005 by Cynthia Parker-Ohene. Reprinted with permission of the author.

Paschen, Elise: "Engagement." Originally appeared in *Ploughshares*, Vol. 30, No. 4, Winter 2004/2005. Reprinted with permission of the author.

Peacock, Molly: "The Flaw." Originally appeared in *River Styx*, 2005. Reprinted with permission of the author and the publisher.

Pollitt, Katha: "The Expulsion." Originally appeared in *The New Yorker*, Nov. 12, 2001. Copyright © 2001 by Katha Pollit. Reprinted with permission of the author.

Porter, Cati: "Pomegranate, Juiced." Originally appeared in *The Bedside Guide to No Tell Motel – Second Floor*. Reprinted with permission of the author.

Powell, Ren: "A Matter of Course." Originally appeared in *Mixed States* (Wigestrand forlag AS, 2004). Reprinted with permission of the author.

Prevallet, Kristin: "The Mother Maker." Originally appeared in *mem2*, Fall 2005. Reprinted with permission of the author.

Queyras, Sina: "A Lilac Begins to Leaf." Originally appeared in *Lemon Hound* (Coach House Books, 2006). Reprinted with permission of Coach House Books.

Rachlin, Ellen: "Night Swim." Previously appeared in *Waiting for Here* (Finishing Line Press, 2004) and *White Crow*, 2004, Vol. 6, Issue 2. Reprinted with permission of Finishing Line Press.

Rainbolt, Beverly: "The Text is Dead—Long Live the Text." Originally appeared in *The Altar of this Moment* (Portals Press, 2001). Reprinted with permission of Portals Press.

Randall, D'Arcy: "Wrong Window." Originally appeared in *The Sow's Ear*, Vol. 4, No. 4, 1993. Copyright © 1993 by D'Arcy Randall. Reprinted with permission of the author.

Rees, Elizabeth: "Talia." Originally appeared in *North American Review*, Vol. 288, No. 6, November/December 2003. Reprinted with permission of the author.

Rhodes, Martha: "Low Ceiling'd." Originally appeared in *The Laurel Review,* 2005. Reprinted with permission of the author.

Rich, Susan: "For Sale." Originally appeared in *Water~Stone*. Reprinted with permission of the author.

Richards, Moira: "Doing my bit agin domestic violence." Originally appeared in *RaW NerVZ*, Vol. 10, No. 3, 2005. Reprinted with permission of the author.

Rifkah, Eve: "Solomon." Previously appeared in *The Worcester Review*, Vol. 24, No. 1 & 2, 2003, and *At the Leprosarium* (Reveler Press, 2004). Reprinted with permission of Reveler Press.

Roberts, Kim: "Fowler and Wells' Phrenological Cabinet." Originally appeared in the *Michle Street Reivew*, No. 15, Summer 2002. Reprinted with permission of the author.

Rodríguez, Aleida: "Apple." Originally appeared in *Paterson Literary Review*, Issue 32, Spring 2003, and *The Face of Poetry,* 2005. Copyright © Aleida Rodríguez. Reprinted with permission of the author.

Roma-Deeley, Lois: "Throwing a Chair through the Hospital Window." Originally appeared in *NorthSight* (Singularity Press, 2006). Reprinted with permission of the author.

Rose, Rachel: "Sheets." Previously appeared in *Poetry*, September 2003, and *Notes on Arrival and Departure* (McClelland & Stewart, 2005). Reprinted with permission of the author.

Roth, Cynthia: "The Sound of Love Failing." Originally published in *Mind the Gap*, Issue 4, 2000. Reprinted with permission of the author.

Ruggieri, Helen: "Jazz on a Summer Afternoon—Newport Jazz Festival, 1958." Previously appeared in *Poem* (University of Alabama) and *Glimmer Girls*. Copyright © 1999 by Helen Ruggieri. Reprinted with permission of the author.

Sage, C. J.: "Sonnet for Carryhouse and Keeper." Previously appeared in *The Spoon River Poetry Review* and the book *Let's Not Sleep* (Dream Horse Press, 2002). Reprinted with permission of the author.

salach, cin: "Ripe." Originally appeared in *RHINO*, 2003. Copyright © 2003. Reprinted with permission of the author.

Sáma, Metta: "Fluid, fecund, forget me not." Originally appeared in *Pebble Lake*, Spring 2007. Reprinted with permission of the author.

Schneider, Ada Jill: "Waiting for You." Originally appeared in *Diner*, Vol. 3, No. 2, Fall/Winter 2003. Reprinted with permission of the author.

Schott, Penelope Scambly: "April, Again." Previously appeared in *The Georgia Review*, Vol. 57, No. 3, Fall 2003, and the book *Baiting the Void*. Reprinted with permission of the author.

Schwed, Margaret Peters: "Penelope." Originally appeared in *Raritan*, Vol. 23, No. 2, Fall 2003. Reprinted with permission of the author.

Sexton, Elaine: "Public Transportation." Previously appeared in *New Letters*, Vol. 67, No. 2, Spring 2001, and *Sleuth* (Western Michigan University, 2003). Reprinted with permission of New Issues (Western Michigan University).

Shehabi, Deema K.: "Lights across the Dead Sea." Originally appeared in *Drunken Boat*, Vol. 8, 2006. Copyright © 2006 by Deema Shehabi. Reprinted with permission of the author.

Shockley, Evie: "possibilities of poetry, upon her death." Previously appeared in *Beloit Poetry Journal*, Vol. 52, No. 1, Fall 2001, and *a half-red sea* (Carolina Wren Press, 2006). Copyright © 2006 by Evie Shockley. Reprinted with permission of the author.

Shumaker, Peggy: "Walker Lake." Previously appeared in *Looking North*, 1998, and *Blaze*, 2005. Reprinted with permission of the author.

White, Ann: "The Two Fridas." Originally appeared in *Kaleidowhirl*, Vol. 2, Issue 3, Summer 2005. Reprinted with permission of the author.

Whittemore, Christine: "The Paper-Wasp." Originally appeared in *Hunger Mountain*, Issue 6, Spring 2005. Reprinted with permission of the author.

Wiley, Catherine: "The Pink Girls." Originally appeared in *Failing Better* (Finishing Line Press, 2003). Reprinted with permission of the author.

Williams, Crystal: "Night Bloom." Originally appeared in *5 AM*, Issue 21. Reprinted with permission of the author.

Williams, Susan Settlemyre: "Linnaeus in Eden." Originally appeared in *Sycamore Review*, Vol. 19, Issue 1, Winter 2007. Copyright © 2007 by Susan Settlemyre Williams. Reprinted with permission of the author.

Williamson, Caroline: "Biographies." Previously appeared in *Eureka Street*, Vol. 14, No. 1, January/February 2004, and the book *True North* (Waterline, Press, 2006). Reprinted with permission of the author.

Williamson, Susan R.: "Nocturne." Originally appeared in *Virginia Quarterly Review*, Vol. 81, No. 3, Summer 2005. Reprinted with permission of the author.

Winslow, Rosemary: "Palomino." Originally appeared in *32 Poems*, Spring 2004. Reprinted with permission of the author.

Yost, Chryss: "Advice for Women." Previously appeared in *Quarterly West*, Fall/Winter 1997/1998, and *La Jolla Boys* (Mille Grazie Press, 2000). Reprinted with permission from the author.

Zawinski, Andrena: "Open Stage." Originally appeared in *Quarterly West*, No. 49, Winter 2000. Reprinted with permission of the author.

Zucker, Rachel: "The Moon Has a Reputation for Being Fickle." Originally appeared in *The Last Clear Narrative* (Wesleyan University Press, 2004). Reprinted with permission of Wesleyan University Press.